D1256857

The Christmas Truce

THE
CHRISTMAS
TRUCE

Myth, Memory,
and the
First World War

TERRI BLOM CROCKER

FOREWORD BY PETER GRANT

UNIVERSITY PRESS OF KENTUCKY

Scholarly publisher for the Commonwealth,
serving Bellarmine University, Berea College, Centre College of
Kentucky, Eastern Kentucky University, The Filson Historical Society,
Georgetown College, Kentucky Historical Society, Kentucky State
University, Morehead State University, Murray State University,
Northern Kentucky University, Transylvania University, University of
Kentucky, University of Louisville, and Western Kentucky University.
All rights reserved.

Editorial and Sales Offices: The University Press of Kentucky
663 South Limestone Street, Lexington, Kentucky 40508-4008
www.kentuckypress.com

Library of Congress Cataloging-in-Publication Data

Crocker, Terri Blom, author.
   The Christmas truce : myth, memory, and the First World War / Terri
Blom Crocker ; foreword by Peter Grant.
      pages cm
   Includes bibliographical references and index.
   ISBN 978-0-8131-6615-5 (hardcover : alk. paper) —
   ISBN 978-0-8131-6616-2 (pdf) — ISBN 978-0-8131-6617-9 (epub)
   1. Christmas Truce, 1914. 2. World War, 1914-1918—Campaigns—
Western Front. 3. World War, 1914-1918—Armistices. I. Title.
   D530.C76 2015
   940.4'21—dc23   2015028404

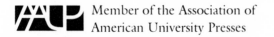

For Mark

It is wishful thinking to suppose that an historical memory can be transmitted without being simplified. The memory is already simplified before people decide that it needs to be transmitted.
—Clive James, *The Crystal Bucket*

Wars that shout in screams of anguish . . .
—Yes, "The Gates of Delirium"

Contents

Illustrations

Foreword

Of all the events in history, surely none has become more mythologized than the First World War, and within this narrative no single episode is more mythologized than the 1914 Christmas truce. Especially in Britain and America, the popular view of the meaning of the war is clear: it comprised the futile slaughter of an entire generation of innocent young men. Despite many recent scholarly attempts to dispel this myth, to which Crocker's must now be added, this view is remarkably persistent.

The centenary of the war is now upon us, and Christmas 2014 saw significant new interest in the truce and its meaning. Several books, many articles, and a controversial TV advertisement brought the truce to wider attention. Even the Football Association became involved, getting every school and every team in the United Kingdom to help commemorate the supposed match between British and German troops in No Man's Land.

Crocker's summation that "the Christmas truce . . . is now viewed as a moment of sanity in the midst of the brutal and senseless lunacy that the First World War comprised" and more specifically as "a soldiers' rebellion against the tragic waste of the war and the stupidity of the . . . politicians and generals" was confirmed, especially in the many comments by members of the public on various websites.

Yet this popular view is, as Crocker ably demonstrates, virtually without foundation. There was no "rebellion," no suggestion that the truce was anything more profound than a welcome break from appalling trench conditions and an opportunity to celebrate the holiday and bury the dead. Her book clarifies what happened, who took part, and what they thought but then goes on to do something far more innovative. The book charts the development of the myth from the events of 1914 through the interwar years and the crucial decade of the 1960s, and on to the present day.

This book marks a major contribution to both the literature on the war and our understanding of it. The scholarship is exemplary, the analysis entirely reasoned and consistent. It follows on from where other books on the First World War and cultural myth, such as Dan Todman's *The Great War: Myth and Memory,* leave off by taking a single myth and following its metamorphosis from event to legend. As such, it fills a major gap in the literature and should lead others to take up the many avenues it opens. It will therefore be of interest not just to historians of the Great War but to cultural historians and those interested in popular culture in general.

Popular myths are not in themselves wrong; they reveal very important aspects of the societies that adhere to them, but they are not history. To understand history, however, we also need to understand how these often deeply held myths formed and persisted. Terri Crocker's book does precisely that.

Peter Grant
City University London

1

"A Candle Lit in the Darkness"

The Christmas Truce and the First World War

> To fraternize was in itself an implicit condemnation of the war.
> —Remy Cazals, *Meetings in No Man's Land:*
> *Christmas 1914 and Fraternization in the Great War* (2007)

> The three Battalions in the line, like the rest of the British Army,
> met the enemy in No-man's-land; exchanged the "souveneer"
> so precious to the hearts of the Private Rifleman; smoked
> German cigars and gave "gaspers" in return; speculated with
> philosophically minded Teutons upon the futility of the whole
> thing, and upon the "rumness" of talking together today
> and killing each other tomorrow; passed Boxing Day in the
> traditional spirit of sentimentality; and resumed the war hammer
> and tongs on the 27th.
> —Reginald Berkeley, *The History of the Rifle Brigade*
> *in the War of 1914–1918* (1927)

"To die tomorrow," proclaims a German soldier in *Joyeux Noel* after the Christmas truce, "is even more absurd than dying yesterday." The 2004 film takes the futility of the First World War as its theme and uses the 1914 holiday armistice, the day when "enemies leave their weapons behind for one night as they band together in brotherhood and forget about the brutalities of war," to advance its theory that the soldiers who participated in the truce were rebelling against the senseless conflict in which they were engaged. *Joyeux Noel* begins with British, French, and German schoolchildren parroting their national attitudes toward their enemies; the British child recites,

"To rid the map of every trace / Of Germany and the Hun / We must exterminate that race." This early scene establishes the film's attitude toward the war: that all combatants were equally culpable for the conflict, and yet equally innocent, as they had clearly been indoctrinated by their governments to hate their enemies. The film then shows French and Scottish soldiers on the Western Front attacking a German trench in December 1914, an assault that results in many casualties but no gain of territory. Soon afterward, on Christmas Eve, the Germans place lit Christmas trees on their parapets, a soldier sings "Silent Night," and the men from all three countries walk hesitantly into the bomb-cratered area between the trenches. The German, French, and Scottish officers share a bottle of champagne and arrange for an evening's cease-fire. The lower ranks exchange drinks, cigarettes, and chocolate, and at midnight a Scottish priest leads them all in a Mass.[1]

On Christmas morning, the officers return to No Man's Land and coordinate the burial of the dead. After the bodies are interred and a service is read over the graves, fraternization resumes with a hastily arranged football match and card playing, and there is even a juggler entertaining the troops. The next morning Horstmayer, the German officer, walks over to the French line. The French officer, Audebert, protests that the truce is over, but the German has not come to extend the armistice. Horstmayer instead warns the French that they will shortly be shelled by German artillery, and he invites the French and Scottish soldiers to take shelter in the safety of the German trenches during the bombardment. Once the German shelling has ceased, the soldiers from all three armies congregate in the French trenches to avoid retaliatory shelling from the French artillery on the German lines. Afterward, the German soldiers return to their trenches on the other side of No Man's Land, while the three officers shake hands wistfully and a Scottish bagpiper plays "Auld Lang Syne."

After the truce ends, the narration shifts to military censors reading the letters that the soldiers have written home about the event, which also announce their intentions of continuing the armistice:

The Scots photographer promised us pictures at New Year's.
Be a chance to get back together.

We and the British decided to accept the Krauts' invitation.
We'll go spend New Year with them.

And above all, drink to the health of all those bastards who, sitting pretty, sent us here to slug it out.

Joyeux Noel then shows the official consequences of participation in the impromptu cease-fire. Audebert is chastised by a superior officer, who tells him that it was disgraceful for his unit to have been involved. "If public opinion hears of this—" the officer warns, at which point Audebert interrupts, "Have no fear, no one here will tell . . . because no one would believe or understand." Audebert also admits that he "felt closer to the Germans than to those who cry 'Kill the Krauts!' before their stuffed turkey!" His unit is then sent back into battle in a different part of the front lines. The Scottish battalion that participated in the truce is disbanded "by order of the King" and its soldiers scattered among other regiments. The Germans are reprimanded for their participation in the truce by their crown prince, who lectures the soldiers briefly on their insubordination before informing them that they are being sent to "East Prussia to take part in an offensive against the Russian Army." As punishment for their fraternization with the enemy, therefore, the Scottish battalion is dispersed, the French soldiers are returned to a brutal sector in the front line, and the Germans are dispatched to the Eastern Front.

Joyeux Noel's depiction of the Christmas truce will be familiar to many. As the reviews it received demonstrate, the film was accepted as an accurate representation of the famous day in 1914 when enemy troops fraternized on the Western Front. The *Times* observed that it was "inspired by the spontaneous ceasefire that occurred in the corpse-strewn no man's land between the trenches in northern France on Christmas Day, 1914." The *New York Times* noted that it "tells the true story of an improvised Christmas truce during the first year of World War I." While it may sound unbelievable, the BBC asserted, *Joyeux Noel* "is actually based on fact." Roger Ebert, the famous film critic, declared that the film's "sentimentality is muted by the thought that this moment of peace actually did take place, among men who were punished for it, and who mostly died soon enough afterward." Christian Carion, the film's director, stated that, although the characters presented in *Joyeux Noel* were fictional, "the detail is historically accurate."[2]

As recounted in *Joyeux Noel* and echoed in many other sources, the story of the Christmas truce is indeed a heart-warming tale—but one that bears little relation to the truth. There may have been British soldiers who rushed out to meet the Germans with peace and brotherhood in their hearts and mutiny on their minds, but for the vast majority of the troops involved, the reality was much different. The truce, which at the time it occurred was largely perceived as an interesting but unimportant event, was not an act of defiance but one that arose from the convergence of a number of factors: the professionalism of the soldiers involved, the unprecedented conditions of static trench warfare, the adaptation of the troops to their new environment, foul weather on the Western Front in the first winter of the war, the absence of major initiatives along that front during the last two weeks of December, and memories of traditional celebrations of Christmas. The holiday truce, in short, was caused by rain, mud, curiosity, lack of personal animosity toward the enemy, and homesickness rather than by frustration and rebellion.[3]

The actual armistice, however, does not have the narrative appeal of the Christmas truce as it is commonly portrayed in historical and fictional accounts. In the popular imagination, the holiday cease-fire, which appeared out of nowhere and ended just as quickly, has left behind the legend of a "candle lit in the darkness of Flanders" and a lingering collective memory of football matches, shared cigars, and camaraderie. In Britain the conventional story of the truce is well known: on 25 December 1914, the soldiers in the trenches, trapped in a pointless war and angry with both the politicians who had deceived them into enlisting and the incompetent generals who commanded them, were eager to show their opposition by defying their officers and consorting with the Germans. The military leaders, outraged by the willingness of their men to fraternize with the enemy, issued harsh orders commanding that the truce end, and the soldiers, now reluctant to fire on opposing troops, had to be coerced into resuming the war and were subsequently punished for their participation in the cease-fire. Some regiments that took part in the truce even had to be transferred to different parts of the line, or to other fronts altogether, as they refused to fight the men they now considered comrades. Soldiers, whose letters were censored, were forbidden to write home about the armistice, and press censorship, imposed by the government to keep civilians ignorant about the truth of the war, prevented the news of the truce from reaching the British public. In any case, the conspiracy that the press barons had willingly entered into with the authorities to promote the war made it impossible, even without government-imposed restrictions, for the newspapers to acknowledge the existence of the truce or the soldiers' attitudes that prompted it.[4]

According to the widely accepted narrative of the truce, since the episode was covered up at the time it occurred, only the soldiers who had been involved in it knew about the holiday cease-fire. The general public supposedly did not find out about it until decades later, when the truce was mentioned in the famous 1964 BBC documentary series, *The Great War*, and memorialized in the antiwar play and film *Oh! What a Lovely War*. As soon as the British became aware of the 1914 Christmas fraternization, the story of the truce and the desire for peace on the part of the soldiers involved that it symbolized became a vital part of the narrative of the war, as the number of books, newspaper articles, and websites devoted to it demonstrate. It has been the subject of television documentaries, plays, children's books, and an opera, *Silent Night*. The truce was mentioned in the last episode of the popular BBC television series *Blackadder Goes Forth,* a cross has been put up in Ploegsteert Wood to memorialize the spot where enemies met and fraternized in No Man's Land, and the centenary of the First World War was celebrated by recreating the truce's most famous feature, "the football match played against German troops which remains one of the most poignant moments of the conflict." As a recent *Guardian* article claims, the story of the Christmas truce is one "that seems to gain in resonance and potency as the years go by."[5]

It is certainly true that the tale of the truce is one that has expanded throughout the years to encompass the changing narrative of the First World War, but as the holiday armistice has gained a cherished position in public memory, myths about it have overtaken its reality. Although the conventional narrative of the truce maintains that soldiers defied their officers to participate in it, this was rarely the case: in fact, Lieutenant Colonel Laurence Fisher-Rowe, commander of the 1st Grenadier Guards, wrote to his wife that the Germans "say they want the truce to go on till after New Year and I am sure I have no objection. A rest from bullets will be distinctly a change." No soldiers were punished for their participation in the 1914 armistice, and no troops refused to fire on their enemies afterward. The military diaries of the regiments involved often reported the truce openly, and numerous accounts of it were published in the British national press soon after it occurred. The truce remained a part of the public narrative of the First World War from the time the conflict ended through the early 1960s, when it was repackaged and repurposed by historians and others who were determined to advance a certain view of the war.[6]

In spite of the readily available information regarding the episode that demonstrates otherwise, the romanticized version of the Christmas truce, with its defiant soldiers, disapproving leadership, and ignorant home front, is one that has increasingly been pressed into the service of the conventional discourse of the First World War. That assessment of the 1914–1918 conflict that came into prominence during the 1960s and is embodied in the works of authors such as Alan Clark, A. J. P. Taylor, Paul Fussell, and John Keegan, is that it was a "stupid, tragic and futile" war. It is famous, first, for the enormous numbers of people who died in it. Gerard De Groot, for example, opens his history of the war with the stark observation that "nine million combatants and twelve million civilians died during the Great War." The sheer scale of the war's destruction and its unprecedented impact on the civilian populations involved greatly surpassed any previous conflicts, as Martin Gilbert notes when he adds the "mass murder of Armenians in 1915, and the influenza epidemic that began while the war was still being fought" to the butcher's bill.[7]

Of course, horrific as these totals are, the number of people killed by the war is not necessarily sufficient grounds on which to condemn it. The judgment of history, however, is that in spite of the millions who died fighting in it, the 1914–1918 war achieved nothing. "The First World War," John Keegan states unequivocally, "was a tragic and unnecessary conflict." The twin themes of tragedy and futility are present in most works about that war, ceaselessly underlining this view of the conflict and propagating the belief that the nations of Europe, through lack of foresight and with insufficient justification, had blundered into a war that they foolishly expected would be localized, short, and relatively easy to win. As Adam Gopnik sums up the attitudes of the countries involved, they went to war in 1914 because "the Germans thought that, more or less, it would be like 1870; the French thought that, with the help of the English, it *wouldn't* be like 1870; the English thought that it would be like a modernized 1814, a continental war with decisive interference by Britain's professional military; and the Russians thought that it couldn't be worse than just sitting there."[8]

The catalyzing event that prompted the British to get involved in the war, the violation of Belgian neutrality, is now perceived as an excuse rather than a reason, and the subsequent emphasis on the atrocities committed against that country by the Germans is also viewed cynically. In addition, many theorize that the British press deliberately published a number of outright lies about the behavior of the German army in Belgium and France in order to sway British public opinion in favor of the conflict and therefore assist with recruiting. Niall Ferguson argues that in Britain "the most commonly aired justification for the war was that it was necessary to defeat Prussian militarism and 'frightfulness,' exemplified by the atrocities perpetuated by the German army against Belgian civilians." John Simpson, the noted BBC reporter, agrees that the situation in Belgium was exploited by the British government, observing that on the basis of the "memory of 1870 . . . there was an expectation that when the Germans invaded Belgium and France they would behave savagely. It was this expectation which the British wartime propaganda services took advantage of."[9]

According to the conventional narrative, the series of miscalculations and pretexts that entangled Europe in the First World War paled in comparison to its sheer incompetence in fighting it. Military leaders on both sides, trained for and expecting a war of movement, proved unable to cope with the conditions of defense-oriented industrialized warfare. As a result, soldiers were slaughtered in the millions on the battlefields of the war simply because of the shortsightedness and callousness of the generals leading them, and those same generals were willing to endure enormous casualties rather than admit to incompetence. On the Western Front, Fussell asserts angrily, "even in the quietest times, some 7000 British men and officers were killed and wounded daily, just as a matter of course. 'Wastage,' the Staff called it."[10]

The battles of the First World War—of which the Somme and Passchendaele are by far the most infamous in British remembrance—are thought of today chiefly in terms of the ineffectual generals who caused the gratuitous death and destruction of the men involved. The combat on the Western Front, with its characteristically static nature, came to embody the typical soldier's experience in the war: endless spells of duty in horrific conditions, interrupted only by orders to "go over the top" and take part in yet another fruitless, and generally fatal, assault. The modern attitude toward the Western Front can be inferred from the titles of the books written about it, including *Eye-Deep in Hell: Trench Warfare in World War I* and *The Killing Grounds: The British Army, the Western Front and the Emergence of Modern Warfare, 1900–1918*. The time spent in the hell of the killing grounds took its toll on those involved, even if they survived the experience; Keegan, for example, notes that the war not only "ended the lives of ten million beings," but also "tortured the emotional lives of millions more."[11]

One factor that contributed to the acceptance by the British public of the continued slaughter and mental torture of their soldiers on the Western Front was the ignorance of civilians about the conflict. "What actually happened," Cate Haste claims, "was that so little information was released that the home front was left in a state of bewilderment about the nature of the war." The public, however, had been made to believe in the war and therefore supported its continuance; as A. J. P. Taylor argued, "It was necessary to rouse public opinion in order to fight the war; and this opinion then made it essential to keep the war going." Because noncombatants, for the most part, did not come under attack, De Groot maintains that "a chasm of experience developed between the home front and the fighting front. Soldiers felt deep antagonism towards civilians who, they felt, could never understand the horrors of the trenches." The hostility that active troops felt not only toward civilians but also toward the military leaders who took great care never to expose themselves to hostile fire and the politicians who chose to sacrifice an entire generation in an unnecessary war only increased the soldiers' alienation from noncombatants and their subsequent disillusionment with the entire conflict.[12]

As a result, British society was divided, in Arthur Marwick's view, between the civilian on the one hand who was "aware of and almost inured to colossal slaughter, but oblivious to the real tortures, physical and mental, of trench warfare, and on the other the soldier who was enduring them." According to Simpson, however, this division was both necessary and deliberate, as "the horrors of frontline warfare were so great that if the newspapers had been free to describe them honestly, it would certainly have been harder to persuade men to come forward and join up in sufficient numbers." It was therefore "better, the politicians and the generals believed, to hide the truth from the British public, so that they would continue to support the war and encourage their sons to join the forces." In fact, as Brian Bond maintains, it was not necessary for politicians and generals to direct the press to hide the reality of war, as the newspapers were only too glad to take on that task themselves. "Censorship of the press was inconsistent and astonishingly lax," he notes, "but this hardly mattered given the press barons' conviction that newspapers had a duty to maintain civilian morale and support the army."[13]

Keith Robbins further contends that, because the truth about the war was hidden from the general public, many soldiers were later unable to talk about their memories of combat with their families and friends and were therefore prevented from coming to terms with what they had been through. He declares that the experiences of the war so traumatized the men who fought it that "no man who took part in the First World War ever completely shook off the experience. . . . For some, the only solution was silence. There was no way in which it was possible to communicate with those who had not been through it themselves." According to the modern narrative, there would be no survivors left to stifle the memories of their experiences in any case, as service in the First World War is now assumed to mean death in the First World War. As Simon Schama notes in his critique of *Downton Abbey*, if the series had been a realistic portrayal of British life during the war, Matthew Crawley, who was wounded during the Battle of the Somme, "would be one of the 750,000 dead." Although the vast majority of British soldiers who fought in the war survived it, Schama admits no other possibility for this fictional character: not "might be" dead, but "would be."[14]

Beyond the boundaries of the war itself, and the damage it caused to the lives and psyches of those who were involved in it, lay the aftermath of the conflict. Barbara Tuchman believed that "the war had many diverse results and one dominant one transcending all others: disillusion." Gilbert asserts that it "changed the map and destiny of Europe as much as it seared its skin and scarred its soul." A major truism of the history of modern Europe is that the First World War, and more particularly the treaty imposed on Germany after that war, was the proximate cause of the Second World War. "One of the tragedies of the Great War," Jay Winter and Blaine Baggett observe, "is that, despite all the suffering it had entailed, war simply begat another war." Gilbert holds the Treaty of Versailles, and particularly the clause in that treaty blaming Germany for the war, responsible for the renewed world conflict only twenty years later, maintaining that "the link between the two world wars . . . was this 'war guilt' clause as perceived by Germany, aggravated by her extremist politicians, and set up as a target to be shot down in flames and fury by Hitler." The final entry in the ledger against the First World War, therefore, is the way it led inevitably and inexorably to the Second World War.[15]

The generally accepted narrative of the Christmas truce as a soldiers' rebellion against the tragic waste of the war and the stupidity of the warring countries' politicians and generals aligns perfectly with this interpretation of the conflict. In fact, by emphasizing the disillusionment of soldiers with the war and the comradeship they felt during fraternization for the enemy troops, their fellow sufferers in the trenches, the holiday cease-fire underlines the moral of the war's orthodox narrative. As Peter Bradshaw inaccurately notes in the *Guardian* review of *Joyeux Noel*, the truce was "supposed to have begun not merely with carols but cries of 'No more war!'" This typical misconception about the impromptu armistice helps explain its overwhelming appeal to many who consider the First World War a futile and senseless conflict and who use the truce to illustrate that discourse by emphasizing the anger that the generals felt toward their rebellious soldiers who had fraternized with the enemy, and the subsequent official cover-up of the story of the truce.[16]

Fussell, for example, believes that the British military leadership was furious about the insubordination of the men participating in the truce, claiming that when "British and German soldiers observed an informal, ad hoc Christmas Day truce, meeting in No Man's Land to exchange cigarets and to take snapshots," the army command was "outraged" and "forbad this ever to happen again." Taylor took the same view, adding an element of irony by including the reaction of the ignorant home front to the event when he observed that "on Christmas Day in France firing stopped in the front line. British and German soldiers met in No Man's Land, gossiped, exchanged cigarettes. In some places they played football. They met again the next day. Then, after strong rebuke from headquarters, firing gradually started again. In the churches at home, prayers were offered for victory and for the slaughter of the men who were exchanging cigarettes." Winter and Baggett share the opinion that the truce was viewed as threatening by the army command and claim that "British generals were appalled at the news of the Christmas truce. Explicit orders threatened serious punishment should any similar incident ever happen again."[17]

Others endow the episode with even greater significance. Malcolm Brown and Shirley Seaton, in *Christmas Truce*, a popular rather than academic history, maintain that the truce is an event of continuing importance and "can be now seen as a small but significant gesture against the tide of international and nationalist rivalry and hatred which was flowing strongly in 1914 and flows strongly—and no less dangerously—as the century moves towards its close." In *Silent Night*, another work devoted to the holiday armistice, Stanley Weintraub argues that the significance of the truce goes far beyond its temporal boundaries; he asserts that "Christmas 1914 evokes the stubborn humanity within us, and suggests an unrealized potential to burst its seams and rewrite a century."[18]

The Christmas truce, therefore, is now viewed as a moment of sanity in the midst of the brutal and senseless lunacy that the First World War comprised. The orthodox narrative of the First World War, which this view of the 1914 holiday armistice underscores, argues that the war killed enormous numbers of people but achieved nothing, that it was caused by an irrelevant assassination in the Balkans, that the violation of Belgian neutrality merely provided British politicians with a convenient excuse to get involved in the conflict, that the stories about German atrocities in Belgium were invented to incite hatred against the enemy, that the war was incompetently fought, that the civilians of the combatant nations blindly supported the war with no idea of its realities, that the few soldiers who survived the conflict were forever haunted by the horrors of the war that festered in their repressed memories, and that the First War World was the proximate cause of the Second World War. To those who subscribe to the conventional narrative of the conflict, the Christmas truce represents a golden opportunity lost: a moment when the two sides met up in No Man's Land in a spirit of peace and fellowship, and the war's madness might have been stopped.

More recently, however, the generally accepted discourse of the First World War, into which this version of the truce fits so cozily, has been challenged. Adrian Gregory, Niall Ferguson, Daniel Todman, John Terraine, and Gary Sheffield, among other modern historians, have examined many of the orthodoxies of the First World War narrative and argue for a more nuanced view of the conflict. Gregory believes, for example, that the more clear-cut goals of the Second World War contributed to the perception that the 1914–1918 conflict was futile. "Both morality and long-term self-interest," he observes, "appear to argue that Britain was right to go to war against Nazism in 1939," but he notes that it is important to remember that the British public "believed precisely the same thing about the Kaiser's Germany." Although current conventional wisdom may maintain that this was a delusion, Gregory argues that the war "was not fought in retrospect and to understand it we must stop re-fighting it that way." Sheffield agrees, stating categorically that, while the war was tragic, "it was neither futile nor meaningless. Just as in the struggles against Napoleon and, later, Hitler, it was a war that Britain had to fight and had to win."[19]

John Horne, the editor of *A Companion to World War I*, claims that the expectations raised by the conflict's magnitude inspired its reputation for futility, observing that "the scale of the effort and the size of the sacrifice inclined many who fought in the war to believe while it lasted that such an experience must have a decisive result, a closure that would be worthy of the conflict." Owing, however, "to the gulf between cause and effect, and to the ways in which it set in motion more than it resolved . . . popular perceptions and official memory have likewise reflected the divisive legacies of the conflict." Terraine advances a more sanguine view of the war, believing that, for Britain, preventing German domination of the Continent was the primary goal of the war, which meant that the country's "victory lay in what had been averted, not in what had been achieved."[20]

Equally, many scoff at the notion that the war was sparked by the assassination of Archduke Ferdinand and his wife, seeing their deaths at the hands of a Serbian nationalist as merely the excuse Austro-Hungary and Germany seized on to begin the desired conflict. *Blackadder Goes Forth* highlights the irrelevance of the actual event in the following exchange between two soldiers:

> PRIVATE BALDRICK: I heard it started when some fella called
>   Archie Duke shot an ostrich 'cos he was hungry.
> CAPTAIN BLACKADDER: I think you mean that it started when
>   the Arch-Duke of Austro-Hungary got shot.
> PRIVATE BALDRICK: No, there was definitely an ostrich involved.

Gopnik observes that the only person who seemed genuinely concerned about the deaths of the Austrian royals, whom he describes as "notably unmourned," was the kaiser, "who had a class interest in protecting Germanic royalty from Slavic terrorists." On the subject of why the British in particular chose to get involved in the First World War, Marwick looks past the German invasion of Belgium to "the growing awareness in Britain that her world economic position was steadily being challenged by Germany [and] the conviction that any German aggrandizement on the European continent would fatally upset the balance of power." Todman agrees, observing that "British ministers in 1914 went to war to maintain the balance of power in Europe," and arguing that it "was in Britain's best interests then, as it had been for centuries, to prevent a single hegemonic power dominating the whole mainland of Europe."[21]

Additionally, many historians now maintain that the outrage over purported German brutality toward the Belgian population was in fact prompted by the existence of real atrocities in that country. Although some of the more inflammatory stories about German soldiers chopping off the hands of children, raping nuns, and tying priests to bell clappers were discredited almost as soon as the war was over, it has been noted lately that a number of the press reports written about German behavior in Belgium were accurate in their descriptions of German soldiers killing noncombatants, including women and children, on flimsy military pretexts and behaving savagely toward the civilian population generally. Gregory observes that the German soldiers in Belgium engaged in both "cold-blooded executions of large numbers of hostages and more spontaneous massacres carried out by units that went on the rampage." Todman contends that German actions against Belgian civilians "were not just the actions of soldiers out of control of their officers: German atrocities were a matter of policy, not just panic."[22]

The idea that the war was incompetently fought is one that has also come under attack in recent historiography. Terraine, for example, protests that too many people think about Douglas Haig in terms of the "grim casualty list" of the battles of the Somme, Ypres, and Passchendaele. Instead, he argues, "what *is* exceptional about Haig is the hundred days of uninterrupted victory by which he did so much to bring the War to an end." Gopnik agrees, observing that recent accounts of the war "conclude that the generals did the best they could" and maintaining that if "a steering committee of Grant, Montgomery, Napoleon, and Agamemnon had been convened to lead the allies, the result would have been about the same." Horne notes that, although the current understanding of the war has "moved decisively" in the direction of a narrative of horror and disproportionate suffering, military historians have emphasized "the 'learning curve' of the British army which, they suggest, achieved one of the finest performances ever on the western front in the last three months of the war."[23]

The view that service on the Western Front consisted of nothing but suffering and death is also one that is, to a certain extent, a creation of modern attitudes. Although no one would deny the horrific number of fatalities that occurred on that front, as well as the misery caused by the conditions of trench warfare, it is important to remember that this was not the overall or even dominant experience of every man involved. One First World War veteran estimated that, while serving with an infantry battalion in France, a soldier would spend approximately one hundred days during a year in the front line, and although sniping and shelling remained almost a daily fact of life in the trenches, actual attacks would occur only a few times a year. The rest of the time was spent in reserve trenches, in billets, in training out of the line, and on leave. This does not mean that time serving in the lines was in any way easy, but the troops passed the majority of their time away from the front, a fact that makes the usual image of soldiers living for the entire four years in the unrelieved mud and misery of the trenches inaccurate.[24]

The famous poetry of the First World War, however, with its stress on the horrors of the front unmitigated by spells out of the line, has influenced the collective British memory of the conflict and shaped its perception of the lives of soldiers who served in it. Samuel Hynes, in *A War Imagined: The First World War and English Culture,* examines literature written during and after the war and traces the myths that dominate the literary narrative of the conflict: the idiotic generals and uncaring politicians sacrificing the brave and idealistic young soldiers who went off so gallantly to the trenches, to be slaughtered there by the millions. Many other historians maintain that the emphasis in British school curricula on the poetry of writer-soldiers, such as Wilfred Owen, Siegfried Sassoon, and Robert Graves, encourages students to believe that this body of literature represents the "truth" of the conflict rather than the specific reactions of a group of nonprofessional junior soldiers to their experiences of battle. As Emma Hanna notes, "In Britain, the idea that the First World War can be understood through its literature has proved particularly enduring. . . . British historians, although they have produced an enormous body of very good work, have had a negligible effect on the way the majority of the nation thinks about the war." Hew Strachan advances a similar argument, observing that the "legacy of literature, and its effects on the shaping of memory, have proved far more influential than economic or political realities."[25]

Other modern portrayals of the war have also influenced the way it is perceived. Lyn Macdonald's popular and compelling books about the First World War use extensive personal narratives to focus on the miseries of the trenches, the high death toll, and the surviving soldiers' subsequent disillusionment with the conflict, and therefore, according to Ferguson, tend "to endorse the idea that the war was sheer hell and the soldiers its victims." In fact, Gregory believes that "it is reasonable to suggest that many working-class men in the armed forces found their experiences less unusual and shocking than might be expected."

It can be argued that it was the very qualities such as patience and a sense of responsibility toward the men with whom they fought that enabled soldiers to survive four years of regular spells of trench warfare, conditioned their postwar attitudes and prompted them to retain a belief in the war for which so many had paid a high price. Gary Sheffield agrees, countering the suggestion that soldiers were disillusioned by their experiences with the observation that "many who fought in the war did not hold the view that it was futile, and maintained their pride in their achievements to the end of their days."[26]

The ignorance of civilians about the horrors of the war, which springs from the belief that press reports during the war consisted of nothing but propaganda and lies, is another First World War truism that has been lately revisited. Horne, for example, notes that neither censorship nor propaganda "was as powerful as was made out by . . . [an] interwar myth, according to which governments and the press deliberately manipulated opinion with mendacious tales." To demonstrate that the public received more information about the war and its associated terrors than is currently acknowledged, Ferguson includes in his work a photograph of a German corpse on barbed wire, which he notes was taken by an accredited press photographer and "reproduced for use in stereoscopic viewers. The horror of war," Ferguson infers, "was concealed less from the public than is sometimes thought." While Gregory does believe that soldiers had trouble expressing the truth about their experiences at the front, he nevertheless concludes that "they tried to recount conditions far more than is sometimes realized, and were listened to by their friends and relatives, much more so than is usually acknowledged."[27]

Finally, the contention that the First World War was the proximate cause of the Second World War has also received considerable attention from revisionist historians. Ferguson, for example, argues that the terms of the Treaty of Versailles did not cripple the German economy or leave its population open to the appeal of fascism: "The reality," he maintains, "was that the economic consequences of the Versailles Treaty were far less severe for Germany than the Germans and Keynes claimed." In fact, Ferguson asserts, the German economy was wrecked by bad economic policies, not reparations. Todman concedes that there were issues with postwar settlements and the Treaty of Versailles but believes that these issues should not retroactively deny the war its meaning. The fact that the treaty was flawed, he observes, does not mean "that the war that preceded it was futile. The First World War stopped the German threat that had erupted in 1914. Perhaps that was enough. The Britons who had gone to war in 1914–18 had achieved their objective."[28]

The existence of blogs with titles such as "Fighting the Myths of the First World War" demonstrates that resistance to the generally accepted narrative has become a battle of its own, pitting the forces of orthodoxy against the insurgency of revisionism. As Todman points out in *The Great War: Myth and Memory*, however, these onslaughts on the conventional discourse have not "made the slightest difference to what most people actually believe." The surprisingly persistent myths that dominate the popular conception of the war have been the focus of many scholars who have tried to elucidate the reasons for the "stupidity plus tragedy equals futility" view of the conflict. Some historians believe this interpretation can be traced to attitudes toward the war prevalent in the 1920s. Nicoletta Gullace, for example, argues that scholarship between the two world wars "subordinated itself to the overriding imperative of turning World War I into a morality tale" with the aim of avoiding future wars by labeling the late conflict the creation of government, press, and commercial lies, and therefore futile and unnecessary. "The moral and ethical imperatives of this interpretation," she observes, "have made it unusually difficult to dislodge." Michael Neiberg, like Gullace, places the narrative shift in the interwar period but provides an alternative explanation. Neiberg contends that the belief that the war, which had been a disaster for all of Europe, should never have happened "built up steam in the comparatively co-operative and pacific atmosphere of the mid-1920s because it moved blame away from Germany in the hopes of creating future peace."[29]

Other scholars situate the attitudinal shift against the First World War in the 1960s. Emma Hanna notes that during that decade, the Second World War became perceived "as a 'good' war, with a relatively low number of casualties, while the memory of 1914–18 was reduced to images of mud, blood and cemeteries." Adrian Gregory similarly credits the changing attitudes toward the First World War to the memory of the second conflict, claiming that in its aftermath the earlier war became "an apocalyptic fall from grace, at best, the definitive *bad* war." Todman, in addition, believes that, during the 1960s and after, the passing of the generations most hurt by the First World War's deaths, the parents, siblings, and wives of soldiers killed and wounded in battle, freed critics of the war from the need to respect the feelings of the bereaved, which therefore allowed a more unfavorable view of the conflict and its aftermath to surface.[30]

Janet Watson sees the narrative shift as more thematic, arguing that the emphasis on trench warfare as the essential experience of the First World War has strongly conditioned its discourse. As a result, the "received history of the war starts with idealistic volunteers and ends with shattered veterans and names carved in stone on memorials." Although all these factors certainly contributed to the First World War's reputation for futility and tragedy, this book will argue that an even more important factor in the construction of the conventional narrative is the fact that a new world war broke out so soon after the first one had ended. The necessity for another global conflict only twenty years later is the most telling argument that, for whatever reasons the First World War was fought, the conflict solved nothing, and the soldiers who died fighting it gave their lives in vain. The national commitment to this interpretation is demonstrated by John Simpson in his work on twentieth-century British journalism, in which he confidently asserts that every appalling event of both the twentieth and twenty-first centuries can be credited not only to the First World War, but, more precisely, to the purported cause of the conflict. The murders of the archduke and his consort, he argues, led

> not just to the start of the First World War five weeks later, but directly or indirectly to many of the most important events of the twentieth century: the Russian revolution, the rise of Stalin's Communism and Hitler's Nazism, the Second World War, the Holocaust, the atomic bomb, the decline of Europe and its colonial empires, the Cold War, the seemingly endless conflict in the Middle East, the growth of militant Islam. If the Archduke's car had not taken a wrong turn and stalled, would any of these things have happened? Perhaps, but they would have happened differently. The balance of Europe could well have been maintained indefinitely, had it not been for one particular chain of events.[31]

As this passage demonstrates, though the orthodox narrative of the war has been continuously challenged by revisionist historians, and numerous myths about the conflict have been thoroughly dissected, British cultural memory remains fiercely loyal to the dominant First World War discourse of waste and futility.

Within these various challenges to the conventional discourse of the First World War, however, the Christmas truce has not yet found its place in the revisionist narrative. If the truce can no longer be used to underline the moral of the war, does it continue to have any meaning? Without a privileged place in the orthodox view of the war, the event appears to become merely a day off for the soldiers involved and a temporary curiosity for the British public, and many historians challenging the war's orthodox narrative write about it in precisely those terms. This dismissive attitude, however, obscures the meaning that the 1914 truce had for those who had participated in it. As the letters, diaries, and memoirs of the soldiers involved demonstrate, the impromptu cease-fire was a significant moment for all those who were involved and remained a cherished memory for veterans long after the war was over. In addition, even within a more revisionist view of the war, the Christmas truce can still maintain an important role: as an episode that illuminates the attitudes of the soldiers who participated in it, including their belief that the conflict had meaning and purpose, their willingness to share information about their experiences with those at home, their adaptation to the conditions under which they fought, and the professionalism they brought to their service on the Western Front. Furthermore, the way the news of the Christmas truce was received by the home front illustrates that the British public was not, as is often argued today, protected from the truth about the war, but was instead aware of the realities of life at the front and what its soldiers had to endure in the trenches.

A new assessment of the 1914 Christmas truce demonstrates that the holiday cease-fire was neither "the only meaningful episode in the apocalypse," as Weintraub would have it, nor "relatively minor and inconsequential," as Neiberg argues. The armistice was an event of significance for those involved, even if its contemporaneous meaning was not the defiant moral that was imposed on it long afterward. The truce meant time off for weary soldiers, providing them with an opportunity to move about in the lines without fear of snipers, rebuild their trenches, and enjoy Christmas as best they could under the circumstances, as well as a chance to satisfy their curiosity about the enemy and write home about something besides the endless mud and shelling. The holiday cease-fire became a valued memory for the participants, as demonstrated by the way it was discussed in letters written by the soldiers, fondly recalled years later in interviews and memoirs describing their service, and featured in many regimental histories. "It will be a thing to remember all one's life," was how R. J. Armes, one truce participant, put it, and most of the men writing home about the impromptu armistice expressed similar sentiments, noting that they would always cherish the memory of the Christmas Day they had spent fraternizing with the enemy in No Man's Land. An examination of the accounts sent home by the soldiers who took part in the holiday cease-fire, as well as the reports of it that appeared in the war diaries of the participating regiments and subsequently in the same regiments' official histories, will refute the legends and fictions that have come to obscure the reality of the truce.[32]

In addition to its personal importance to those involved, the episode is significant for another reason, which is that attitudes toward the Christmas truce have tracked the evolving popular narrative of the war. Examining works written about the war and the way they deal with the truce illustrates how the discourse of the conflict has evolved since the firing stopped on 11 November 1918. In the century that has passed since it took place, the 1914 Christmas truce has been invoked by many as confirmation that their assessment of the war is accurate. The episode has been employed by a number of historians and writers who believe that their view of the conflict can be proven, or at the minimum highlighted, through reference to the impromptu armistice. In the 1960s the truce became and has since remained a historiographical touchstone for the conventional narrative of the First World War and an enticing shorthand for the view that the conflict was futile and senseless. As Emma Hanna has noted, the holiday armistice has proved to be "a historical soft spot," engaging emotions "which render the audience uncritical" and therefore much less likely to question the point that the truce is being used to prove.[33]

The myth of the 1914 armistice, like the conventional view of the war, has its roots in the "lions led by donkeys" interpretation of the First World War promoted so strongly in the 1960s, and the parallel discourses of the war and the truce demonstrate the power of an appealing and simplistic narrative to drive out the voices of dissent, even if in this case the "dissenting" voices are those of the original participants in the event. Now that more than a century has passed since the 1914 Christmas truce took place, it is past time for the opinions of soldiers who were involved in the cease-fire to be heard.

Joyeux Noel and other similar works use a romanticized Christmas truce to advance their view of the First World War as a futile conflict, but this book will instead engage with the reality of the 1914 holiday armistice as a means of challenging the popular perception of the war. Rather than reacting to the Christmas truce in the monolithic manner now embraced by historians who subscribe to the conventional view of the war, the soldiers who participated in it brought a range of feelings, from elation to suspicion, to the event. There were officers who joined in the truce and commanders who were willing to allow its temporary continuance. No one was punished for participation, and very few of those who took part allowed the event to alter their view of the war. The truce did include shared drinks and spontaneous games of football, but it also featured solemn burial parties and moments of treachery. Furthermore, the manner in which the details of the truce were accepted by the British public demonstrates that the home front was ignorant neither of the conditions on the Western Front nor the attitudes of the soldiers who served there. Consequently, the holiday armistice, in itself a fascinating and complex episode, also serves as a means of achieving further insight into the experiences and attitudes of soldiers on the Western Front, the views of the British public toward the war, and the way the discourse of the war has evolved over the past century. As a result, the 1914 Christmas truce, an event that at first glance appears to confirm the popular interpretation of the First World War, can be used to challenge that view and contribute to a more complete understanding of both the conflict and the development of the war's orthodox narrative.

2

"Absolute Hell"

The Western Front in 1914

It was almost impossible for a man to convey the reality of life
at the front to family or friends, even if social convention had
permitted such frank discussions.
> —Gary Sheffield, *War on the Western Front* (2007)

The firing died down and out of the darkness a great moan came.
People with their arms and legs off trying to crawl away; others
who could not move gasping out their last moments with the
cold night wind biting into their broken bodies and the lurid red
glare of a farm house showing up clumps of grey devils killed by
the men on my left further down. A weird awful scene; some of
them would raise themselves on one arm or crawl a little distance,
silhouetted as black as ink against the red glow of the fire.
> —Captain H. M. Dillon, 2nd Oxfordshire
> and Buckinghamshire Light Infantry,
> to his sister Kathleen, 24 October 1914

To understand what motivated British soldiers to become involved in
the Christmas truce, it is necessary first to examine their attitudes during the first year of the conflict and, in particular, one of the most persistent tropes of the First World War, which is the belief that men fighting
in it did not share the truth of their experiences with the home front.
This theory, coupled with the perception that the civilians in Great
Britain had absolutely no idea about the conditions in which their soldiers fought, including the mud, miseries, and dangers of the trenches,
colors the approach of many historians and other writers toward the
war and helps explain the conventional narrative of the holiday armistice. "What people at home had heard of the fighting man's war was
only a confused murmur," the historian Arthur Marwick wrote about
British noncombatants during the 1914–1918 conflict. "They knew

the statistics of death . . . but not the foul horror of it; they saw the glory, but not the sordid filth of trench life. Fighting men, appalled at the nature of the war in which they found themselves, were unable to convey the unbelievable substance." This narrative was heavily featured in First World War historiography during the 1960s but was by no means limited to that period. John Terraine similarly theorizes that "the inexhaustible patience and cheerfulness of the troops . . . cut them off from communication with their relatives," and Modris Eksteins also notes that "soldiers were inclined to hide the gruesome reality of the war from their loved ones at home." Even Dan Todman, otherwise adept at skewering First World War myths, maintains that, in addition to the restrictions imposed on the soldiers by army censorship, "more powerful was a self-censorship which was designed to protect those at home from the worries they might have experienced if they had known the dangers that their correspondents were facing."[1]

This theme runs through many works on the war. In *Eye-Deep in Hell: Trench Warfare in World War I*, John Ellis contends that "the men were always at pains to conceal the reality of what was happening from their loved ones" when writing letters home. Anthony Fletcher, in "Between the Lines," an article on communications between front-line soldiers and their friends and relations, concedes that "messages sent by British soldiers of the First World War to their loved ones back home have long been valued for what they tell us about daily life in the trenches," but he notes at the same time that "their authors were often at pains not to reveal too much of the horror they endured." Robert Graves, whose memoir, *Good-bye to All That*, greatly influenced the orthodox narrative of postwar veterans' disillusionment, sharply underlined the division between soldiers and their families when he described the emotions he felt upon returning home on leave. "England looked strange to us returned soldiers," he wrote in 1929. "We could not understand the war madness that ran about everywhere, looking for a pseudo-military outlet. The civilians talked a foreign language, and it was newspaper language. I found serious conversation with my parents all but impossible."[2]

Recent studies that have used soldiers' writings as the focus of their analysis have chipped away at this dominant narrative; however, the emphases of their work have prevented the myth of soldierly reticence from being completely exposed. Michael Roper's monograph on soldiers' strategies for emotional survival, which takes a psychoanalytic approach to their writings, seeks to "discern states of mind from the often oblique clues given in letters, diaries and memoirs." He describes the information found in their letters home as "opaque," which forces scholars "to read between the lines" to discern its meaning. Jessica Meyer, on the other hand, acknowledges in *Men of War: Masculinity and the First World War in Britain* that soldiers were more forthright in their letters home than is commonly believed, but her focus on manifestations of masculinity leads her to concentrate on the correspondence of soldiers who "manfully" attempted to reassure their families about their safety in preference to those who wrote openly about the experiences of battle.[3]

The British soldier suffering in the mud and danger of the trenches, therefore, is now assumed to have been writing home cheerfully mendacious letters assuring his relatives that he was warm, dry, and relatively safe, that he remained a patriotic supporter of the war in which he fought, and that he confidently expected that he and his fellow soldiers would thrash the cowardly Hun with the next big push. According to this narrative, the British civilian, safeguarded from the ghastly truth by his protective soldiers, as well as the government and press conspiracy to keep him ignorant of the war so he would continue to support it, was therefore able to give the conflict his wholehearted backing and by doing so prolong both the war and the agonies of those frontline soldiers. By creating the perception that the troops on the Western Front did not share their experiences with their friends and relations, which reticence in turn increased the soldiers' alienation from civilians and their disgust with the strong support for the war by noncombatants, the theory about the supposedly fraught relationship between the home and fighting fronts has strongly influenced the war's discourse and has indirectly provided a convincing rationale for the generally accepted narrative of the Christmas truce. If in fact, as John Morrow argues, "front soldiers' writings reflected a stark division between the fighting and home fronts and their anger and hostility toward the latter," it is only natural that the British troops, when presented with an opportunity to do so by the convenient excuse of holiday celebrations, would have turned to their brothers-in-arms in the opposite trenches, who were the only ones who understood the miseries with which they had to deal daily.[4]

An examination of letters written home by British soldiers during the first year of the war, including both those kept privately by the families who received them and those forwarded to nationally circulated newspapers for publication, however, shows that, at least in the first year of the war, this great divide between soldiers and civilians did not exist. The horrors of frontline warfare were exposed from the moment the guns started firing, and soldiers freely shared information about the war with their families and friends, writing letters about the dangers of battle, the ghastly trenches, and their attitudes toward their enemies. In addition, soldiers' letters openly discussing the conditions at the front were published in nationally circulated British newspapers. Men serving on the Western Front were surprisingly forthright about the war and the conditions under which they fought, and, as censorship of letters home appears to have been minimal, those attitudes were communicated freely. In a 1985 interview, George Ashurst, who served with the 2nd Lancashire Fusiliers, dismissed the idea that there was any military suppression of news in letters written home by soldiers. "We give 'em to the officer," he said, "but I don't think he bothered any further. You had to give it to the officer, you know, your letter . . . he didn't bother to look at them, no." Of course, officers' letters were subject only to self-censorship and were quite frank as a result. Because of the flow of information from the battlefields of France to the home front, civilians were much better informed about the conditions of the war than the current narrative allows.[5]

In addition to these private sources of information, the British public as a whole was able to attain a certain level of understanding about the Western Front through its newspapers, which were not always as deceptive about the reality of war as is now believed. From the first days of the war, the surprising amount of information available to the home front through soldiers' letters published by the mainstream press, including stories not only about the horrors of the war but also about the occasionally friendly relations between the opposing sides, helped give the British the sense that they understood what life in the front lines was like. The reports that were shared with the home front through these letters included information about the changing nature of war, the dangers of battle, the ghastly trenches, the proximity of the Germans, and soldiers' attitudes toward their enemies. By providing those back at home in Britain with vivid firsthand accounts of the lives of their soldiers in the trenches, the press conditioned the public to accept the stories of those who served on the Western Front as the "truth" of the war, paving the way for general acceptance of the seemingly incredible story of the truce.

By the time the truce occurred, the war was nearly five months old. One of the many tropes of the conventional narrative of the First

World War is that everyone expected it to be over quickly. Though this assertion is not altogether correct, what no one involved predicted was that it would be a war of stalemate rather than mobility; the stationary trenches of the Western Front, although not a new development in modern warfare, were one obstacle that the military leadership on both sides struggled to overcome. For almost four years every new offensive, whether undertaken by the Entente or the Central Powers, was supposed to produce the breakthrough that would decide the conflict, but for four years those offensives failed, at the cost of millions of lives over the course of the war. Generals were trained in, and trained their troops for, wars of movement, and the conditions of static warfare were a reality to which both military leaders and common soldiers had to adapt. "It's a war with no glamour or glory such as one expects in a huge world-wide show like this," John Liddell, who served on the Western Front with the 2nd Argyll and Sutherland Highlanders, wrote home to his father. "Modern weapons are too deadly, and the whole art of war, and all tactics as laid down in our books, and in the German dittoes, has been quite altered. No advancing across the open by short rushes." Liddell, like many other soldiers, found his expectations of war confounded by the enforced shift from standard offensive campaigns to tactics that favored the defense. No one knew in 1914 that the stalemate on the Western Front would continue for four long years, but soldiers nevertheless quickly became aware that war, as everyone previously understood it, had changed dramatically.[6]

In addition to the restrictions imposed by a static war, men also had to adjust to the conditions they found at the front. Unfortunately, as the historian Charles Cruttwell pointed out, those conditions were dreadful: the trenches "had not been deliberately sited; they were more often an elaboration of the holes into which the combatants had dug themselves when unable to advance." As a result of their haphazard placement, the trenches were generally hastily constructed, situated in muddy and flat areas, prone to flooding, and always uncomfortable. In fact, the soldiers serving on the Western Front often found the Flanders mud to be as persistent an enemy as the Germans, and that mud and its attendant discomforts featured largely in soldiers' letters home.[7]

"I have been up to my knees and over them at times in this horrible cold mud—the awful part is having to stand there until the frost comes and binds all together into one congealed mass," Tom Lucey, of the 1st Loyal North Lancashires, wrote to his mother. Arthur Pelham-Burn, with the 6th Gordon Highlanders, echoed that assessment, remarking in a letter to England: "I used to think I knew what mud was before I came out here but I was quite mistaken. The mud here varies from 6 in. to 3 and 4 ft. even 5 ft. and it is so sticky that until we were all issued with boots, half my men used to arrive in the trenches with bare feet." Lieutenant Edward Berryman, who served with a Garhwali regiment, described the physical effect of living in such conditions, observing how "after standing in water and mud" for days, "you can't imagine the state your feet get into, soft and swollen and no good for walking on, just good enough to stand upon and no more." In fact, he even provided a drawing to help his correspondent understand the miseries of the trenches. (See figure 1.) Similar vivid portrayals of the physical discomforts of the front featured prominently in the letters written home by many soldiers and left their friends and relations in no doubt about the conditions in which they were living.[8]

Far from protecting those at home from the horrors of the trenches, soldiers instead kept their correspondents very well informed about their daily experiences, including the dangers to which they were exposed. Frank Black, an officer with the 1st Royal Warwickshires, wrote to a friend in early December 1914 that his unit was "having an easier time now, spending four days in the trenches and four days out." This "easier" time, however, consisted of trying to hold "a very warm corner" where "shots are flying up the trenches, down the trenches and across them all day, and most of the night; and all of us except the sentries sit tight in our dug-outs all day, and only venture out when it is absolutely necessary." Captain Harry Dillon, who served in Flanders with the 2nd Oxfordshire and Buckinghamshire Light Infantry, sent his sister grim details of an attack on the Germans: though first taken by surprise, the enemy "must have seen us as from then on it was absolute hell let loose, one could not move a finger and the opposite bank was plastered with shell and shrapnel. One high explosive burst right above where I was and the 2 poor devils on my right got a piece of it between them. It tore the flesh clean away from the bone of one of their legs, and there was a piece of bone 6 inches long with the flesh hanging over the heel." E. Daniell, a major with the 2nd Royal Irish Rifles, told his mother at the end of September 1914 that his battalion had "not had a day's repose since we started the campaign; previous to this it has been march, fight, hell-fire from shells continuously." Pelham-Burn also noted in a letter written home that the "hardships to be suffered in the trenches are really quite beyond anything I could have imagined while still in

Figure 1. A soldier leaving for and returning from the trenches. Drawing by E. R. P. Berryman, 2/39th Garhwal Rifles. (Used by permission of Tamsin Baccus.)

England. The cold, the wet, the mud, are awful, also the frequent lack of water means continual risking of life."[9]

Percy Jones, with the 1/16th Queen's Westminster Rifles, described the trenches in a letter to his brother as "a wet hell." Wilbert Spencer of the 2nd Wiltshires agreed, writing to his mother that he wondered "how many people realize what Hell the trenches can be. No shelter from rain or cold and in some places mud right over one's knees nearly always over one's ankles." Lieutenant John Aiden Liddell reported in a letter to his mother that the soldiers heard gruesome stories about "trenches where both sides have sapped forward until they are about 20 yards from each other." He explained that because "the ground is full of dead bodies . . . when the walls of a dug-out or part of the trench falls in, there is generally a body exposed." Liddell ended his macabre tale with the information that a soldier "wanted to cut some ends of roots that were sticking out of his dug-out wall, and discovered they were a corpse's fingers!" Even the most shocking details about the horrors of active service in the line, it appears, were considered appropriate subjects for inclusion in letters home.[10]

At the same time that these gruesome depictions of the war were keeping the soldiers' correspondents well informed about conditions at the front, the men also wrote home about the enemy whose trenches were so close to their own. The fiancée of Maurice Mascall, who served in the Royal Garrison Artillery, must have been concerned to receive a letter from him stating matter-of-factly that he was "in trenches at the edge of a large wood, with the German trenches only about 70 yards distant." Captain Dillon reported to his sister that in his battalion's position, "the German trenches were 25 yds in front of us, i.e. about the length of a tennis court," although he did add the reassuring fact that between the two lines was "a fairly thick wood." Captain Lucey wrote to his brother that his battalion's place at the front was "slap up against the Germans," noting that "in some cases only 30 yards separates the two lines and we chuck bombs at one another." As alarming as these descriptions of the nearness of the enemy must have been to those at home, it should also be noted that the proximity of the trenches of the British and Germans had an unexpected result for both armies: that of a better acquaintance with the soldiers in the opposing trenches.[11]

Soldiers, even in the early days of the war, became used to their places in the line; as both armies on the Western Front dug in for the long haul, they could not avoid growing familiar with the troops opposite them. Under these conditions, whatever the men in the front lines felt about the enemy as a political entity, they recognized that the soldiers whose trenches they were facing, and whose daily activities not only mirrored theirs but could also be observed, were enduring the same discomforts and fears as they were. As a result, the two sides developed, in addition to a certain amount of familiarity with each other, a surprising level of acceptance, considering the natural antipathy that must have been felt as a result of the terrible death toll of the first months of the war.

Contributing to this atmosphere of mutual tolerance was the fact that almost all the men in the trenches in winter 1914 on both sides of the line were professionals, previously conscripted soldiers, or from reserve units, all of whom had enlisted in or been drafted into the army before the war. As a result, their service was generally motivated by reasons other than hatred of the opposing side, as opposed to the attitudes of at least some of the men who enlisted once the war had started. With its small all-volunteer army, Britain was initially able to send only a small number of men to France, in the form of the British Expeditionary Force (B.E.F.). Though both the Germans and French were subject to conscription, the armies who were sent to the front during the early winter of 1914 were composed mainly of men who were in service before the war began, as it took time to train and equip those who joined or were drafted at the beginning of the conflict. The British forces did receive supplements in the form of newly enlisted men throughout the late autumn and early winter, but those recruits were absorbed into already formed units; thus, the men who joined up early in the war served with career officers and soldiers, and the presence of newly recruited soldiers in a particular unit would therefore have been diluted.[12]

The fact that so many of the men, and particularly the officers, in the British front lines during the winter of 1914–1915 were prewar professionals contributed to the relative lack of personal enmity between the opposing lines of trenches at that time. The historian B. H. Liddell Hart, in particular, credited at least part of the tolerance that developed toward the enemy during the first winter of the war to the fact that the British Army, because of its professional character, was "relatively immune" to "the natural ferocity of war accentuated by a form of mob spirit which is developed by a 'nation in arms.'" As Robert Graves observed colloquially in a story about the Christmas truce, "'Regulars, you see, know the rules of war and don't worry their heads about politics or propaganda.'" This resistance to partisan hatred by the troops who fought on the Western Front in 1914 created more opportunities for the opposing sides to develop a respect for the professionalism of their enemies. An example of this was provided by Edgar Cox, an intelligence officer at General Headquarters, who wrote to his wife in September 1914 that "the Germans are making a splendid stand. They are wonderful soldiers." Such mutual esteem, even among the fierce battles and debilitating conditions of the trenches, informed the attitudes of the soldiers on both sides, and British troops, as a result, spoke in their letters home about the Germans in a way that made it clear to their families and friends that the enemy was not the stereotypical "fiendish Hun" of the more sensationalist British press.[13]

The professional soldier's resistance to "politics and propaganda" created more chances for the opposing sides to develop a respect for their enemies' positive qualities, leading Major Daniell to write to his mother about the consideration shown by the enemy to the British who were injured in battle, which he contrasted to anti-German propaganda. "All these stories of cruelty to our wounded are I think a pack of lies," he observed. "Our information is very reverse, because we have direct evidence repeatedly of the extreme kindness extended to our wounded." After one battle, he noted, the British had "to leave our wounded . . . and when our Dr. went out to bring them in he found they had been bandaged by the Germans, given them water and removed them to a comfortable place. Many of the Germans said you English treat our wounded well and we do the same for you." In fact, two postcards available to Commonwealth soldiers through the Daily Mirror Canadian Official Series show British soldiers "Dressing the Enemy's Wounds" and German troops carrying a stretcher with an injured British soldier, entitled "Fritz Is Glad to Bring in the Wounded," which demonstrate not only that such vital courtesies were performed by soldiers on both sides of the line, but that the public was equally well informed about them. (See figures 2 and 3; printed on the back of these postcards is the information that the photograph had been "passed by Censor.") Cuthbert Lawson, who served in an artillery unit, also praised the abilities of the enemy, telling his mother in October 1914 that the war "is going to last a jolly long time unless something unforeseen happens—the German army is a highly efficient fighting machine, and the German staff is very nearly perfect, and certainly the best in the world—they won't make any silly mistakes, and can only be decisively beaten by really superior numbers." Such

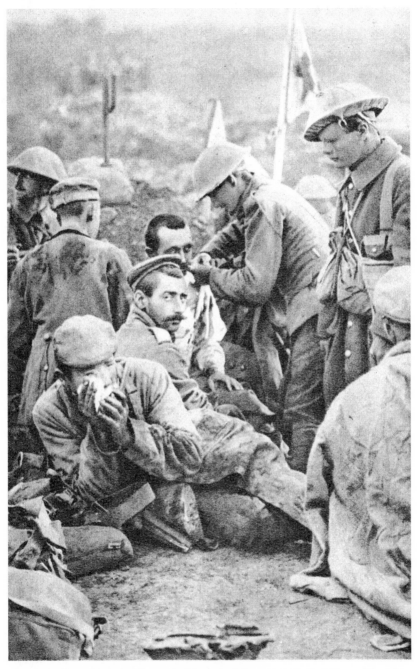

Figure 2. "Dressing the Enemy's Wounds." Postcard, Daily Mirror Canadian Official Series. (Courtesy of Mark Crocker.)

Figure 3. "Fritz Is Glad to Bring in the Wounded." Postcard, Daily Mirror Canadian Official Series. (Courtesy of Mark Crocker.)

observations reflected the way these professional soldiers viewed their enemies, and many of the British troops showed no hesitation about reporting these opinions to the civilians at home.[14]

Because of the proximity of the two lines of trenches, soldiers on both sides not only shared respect and common miseries, but also were able to appreciate mutual jokes and entertainment. Alfred Chater of the 2nd Gordon Highlanders, for example, reported in a letter how the British troops used a German's tin chimney as a target for rifle practice: "After each shot the German waved a stick or rang a bell according to whether we hit the chimney or not! There are lots of amusing incidents up there," he continued, "and altogether we have quite a cheery time our worst trouble is the wet and mud which is knee-deep in some places." Liddell also talked about friendly relations with the enemy, writing to his mother that he had heard about some British officers who "were reported to have made a practice of going over to the Germans' lines by day for a chat with the men, the latter warning them when one of their officers was approaching, and helping them over the parapet so that they could get back."[15]

Foreshadowing the carols on Christmas Eve that ushered in some truces, singing in the trenches often occurred on quiet evenings in the line, and both British and German troops enjoyed the impromptu performances. Michael Holroyd, a subaltern in the 1st Hampshires wrote about a battalion "who had a fine singer among them, whom both sides delighted to honour: so the Germans just shouted 'Half time, Wessex,' when desiring music, and everyone stopped firing. The songster climbed on the parapet of the trench, and both sides joined in the chorus." F. E. Packe, a company commander with the 2nd Welch, also reporting singing across No Man's Land, writing to his mother in October 1914 that some cheering from the German trenches "was followed by singing, the tune being the Austrian National Anthem—do they sing 'Deutschland Deutschland Uber Alles' to that tune I wonder? Our men responded with 'counter cheers' and sang 'Who Killed Cock Robin' and 'Down by the Old Bull and Bush'—so very characteristic of Atkins." As these excerpts demonstrate, the two armies certainly had the miseries of trench life in common, but jokes and music were also shared with the enemy—and, through the soldiers' letters, with the British home front.[16]

Besides noting the details of daily life on the Western Front, soldiers also wrote home occasionally about the larger topic of the war or, more explicitly, their perceptions of the conflict's rationale. Their thoughts on the war itself did not constitute a large portion of their letters: as Ashurst explained years later, soldiers did not tend to write about the conflict generally because "they really weren't interested in that, your parents, you know what I mean, they just wanted to know how you was." While the British troops were able to admire the Germans soldiers' professional abilities, they still felt anger over their behavior toward the Belgians. An examination of British soldiers' writings demonstrates that, contrary to modern cynicism about atrocity stories, many of them found the sufferings of Belgium sufficiently compelling, even without any propagandistic embellishments, to serve as a reason for fighting.[17]

As temporary residents of Belgium, the British troops were in a position not only to see the effects of the war on it, but also to tell their relatives and friends about what they had observed. Cox told his wife that although he tried to be tolerant toward the enemy, "since reading a German officer's diary yesterday, I feel I only want to get into Germany and raze everything to the ground and let their people feel the effects of the war to the very utmost limit. They are incredibly brutal and should be treated as they have treated the Belgians." Dillon, who was fatalistic about his eventually being wounded or killed during the war, felt that his sacrifice would be worthwhile: "I don't care one farthing as far as I am concerned," he wrote to his sister in October

1914, "but the whole thing is an outrage on civilization. The whole of this beautiful country devastated. Broken houses, broken bodies, blood, filth and ruin everywhere. Can any unending everlasting Hell fire for the Kaiser, his son and the party who cause this war repair the broken bodies and worse broken hearts which are being made." Lieutenant Chandler shared Dillon's sentiments, writing that, while he didn't know "which is the worst—high explosive shells, shrapnel or rifle bullets," what "upsets me most of all is the plight of the civilians and hearing the kiddies crying with fear. It is a strange and awful state of things." These statements, while firmly contradicting the idea that German atrocities in Belgium were concocted to provide fodder for the sensationalist press in Britain, demonstrate that British soldiers felt strongly that the war was worth fighting, and also that they believed that there were clear differences between the actions of the two sides, however much they might admire the professionalism of the troops opposite.[18]

As revealed by the letters that they wrote home from the Western Front, British soldiers found the conditions of the trenches and the defensive warfare they faced both horrific and challenging but were forthright about sharing with their correspondents details of their lives in the front line. As a result, those on the home front were able to receive information about the war from unimpeachable informants: the soldiers themselves. At the same time, if individual letters from the trenches were its only source of such information, the British public as a whole, particularly those households that did not have a near relation at the front, would have found itself largely ignorant about the war. An examination of British newspapers published during the first five months of the conflict, however, shows that they in fact revealed much more about the conditions on the Western Front and attitudes of the soldiers fighting there than the orthodox narrative customarily allows.

When discussing the way the First World War was reported in the British press, it must be remembered that access to the Western Front was strictly controlled by the military and that before the middle of 1915, there were no journalists at the front at all. As a result, the accounts of the war that the newspapers published during 1914 were based entirely on official briefings and therefore tended to run along the now familiar lines of how splendidly the Allies were fighting, and how easily the treacherous and brutal Germans were being beaten. A report in the *Daily Telegraph* on 12 December 1914, for example, flatly insisted that no other outcome was imaginable, except on a temporary basis. "A few days ago," the article began, "there was suddenly a rumor that a repulse had been met with, and this was rather a shock, considering that a repulse anywhere along the Franco-British front is, according to a foregone conclusion, impossible, and it was received, therefore, with incredulity." The report went on to state that this incredulity was "entirely justified, for the so-called repulse consisted simply of the loss of one advanced trench, which had been insufficiently guarded, and which the French immediately recaptured the following day, and to the success of which they added by capturing several other trenches in the same district from the enemy." Lest the *Telegraph*'s readers worry that there was more to this enemy assault than the French merely being caught temporarily off-guard, the paper went on to reassure them that this was just another example proving "that the Franco-British ascendancy is asserting itself more and more over the enemy, who may sometimes capture a trench, but is never able to hold it long, whereas the Allies thoroughly maintain themselves in every position conquered."[19]

If all the newspapers had to rely on were official sources, it is unlikely that their war reporting would have gone beyond these types of clichéd and misleading accounts. In an effort that was probably aimed at providing "human interest" for readers while simultaneously filling column inches about the main subject of the day, however, all the major daily newspapers regularly solicited and printed letters received from soldiers' families. Columns featuring this type of correspondence were not printed as prominently in the newspapers as the war news itself, but neither were they tucked away in small print on the back pages. Although not all these letters were completely forthright about the war—there were examples printed from soldiers who were anxious to get to the front before the conflict reached an untimely end, and missives that echoed such blithe phrases as "But are we downhearted? No!"—the majority of soldiers' writings included in the "Letters from the Front" columns presented sober and detailed descriptions of the realities of war. Through these letters, the British public was able to catch glimpses of the horrors of the conflict beyond the military's heavily censored and often fantastical accounts. A sampling from the "Letters from the Front" columns featured in all the major British newspapers demonstrates that this correspondence featured a remarkable amount of information, given the papers' commitment to self-censorship and the desire on the part of the British press to keep accounts of the war positive. It was in these columns of letters that the truth about the war, at least as far as soldiers' experiences of it, was told, and these same columns later provided the medium through which the details of the Christmas truce would be transmitted to the general British public.[20]

The "horrors of frontline warfare" that were supposed to be so carefully kept from the home front were in fact freely shared with the readers of the *Daily Mail,* who learned through a letter from an officer that "we do endure ghastly tortures in this war. The cold is perfectly appalling, however many clothes one wears, and I haven't slept for nearly a fortnight, so I am awfully tired and done up." The *Mail,* which was the British newspaper with the widest circulation at that time, published a letter in December 1914 under the headline "What Modern Shell Fire Is Like," from an officer with the Army Service Corps who described the troops coming out of the line. "The experiences in the trenches are sometimes so terrible that those who come out sound in body look absolutely indifferent to all their surroundings; they are always covered with mud from head to foot, clothes torn, tired out through lack of sleep and having in many cases seen half their pals killed or wounded alongside of them and in all cases having existed for days under a continuous shell fire," the officer reported. "This is the kind of thing all our fellows in the firing line are going through to keep the Germans back, and in many instances it is enough to send them out of their minds." The letter concluded with a bitter observation: "People say the Army is paid to do this job. No pay can ever compensate a man for a few days under modern shell fire."[21]

Another letter printed in the *Daily Mail* from a soldier in a West Yorkshire regiment described an attack on a British trench. "We were subjected to a murderous fire from machine guns and shrapnel, and our men fell like sheep in this terrible rush, and the few who arrived in the firing line found very few of the original line alive," Sergeant Woodcock's letter reported. "We had to get in the trench somehow, and in places dead, wounded, and living piled on top of each other." In case the *Mail's* readers failed to understand how badly the British troops suffered in this attack, the letter was printed under the headline "Letters from the Front / 204 Left Out of 1,250," a reference to the number of soldiers able to answer the battalion's roll call the next day. The *Mail* also printed many soldiers' letters that tried to sum up the entire experience of the conflict. Echoing Liddell's observations to his father, one staff officer wrote to his wife that "the war is absolutely different from what I expected it to be. There is no what I call glamour about it or any kind of chivalry." A letter written by a lieutenant in a Northamptonshire regiment to his mother summed up the experience of life on the Western Front even more succinctly: "It's awful," he wrote. "Nothing can describe it but the two words, 'absolute hell.'" His assessment was echoed by an officer from a Cheshire regiment: "If there is such a thing as hell on earth this must surely be it."[22]

Other newspapers provided equally honest views about the trenches in the letters they chose to print. In December 1914 the *Manchester Guardian*'s "Letters from the Front" column featured a letter from a sergeant in the Stalybridge Territorials that provided a frank assessment of the conditions at the front. "The trenches are awful," the sergeant wrote. "In some parts they are up to the waist in water and slush, and we were practically doubled up for 60 hours. The men were absolutely done when they were relieved." A captain in the East Kents presented a somber description of life at the front in the *Daily Telegraph*. "It is the poor devils in the trenches who get shelled day and night, who sit in mud, and seldom get a hot meal, and who then, disheartened and cold, are asked to run over a sea of mud under a hail of lead to capture another mud ditch," he wrote. "Depend upon it, in the present show the country's thanks and compassion should be to the sufferers in the trenches. Poor devils!"[23]

The *Times*'s "Letters from the Front" column also contained frank accounts of the horrors of the war. A letter from a "general officer," published in November 1914, talked about life in the trenches under fire, noting that his troops were "shot at all day and night by bullets and shells. The latter do far the most damage, but the bullets are particularly deadly, being all fired by picked marksmen, who lie in wait to pick off heads moving in the trenches." On the same day, the *Times* also printed a letter from an infantry officer who described a battle in which he had led some troops. The German heavy guns were trained on their trenches, and "more than once" the shells "buried whole sections of men in the earth of the parapet. Some of these took no harm, and we dug them out and used them again. Others died, being torn to fragments. Shrapnel killed others, and then as the infantry crept nearer rifle bullets made their mark." The letter went on to describe the confusion of battle, when at one point the British soldiers stopped firing at advancing Germans, with catastrophic results, because they believed the soldiers were British; how multiple messengers were sent to fetch reinforcements and killed in the attempt; and a final retreat after no support for the British troops was made available, owing to the prevalence of enemy fire and overall muddle. It seems incredible, in the face of such readily available public information, that historians can continue to argue that only "sanitized" reports of the war were presented by the British press to the public, when it is clear that civilians were frequently exposed to graphic accounts from soldiers serving on the Western Front.[24]

The *Times* also freely printed letters that praised the abilities of German soldiers and directly contradicted the information routinely found in the major British newspapers, including its own columns. One letter published in November 1914 came from a major in a Highland regiment. Bemoaning the slowness of recruiting, he blamed "the home papers tremendously for publishing articles saying the Germans cannot shoot straight, that they run away, that their armies are now composed of old men and boys, &c." The major also noted that "such things are not true, or, if they are, their old men and boys fight wonderfully well" and finished his account with the sobering prediction that the British were "up against a thundering good army, and it will take us all our time to break 'em." In the same edition of the *Times,* the officer who found life in the trenches so deadly remarked that he was "disgusted by the accounts I see in the papers of the inferiority of Germans as soldiers; don't believe one word of it. They are quite splendid in every way. Their courage, efficiency, organization, equipment and leading are all of the very best, and never were surpassed by any troops ever raised." A private from a Cheshire regiment, in a letter published in the *Manchester Guardian,* agreed with this assessment. "It is no use saying the Germans are a 'rotten lot' as fighters, because I think their artillery is very fine," he wrote. "German aeroplanes were on top of us, and found us out every time. They worked well, helping their troops and giving the guns the range."[25]

The British press also, rather astonishingly, printed some letters discussing friendly relations between the British and Germans in the trenches. The short distances between the opposing armies increased not only the danger of exposure to rifle fire, but also the opportunities to eavesdrop on the enemy. The *Daily Mail,* for example, published a letter from Private Rogan in the Seaforth Highlanders, who wrote that his unit was in trenches so close to the Germans "that we can hear them talking and sometimes singing." He also reported that they had a gramophone, which "must have broken down, for one of them shouted across to us in quite good English, 'Hey, you chaps, can any of you mend a gramophone? This one has got broken.'" One of the British soldiers even volunteered to fix it. "So you see," the soldier concluded, "we are on quite friendly terms with them." The *Daily Mail* also printed a letter from a major serving on the Western Front who recounted a story he had heard about two opposing regiments whose "trenches are only fifty yards apart." They "have established very friendly relations with one another," he claimed, and "hardly ever snipe at one another now, although they attack each other vigorously when they are required to do so."[26]

The *Manchester Guardian* also published letters describing friendly behavior between the two sides. A private in the King's Own Royal Lancasters wrote in a letter to his wife, published in December 1914, that a "German patrol shouted out to a party of our transport bringing rations to us, 'Halt, you fools; you are going right into the German trenches.'" The contrast between the German soldiers presented, through these letters, as capable of sharing a joke and establishing friendly relations with the British, or warning off a group that was headed into the wrong trenches, and the Germany that the same papers referred to as "a jack-booted Colossus seeking to stamp out the liberties of Europe" shows that the coverage of the war in the British press was not nearly as monolithic as is often believed; in fact, those newspapers did not hesitate to present the soldiers' point of view, with all its divergence from the official line, in the same editions as their censored and stereotypical accounts of the war.[27]

It is, therefore, not altogether surprising that the *Manchester Guardian* felt able to publish an editorial on 24 December 1914 that reflected on the approach of Christmas and the sad irony that the holiday, which "celebrates the coming into the world of the religion of peace," still "finds half the world at war." The editorial argued that any settlement of that war must include the defeated nations; therefore, blind hostility, "however natural and even justified the strongest hostility may be," would not give "the results we seek, and is not in place any more during the continuance of the struggle than it will be at the close. Nor is it necessary even as a condition of the hardest fighting. For in this we may take example by the conduct of our own troops." These troops, the *Guardian* contended, fight with "no fury" but rather with professionalism, endurance, military pride, and patriotism, and "coupled with this a great deal of good humour and respect for and even a kind of queer sense of comradeship with the soldier on the other side of the trenches who is enduring the same hardships and daring the same dangers with feelings and from motives largely similar to [their] own."[28]

The *Manchester Guardian*, it appears, had no qualms about admitting that British soldiers did not hate the dreaded Hun of newspaper clichés, but rather felt respect for, and even a certain kinship with, the enemy. In addition, the paper felt justified in setting before its readers an image of a peace that included the defeated powers. Of course, the *Manchester Guardian* was assuming that the Allies would win the war, but its argument at this time against the atmosphere of hatred and propaganda that characterized much of the British reporting on the conflict shows that there were newspapers, and therefore members of the public, who were able to view the war in a more balanced way. By echoing the attitudes toward the enemy expressed in letters written home by men serving in the trenches, the editorial demonstrates that the soldiers' views about the war were reaching British civilians.

Although the conventional narrative of the First World War emphasizes that soldiers were deceived into fighting it through deliberate propaganda and programmed blind hatred of the enemy, an examination of their letters shows they had a much more complex and nuanced view of the war and their German opponents. In addition, contrary to the orthodox view that the British public was kept entirely in the dark about the course of the war and the conditions under which its soldiers were fighting, even a cursory examination of the newspapers in 1914 demonstrates that information that provided a more accurate picture of the fighting conditions was readily available. In fact, papers such as the *Daily Mail*, the *Times*, and the *Manchester Guardian* had no compunctions about publishing letters and articles that discussed the falsity of atrocity reports, the respect the British troops felt for their German counterparts, and their occasional acts of friendliness toward the enemy.

The fact that realistic information about the Western Front was readily available to civilians has, however, had no discernible effect on the conventional narrative of the war, which continues almost uniformly to insist on a discourse composed of soldierly reserve and public obliviousness. The reasons for the claim by many scholars of the Great War that soldiers kept their experiences from their correspondents, and that those on the home front were unaware of their sufferings, can be credited to a view of the war that has caused the contemporaneous testimony of the soldiers who fought in it to be overlooked in favor of an insistence by the war's poets, memoirists, and historians on a more monolithic interpretation of the conflict. "And when they ask us, how dangerous it was / Oh, we'll never tell them, no, we'll never tell them," sang the soldiers in the 1969 film *Oh! What a Lovely War,* which helped reinforce the myth that the home front was protected from the facts of the conflict and the miseries their soldiers had to endure, a discourse that may, at least unconsciously, have been adopted by postwar civilians as a way to deflect criticism for their support of the war.[29]

Such views, however, are firmly contradicted by the available evidence. Even if the later inhabitants of the trenches on the Western Front, the volunteers of Kitchener's Army, were more circumspect about their experiences, and newspaper censorship became more prevalent later in the war, this was a bell that could not be unrung. Anyone with access to a British national newspaper during the first six months of the war—at a time when it could be argued that interest in the conflict was at its height—could not, with any amount of conviction, claim ignorance of the conditions on the Western Front. As a result of the forthright manner in which British soldiers wrote home about their experiences, and the extent to which the press was willing to circulate accounts from the front that ran counter to its stereotypical war reporting, the British public was in a better position to understand the truth of the war than someone who read only typical newspaper reports. By presenting the firsthand accounts of life on the Western Front to help the home front understand the circumstances under which their men lived, fought, and even died, the British press certified the authenticity of the soldiers' statements and prepared the public to accept a reality from the front lines that deviated from the official reports.

The Christmas truce, which can be understood only through an examination of the circumstances prevailing on the Western Front during the first five months of the war and the attitudes of the soldiers who served in the trenches during that time, grew out of those conditions. Although it is true that the impromptu cease-fire was, as is currently believed, a response by those soldiers to the war and the way it was fought, the nature of that reaction diverges sharply from the conventional view, firmly lodged in the public imagination since the 1960s, that the men involved perceived the war as futile and senseless. Instead, the truce was a consequence of the professional attitudes of the troops involved and the adaptation of the troops to a relatively new type of warfare that, at least initially, promoted an altered relationship with the enemy based on proximity and shared experiences. As the letters they sent home demonstrate, soldiers who were faced with a static military situation learned how to cope with the uncomfortable and dangerous conditions they found on the Western Front, and while doing so they developed a type of understanding with those who shared in the miseries of life in the front lines. Although their motivations for fighting did not change as a result of their increased familiarity with the enemy, the lack of personal animosity most British soldiers felt toward the German troops enabled them, while under the influence of the Christmas spirit, to approach the enemy with a surprising level of tolerance and understanding. The sense of shared experiences and mutual professionalism that contributed to the unofficial cease-fire was displayed by soldiers on the Western Front long before the truce occurred, and placing their participation in the truce within the context of those early war experiences helps explain its occurrence.

Because the home front was exposed to realistic portrayals of what its soldiers endured in the trenches and the way those troops viewed their enemies, the British public was better prepared for the news of the Christmas truce than would have been possible had it been less well informed about the war. As a result, the understanding that civilians attained in 1914 through reading letters and newspaper accounts about the conditions in which their soldiers were fighting and living, and the way that the same newspapers promoted the firsthand accounts of soldiers as the authentic voices of the war, contributed to the way the story of the truce would be presented by the soldiers involved and received by the British public.

3

"A Great Day with Our Enemies"

The Christmas Truce

> The impromptu truce seemed dangerously akin to the populist politics of the streets, the spontaneous movements that toppled tyrants and autocrats.
> —Stanley Weintraub, *Silent Night*

> Spent a very quiet Xmas day. Troops fraternized with enemy on 6th Div. front and held a concert and football match. Pork for dinner.
> —J. S. Fenton, 2nd Field Company Royal Engineers, diary entry for 26 December 1914

"But who would have guessed that, on December 25," the jacket copy of *Truce: The Day the Soldiers Stopped Fighting* asks rhetorically, "the troops would openly defy their commanding officers by stopping the fighting—and spontaneously celebrating Christmas with their 'enemies.'" Jim Murphy's 2009 children's book focuses on the motivations of the soldiers involved in the Christmas truce and takes a far different stance on the cause of the First World War from *Joyeux Noel*'s: while that film identified deliberately incubated nationalist hatreds as the source of the conflict, *Truce*, as a way of emphasizing the war's futility, also stresses how easily it could have been prevented. The book describes the First World War as "this calamitous conflict that could have been avoided," and the first chapter of the work, entitled "Those Stupid Kings and Emperors" after a quote from Winston Churchill, lists the putative reasons that the world went to war in 1914, apportioning blame among all the countries involved but focusing on the flimsiness of their motives: Germany fearful and jealous of other nations' dominance, Austria concerned about Serbia's growing power, France "tensed and anxious" while still nursing a grudge over the Franco-Prussian War, England nervous about Germany's naval fleet, and Russia worried about the prospect of a German invasion of Poland. In the shadow of every country's culpability, the war that did not have to happen began and almost immediately got bogged down in the trenches of the Western Front.[1]

Murphy contends that the barriers between the enemy troops began to break down in the early months of the war because of the physical proximity of the two armies fighting in France and Belgium. Germans and British soldiers "had been induced to fight in part because they'd been led to believe the enemy was inferior to them or a mindless monster," *Truce* argues, but under the conditions of prolonged trench warfare, the "more friendly contact they had with the enemy, the less anger they felt toward them." As a result, according to Murphy, on Christmas Eve, although commanders on both sides told the men to keep "on alert, hoping to discourage fraternization," such warnings were in vain. The desire on the part of the soldiers involved to defy their officers and implicitly condemn the war by celebrating Christmas with their enemies resulted in the Christmas truce that took place "all along the Western Front" on 25 December 1914. According to Murphy, the episode "demonstrated that the combatants were more alike than not." While it was only "a very small step toward peace on earth, a tiny bit of light in a vast and threatening darkness," the armistice, Murphy believes, still "offered reassurance and hope that a kinder, humane spirit could prevail amid the horrible brutality of war."[2]

The cease-fire presented in this book conforms to one of the main myths of the 1914 truce: that the troops who participated in the holiday armistice did so as a form of rebellion against a war they had come to see as a farce, and in fact deliberately disobeyed their leadership's commands so they could fraternize with the soldiers who, within just a few months of the war's starting, had been transformed by the conflict's futility from opponents into "enemies." *Truce*'s reception bears out the acceptance of this narrative: *Kirkus Reviews*, for example, observes that the book describes "that magical, spontaneous Christmas truce of 1914, when peace broke out all along the Western Front." In an interview after the publication of *Truce*, Jim Murphy emphasized the research he had undertaken while writing the book, noting that he would trace participants' names back to the original sources, "usually museums or military organizations in England, France, or Germany," thus suggesting that his view of the Christmas truce has a factual basis.[3]

The reality of the war and the holiday armistice, as attested to by the soldiers involved in it, however, varies widely from Murphy's simplistic and clichéd account. As already noted, the letters and diaries of British soldiers fighting in Flanders in 1914 demonstrate that they felt no blind hatred toward the enemy, and that while they found trench warfare dangerous and the conditions under which they fought horrific, they did not feel that they had been tricked into fighting the war or find it futile. Although the holiday armistice can indeed be attributed to a number of causes, including, as Murphy notes, a familiarity with the troops opposite and the short distances between the opposing trenches, he erroneously contends that the increased knowledge of the other side led to the unmasking of the myth that the enemy was an "inferior" being or a "mindless monster." In fact, in the first months of the war, any British or German soldiers who might have volunteered out of hatred toward the enemy were still back at home drilling and preparing for later battles. The soldiers in the trenches at Christmas 1914, both regular and territorial troops, were fighting because fighting, if their country was involved in a war, was the job for which they had signed up, and their letters reflected this professional attitude long before the truce began.

At the same time, the Christmas truce was not, as Murphy does admit, an unprecedented event. Although it did occur on a much larger scale than any armistices in previous wars had, military history shows that soldiers often established temporary cease-fires, particularly after battles, for the purpose of burying the dead or giving both sides a brief rest. There were cases of fraternization between the French and British soldiers during the Peninsular War of 1807–1818, truces arranged between French and Russians during the Crimean War, and a football match between Boer and British troops during the Second Boer War. Brown and Seaton, in their work on the truce, point out that localized cease-fires in wartime were common enough occurrences and cite examples from the Peninsular War, the American Civil War, the Boer War, and the Russo-Japanese War to prove their case. "So the Christmas truce of 1914," they concede, "does not stand alone," at the same time maintaining that "it is undoubtedly the greatest example of its kind."[4]

To speak of the Christmas truce so monolithically, however, is fundamentally to misunderstand the holiday armistice. The separate truces that occurred on 25 December 1914 and for a few days afterward were not prearranged, centrally coordinated, or consistent, but rather were composed of individually negotiated armistices, entered into at different times, ranging from early Christmas Eve through Christmas afternoon, and widely divergent in nature. As a result, they were really no different in intent or effect from the isolated friendly instances that had occurred both in previous wars and earlier in the First World War. Only the fact that so many battalions participated in separate truces on 25 December 1914 caused the collective cease-fires to be much more well known than any amicable episodes between opposing troops that had already taken place during the conflict. There had already been, for example, some instances of friendly British interactions with the Germans before the holiday season began. The 2nd Essex reported in its official battalion diary that on 11 December 1914, "Officers & men of A & B Co. meet Germans ½ way between the trenches." The diary further noted that the "Germans said they were fed up" and observed that their trenches were in the "same state" as the British ones, indicating that there was conversation between the two sides, and that some British soldiers got close enough to the German lines to note the conditions there. Closer to Christmas, the 2nd Queen's Royal West Surreys' diary recorded a "little armistice" on 19 December, the day after a bloody and unsuccessful British attack on the German trenches. "At daybreak Germans were seen beckoning to our men to come out and collect wounded and bury dead," the diary reported. "Several of our officers including the M.O. and 30 men went out. About 50 Germans and 10 German officers also came out." The Germans helped bury the British dead and collect the wounded, and the cease-fire ended only when a British gun started shelling the enemy trenches.[5]

While in terms of the numbers of soldiers on both sides who were involved in the holiday cease-fire, the description of the truce as "greatest" certainly applies, even those British soldiers who participated enthusiastically in the event had no idea that many others were doing the same on other parts of the front, which indicates that there was no overall coordination of the separate truces. J. Selby Grigg, for instance, described the armistice in which he was involved as "quite 'unofficial' and local," apparently believing as late as 27 December that it had been confined to his unit's area of the line only. As the historian Keith Robbins observes, "There was no single war shared by all who took part in it"; similarly, there was no single truce, and any attempt to impose a uniform interpretation, as Jim Murphy does, on the motivations of the troops who took part in the various armistices on Christmas 1914 on the Western Front is doomed to frustration by the actual experiences and reports of the soldiers involved.[6]

Interestingly, the idea of a truce for Christmas did not necessarily originate spontaneously in different areas on the Western Front, but was first suggested by Pope Benedict XV earlier in December 1914. His proposal that all combatant countries should cease warfare for the Christmas season as a precursor to searching for a peaceful solution to the conflict was not, as the *Times* delicately put it, "crowned with success," but the suggestion must surely have inspired at least some soldiers to create their own version on the ground. When Michael Holroyd, an officer with the 1st Hampshires, wrote to his parents describing his "very remarkable" Christmas, he noted that it included a "peace on earth that really happened, in spite of the Pope's failures," demonstrating that the pontiff's proposal was known by at least some soldiers serving on the Western Front.[7]

The Christmas truce, being driven by the specific situation existing on the front lines at the end of December 1914, including perhaps the seed planted by the pope's suggestion, owed both its existence and its grand scale to those circumstances. The attitudes toward the truce of the soldiers who participated in it reveal a great deal about their opinions on the war and the enemy, and the way they wrote about the temporary cease-fire, both in their diaries and in letters home, shows that their views of it were much more complex than the conventional narrative, as depicted in recent works such as *Truce* and *Joyeux Noel*, allows. Although it is true that some of those involved expressed regret that the truce would eventually come to an end and the war continue, these sentiments appear to have been motivated by distaste for being shot at rather than an expectation that the temporary cease-fire would result in any lasting peace. Even in the middle of the truce, none involved expected the episode to end the conflict—and few even expressed a hope that it would.

Even though many of the soldiers involved made the holiday armistice the main feature of their letters home on or immediately after Christmas or wrote at length about fraternization in the diaries they kept, they were clearly focusing more on the event's novelty value than on its significance. In a month when there was little besides mud and rain to discuss, the truce must have come as welcome fodder for the otherwise monotonous subjects covered in letters written by weary and homesick soldiers. Most important, although the British soldiers all described the truce as "weird" or "unbelievable" when writing home about it, they apparently felt no need to apologize for or explain away their participation in the event. The lack of excuses or justifications offered for fraternization with the enemy makes it clear that they expected their friends and relations to situate the episode within the contemporaneous narrative of the war already jointly assumed and endorsed by those on both the Western and home fronts.

In scale alone, the 1914 truce was indeed great, covering (albeit sporadically) more than fifteen miles of the twenty-mile front fought over by the B.E.F. and the German forces. Brown and Seaton estimate that two-thirds of the British troops along this front, which at the time stretched from Ypres south to the town of La Bassée, participated in some type of Christmastime cease-fire. In total, fifty-four British battalions that were in the line either on or immediately following Christmas joined in a truce with their German opponents opposite. In spite of the widespread nature of the various cease-fires, however, the form the truce took varied widely in different parts of the British-German line. In some cases the holiday armistice was foreshadowed by carol singing on both sides on Christmas Eve and the placing of lit Christmas trees on the German parapets, but in others the night before Christmas was merely a bit quieter than usual. On the day itself, firing still took place in certain areas along the line; for a few battalions the truce consisted of nothing more than a general cease-fire accompanied by no interaction between opposing sides; some units arranged for a collection and burial of the dead in No Man's Land before returning to their respective trenches; and a number of troops engaged in what is now thought of as a conventional "Christmas truce," including full-scale fraternization between the lines.[8]

When fraternization occurred, the soldiers on both sides would gather in No Man's Land and exchange pleasantries, cigars, cigarettes, food, and drink. Often, as soldiers reported in their letters home, the two sides discussed the war, although in the most simplistic terms; these communications were aided by the presence, among the German troops, of soldiers who in civilian life had worked in Great Britain as waiters, cabdrivers, barbers, and hotel attendants and spoke English well. There were even some football matches between the opposing sides, although not nearly so many as would later be believed. Photographs, which often became valued keepsakes, were taken, and souvenirs, such as regimental tunic buttons, were swapped. In some cases the truce lasted for little more than an hour or two, whereas in quieter parts of the line, a general cease-fire and noticeably friendly feeling between the opposing troops persisted until New Year's Day and even afterward. Although there were a few soldiers who wondered whether the temporary armistice would have any effect on the war, the majority of the participants viewed the truce as merely a welcome holiday after a difficult and exhausting five months of fighting and obviously expected the recipients of their surprising news to appreciate the event in the same spirit.[9]

In their letters home, soldiers often introduced the story of the Christmas truce by indicating that they were about to share something unexpected. "We have just had the most extraordinary experience of our lives," Jack Chappell wrote to his mother and father two days after Christmas. Alfred Chater tried to place the cease-fire in context, noting that it was "really very extraordinary that this sort of thing should happen in a war in which there is so much bitterness and ill feeling." Sergeant Hancock, with the 1st Royal Fusiliers, wrote to a school-age pen pal that he had spent an "interesting if not a happy Xmas" in "a truce with the enemy opposite us." The letters home rarely provided more than one line of preamble before launching into the news of the truce: while soldiers were free with their use of the word *extraordinary* to describe the cease-fire, they apparently believed their friends and relations could easily withstand, without a great deal of preparation, the surprising news they were about to impart.[10]

Having briefly primed the way for "a Christmas Day which I shall never forget in all my life," the soldiers then recounted the details of their respective truces. The cease-fires were often arranged by meetings in No Man's Land between representatives of both sides, although British participants generally agree that the Germans initiated the negotiations. Wilbert Spencer, for example, wrote home that "on Xmas Day we heard the words 'Happy Christmas!' being called out, wherefore we wrote up on a board 'Gluckliches Werhnnachten!' and stuck it up. There was no firing, so by degrees each side began gradually showing more of themselves, and then two of their men came halfway over and called for an officer." J. Selby Grigg reported a similar experience, writing that early on Christmas Day, "small parties on both sides ventured out in front of their trenches all unarmed and we heard that a German officer came over and promised that they would not fire if we didn't." Lieutenant Chater wrote to his mother that on Christmas morning, "I was peeping over the parapet when I saw a German, waving his arms, and presently two of them got out of their trenches and came towards ours—we were just going to fire on them when we saw they had no rifles so one of our men went out to meet them." The differences in the way various truces began demonstrate the lack of coordination among the cease-fires, as soldiers from different battalions all reported dissimilarities in the approaches taken.[11]

In a number of cases, the Christmas truce was preceded by German soldiers placing traditionally lit Christmas trees on the parapets of their trenches the evening before. Both German and British troops indulged in carol singing, sometimes in harmony with each other. Private Squire reported to his parents that "on Christmas Eve they were singing away as hard as they could go and they had lights all along their trench in front of us," and Ted Lack told his niece that the British soldiers "listened to the nasty Germans singing carols on Xmas Eve night and we sung some to them." The songs drifting across No Man's Land often invited responses from the opposing trenches: as John Wedderburn-Maxwell, a second lieutenant in the artillery, wrote in a letter to his father, upon seeing the trees and hearing the Germans singing on Christmas Eve, "of course we stopped firing and both sides sang carols." Captain Armes heard reports that "the Germans had lighted their trenches up all along our front," so he went out on top of the parapet to view a scene that had "somehow" become peaceful. As men from both sides sat on top of their trenches throughout the evening of 24 December, enjoying the Christmas lights and the quiet countryside, Armes "talked German and asked them to sing a German Volkslied, which they did, then our men sang quite well and each side clapped and cheered the other."[12]

Many of the British soldiers hoped that the presence of Christmas trees and singing that night would portend a peaceful holiday, and "sure enough," as Holroyd wrote in a letter to his parents, "the carols of Christmas Eve were followed by friendly exchange of greetings on Christmas morning. During the day both sides came out and fraternized in between the lines, buried stale corpses and reconoitred the ground." Holroyd's experience, while not universal, was certainly not unusual: on Christmas Day itself, many truce participants left their trenches and went out into No Man's Land to meet with the enemy. Sam Lane recorded one such encounter in his diary, noting that on Christmas Day, after an agreement with the troops opposite to cease firing for twelve hours, "some of our fellows went over and met the Germans who came out of their lines, and shook hands with each other this seems hardly believable but it is true." Percy Jones similarly observed that for the entire day "the ground between the two lines was simply swarming with little knots of Saxons and English." Grigg, coming up on Christmas afternoon from the reserve line to the front, found "a crowd of some 100 tommies of each nationality holding a regular mothers' meeting between the trenches." Although not all cease-fire agreements involved meetings between the two sides, many participants in those truces that featured fraternization reported a general lack of hesitation in venturing forth from the relative safety of the British trenches and joining the enemy in No Man's Land.[13]

Those who took part in the fraternizations generally did not go out to meet their opponents empty-handed: soldiers from both sides brought food, tobacco, and other items to share with the enemy soldiers. Private Squire wrote home that, after the British left the trenches, the "Germans came out of theirs and we met halfway and talked and exchanged souvenirs our own bullets for theirs and they also gave some of our fellows cigars of which they said they had plenty and we gave them tins of bully beef as they said they had very little food." A soldier from the 1/16th Queen's Westminster Rifles reported in his diary that, when visiting the front lines on Christmas Day, he "found about 200 English drawn up across it & 20 yds further down about 300 Germans looking at each other in the end they all mixed up & started exchanging fags & buttons. I got some fags a cap badge a button & some cigars." Frank Black had a similar experience: while negotiating terms of the truce with some German officers, he told a friend, "crowds of Germans came out and more of my men, till we formed a group of about 100, all shaking hands, and trying to make each other understood and exchanging souvenirs."[14]

In addition to the exchange of food and souvenirs, another standard element of many individual truces was a proposal to engage in a football match. Considering that both the British and Germans were enthusiastic footballers, and that international fixtures had been recently regulated after the creation of the Fédération Internationale de Football Association (FIFA) in 1904, it is hardly surprising that the thoughts of the opposing troops would turn to the possibility of a game. Although in most cases a proper match was impractical for many reasons, including lack of a ball and a suitable patch of ground, it was apparently frequently suggested. Wedderburn-Maxwell, for example, wrote that the two sides "wanted to have a football match yesterday afternoon but couldn't get a ball." Lieutenant-Colonel Diggle, a staff officer with the 8th Division Headquarters, reported that he heard "that there was a football match between the trenches on one part of the line against the Germans. The Germans got beaten again 1–0." J. A. Liddell wrote to his mother that the Germans "were awfully keen to get up a football match against us; whether it will come off or not I don't know." Sergeant H. D. Bryan with the 1st Scots Guards did report an actual match, which he claimed his men had won "easily by 4–1." Although most of the stories of football games were rumors rather than reality, the fact that so many soldiers either mentioned matches being proposed or reported hearing that they took place has given the mostly mythical games an air of reality and embedded them firmly in the collective memory of the truce.[15]

Thus far, the event these soldiers experienced conforms closely to the Christmas truce of the conventional war narrative, including nego-tiated cease-fires, cheerful fraternizing, proposed football matches, and sharing of food, drink, cigars, and souvenirs. Where these accounts diverge from the standard truce discourse is in the lack of rebellious motives on the part of disaffected soldiers. In fact, these reports are notable mostly for the cheerfully matter-of-fact way the British troops approached these individual cease-fires, viewing them as opportunities to have a good time without any significance beyond the celebration of a holiday with other soldiers—who, in this case, happened to be from the opposing army.

At the same time, further examination of accounts of the truce reveals other, more nuanced interactions, many with mournful or omi-nous undertones that often do not find their way into the standard discourse. A number of battalions involved used the cease-fire as an opportunity to retrieve bodies from previous battles that had been lying in No Man's Land; in some cases, the dead were soldiers who had been killed long before Christmas. Sergeant Richard Lintott, for example, recorded in his diary walking up to the front line of trenches to find the two sides "burying some dead which had been lying about since Oct. 21st." After the burial, "we all (Germans and English) stood bareheaded round the grave while a German officer read the service." Grigg participated in a similar ceremony, which occurred after the Brit-ish retrieved the body of a dead German. At the burial, a German offi-cer led a brief prayer service over the grave. Afterward, the Germans thanked " 'our English friends for bringing in our dead,' and then said something in broken English about a merry Xmas and happy New Year. They stuck a bit of wood over the grave—no name on it only 'Fur Vaterland and Freheit' (for Fatherland and Freedom)." Captain Armes wrote home that he gave the German officer in command of the troops opposite "permission to bury some German dead who are lying in between us, and we agreed to have no shooting until 12 midnight tomorrow. . . . We saluted each other, he thanked me for permission to bury his dead, and we fixed up how many men were to do it, and that otherwise both sides must remain in their trenches." Negotiations between officers regarding the parameters of individual truces, including how many men could participate and the time an armistice would cease, were common, which illustrates the transient nature of the episode.[16]

For some soldiers, the burial of the dead seems to have been the primary reason for, and the main feature of, the Christmas Day cease-fire. D. Lloyd-Burch, who served in France with an ambulance corps, wrote in his diary that upon hearing of a truce, he "went to the East-Lanc trenches and found the German and English troops burying the dead between the trenches cigarettes and cigars were exchanged." Cecil Lothian Nicholson of the 2nd East Lancashires also reported the same incident in his diary, noting that, upon moving toward the opposing trenches, he discovered that the Germans "wanted leave to bury the dead of which there were a good many lying in No-Man's land." Nicholson offered the Germans "an hour and a half," for both sides to "bury all the dead lying close to our line and they could do the same with theirs." This offer was "subsequently extended for another hour in the course of which we buried all the dead and Sanders went out from the Adv. Post in the 3rd Sector and recovered the body of Dilworth Sher. For. who had been killed about a month before." Pelham-Burn, with the 6th Gordon Highlanders, wrote that he found the joint burial service for the British and German dead, some of whom "had been there 6 weeks or more," a very moving experience. "Our Padre who was up in the trenches for a few hours arranged the prayers and Psalms etc. and then our interpreter wrote them out in German," he reported. The service was "then read first in English by our own Padre and then in German by a boy who was studying for the ministry. It was an extraordinary most wonderful sight. The Germans formed up on one side the English on the other the officers standing in front, every head bared."[17]

While some British soldiers found the improvised ceremonies consisting of men from both armies united in memorializing their fallen comrades a meaningful and at times heartwarming experience, others were more distressed, particularly by the sight of the dead. Percy Jones described in his diary how, in No Man's Land, there was a "long ditch about four feet wide and four feet deep. It was simply packed with dead Germans. Their faces, brown and leather-like, with deep sunken cheeks, and eyebrows frozen stiff, stared up horribly through the clear water." Some of the soldiers had been killed in a battle that took place on 18–19 December, and the sight of their recently slain comrades strongly affected the troops who had to bury them. A diary from an unidentified soldier in the 2nd Borders recorded on 25 December that an officer told his unit "that we were to Bury our Comrades that fell in the Charge on the 18th of Dec. so we all started diging and Burying them side by side and made them a Cross out of the wood of a Biscuit Box and layed them to rest on Xmas day." When the soldiers had been buried, "we all kneled and offered up a Prayer to God above for our Comrades who fell in Honour."[18]

Second Lieutenant Spencer's unhappy truce consisted of a four-hour armistice, during which the Germans carried "dead men back halfway for us to bury. A few days previous we had an attack with many losses." Spencer noted bitterly in a letter home that he did not want to describe "the sights I saw, and which I shall never forget." After burying the dead "as they were," Spencer wrote, he went "back to the trenches with the feeling of hatred growing ever stronger after what we had just seen." The truce provided some soldiers with the welcome relief of being able to collect and bury the bodies of their comrades as well as honor their memories, but the grisly remains reminded others of the horrors of the war and the reasons they had to hate the enemy. Even Pelham-Burn, who found the joint burial party in which he joined "a wonderful sight," described the collection of the dead for burial as "too awful to describe so I won't attempt it."[19]

In addition to the burial parties, however peaceably conducted, which reminded the soldiers of the presence of the war, there were also signs of continued fighting throughout the holiday week. Grigg, for instance, noted ironically that, though Christmas Eve had been quiet in their trenches, "there has been a little sniping on our right where the Germans are evidently not quite such good friends with their enemies." Captain Wellesley, who served with the 2nd Lincolnshires, the battalion that relieved the 1st Royal Irish Rifles on 26 December, similarly remarked that "on our right and left they have been going on fighting as usual," and William J. Chennell, with the 2nd Queen's Royal West Surreys, observed that during the truce "the most peculiar thing was that on our right and left the Germans and English were still fighting." In spite of the temporary armistice, many soldiers involved were unable to forget the war entirely and remained aware that, while they were fraternizing with the Germans, other British troops nearby in the front lines were still fighting them and perhaps being wounded or killed.[20]

Even without the reminders of dead bodies or adjacent fighting, however, there were soldiers who were still not able to overlook their distrust of the Germans during the cease-fires. Although the modern narrative of the truce has everyone participating happily in the event, many could not, even for Christmas, forget the war and their resentment of the enemy. Spencer's sight of the dead British soldiers, as already noted, upset him badly, and he was not the only soldier who found that the truce aroused negative emotions. Lieutenant Colonel Diggle, who reported in a letter home that the Germans in his area had asked for a truce on Christmas Day, remarked on the treachery of the enemy, who shot "one of our officers dead who was doing his half of the truce." Diggle concluded angrily that the Germans "are dirty dogs and you can't trust them." Frank Black was very nervous during the 1st Royal Warwickshires' truce: when fraternization took place between "crowds of Germans" and his men, during which they shook hands, tried to converse, and exchanged souvenirs, he observed that "the Germans outnumbered us by 4 or 5 to 1." With understandable caution, Black "told the Captain I thought we had better get back to our trenches, which we did after a great deal of bowing."[21]

Bernard Brookes, who served in France with the 1/16th Queen's Westminster Rifles, recorded a similar watchfulness among his battalion, observing that, when an officer went out to meet a German emissary, we "stood at our posts with rifles loaded in case of treachery." Captain Armes reported that although he believed that the German offer on Christmas Eve for a mutual cease-fire was sincere, and that they "mean to play the game," he intended to be "awake all night so as to be on the safe side." The next day, he and the German officers fixed up between them "that the men should not go near their opponents' trenches, but remain about midway between the lines." This was a standard truce precaution, designed to prevent the enemy from learning too much about the opposing sides' defenses, which demonstrates that, even in the free atmosphere of fraternization, reasonable care was taken to prevent the collection of information that could assist their opponents in the next attack. Although under the conventional narrative of the holiday cease-fire, soldiers were supposed to feel confident about the motives of their "comrades" on the opposing side, similar caution was displayed by many truce participants, as their distrust of the enemy was never completely subsumed in the general holiday atmosphere.[22]

Along with a very understandable suspicion of the Germans, many British were also startled to discover how misinformed they were. Instead of making common cause by bonding over their shared dislike of their leadership and the futile war, the two groups sometimes discussed the conflict during fraternization—or rather, as the British often reported, they listened politely to the Germans' confidence about their country's eventual victory. Captain Liddell, for example, wrote to his parents that the Germans he met "were quite convinced that the Russians were absolutely beaten, and also the Servians. Also that they would win, and the war would be over in about 6 months at most." Ernest Morley, who served with the 1/16th Queen's Westminster Rifles, said that one German asked him about the sentries "posted around Buckingham Palace," as he was under the impression that German troops had reached England. Another soldier recorded in his diary that, during fraternization, the first thing the enemy asked "was when are you going to give in you are beat." The Germans further claimed that their newspapers reported "they had troops reviewing in Hyde Park and also troops in Calais." The soldier responded, "Well I must admit that you have got troops in London But they are Prisioners of War"; however, the Germans "would not take that so my Chum gave them the News of the World." Leslie Walkinton, also with the 1/16th Queen's Westminster Rifles, was apparently tactful with his particular group of Germans: although he met some who came from London and hoped to return after the war, "of course we did not talk about who was going to win or anything touchy like that."[23]

In spite of the confidence with which the Germans presented their tales of conquest and impending victory, none of the British soldiers recorded any doubt about the progress of the war and the possibility of Allied defeat. Perhaps the generally outlandish nature of claims about German soldiers standing guard at Buckingham Palace were too ridiculous to contemplate seriously, but at the same time, for the conventional narrative of the First World War and the Christmas truce to retain any credibility, the soldiers at this point in the war should at the very least have begun to question the lack of progress in the conflict. After all, the war had not ended as quickly as some had expected: at the time of the truce the Allies had been fighting for five months and yet the Germans still occupied Belgium and all of northern France, while the British troops were stuck firmly in the mud of the trenches and apparently going nowhere fast. Instead of harboring doubts about the meaning and progress of the conflict, however, British soldiers appear to have cheerfully listened to the Germans brag about their war news, including one soldier who, as Ralph Blewitt reported, refused to contradict a German who had great faith in his country's victories, "as he didn't like to hurt his feelings!!" It seems incredible that, after the retreat of the Allied forces before the German onslaught in the autumn, and their experiences with the miseries of trench warfare, British soldiers continued to feel confidence and optimism about the course of the war and its eventual outcome, but their opponents' display of similar confidence and optimism does not seem to have shaken their belief that the Allies would ultimately prevail.[24]

Many British also reported that the Germans with whom they fraternized confessed that, while they were confident about their country's progress in the war, they also felt tired of the conflict. Ralph Blewitt, for example, wrote to his fiancée that the Germans "were all fed up with the war and wanted to know when we were going to give in!" In some cases, the weariness with war (without a corresponding loss of faith in its prospects) was shared by both sides: Frank Black noted that the Germans "are just as tired of the war as we are, and said they should not fire again until we did." Chater agreed, writing home that "from what I gathered most of them would be as glad to get home again as we should." Grigg claimed that none of the Germans with whom he had fraternized "seemed to have any personal animosity against England and all said they would be jolly glad when the war was over." Although these statements appear to track the conventional truce narrative, emphasizing the bond formed between the opposing sides over their dislike for the war and reluctance to continue fighting it, closer examination of the letters and diaries of the men involved shows that these were standard soldiers' complaints about army service, exacerbated by the holiday season, which would naturally be the occasion for additional homesickness.[25]

It is worth noting that many of the cease-fires ended with firing that had been prearranged, which indicates that both sides understood that the truce was a temporary measure and that the war would resume at a set time. J. Fenton, who served in the Royal Engineers, provided a case in point, recording in his diary that the Germans "threw a message over to say they are going to start firing at midnight and that they take it as an honour to inform us of the fact." John Ray, with the 1st Duke of Cornwall's Light Infantry, which was out of the line on Christmas but relieved the 1st Devonshires in the trenches on 28 December, noted in his diary that the Germans had signaled the British "that they were going to shell us." Harold Atkins of the 1/5th London Rifles wrote that "it is understood that when hostilities must recommence they will be preluded by a volley in the air." These courtesies enabled the truces to end in many areas with fewer hard feelings than they might have had the firing started without any warning and further demonstrate how many soldiers in the line understood that the truces into which they had entered were finite arrangements, which were to last only as long as the holiday period itself.[26]

Another interesting aspect of the truce was the observation by the British of the origins of the soldiers opposite them. Whereas the phrase *the enemy* in modern discussions of the war now refers to all Germans, the men on the front line at that time clearly drew a distinction between Saxon and Bavarian soldiers and Prussians. As Brown and Seaton note, the onus of dislike toward the enemy fell mostly on one subgroup, and "the Saxons were assumed to have had no hand in excesses blamed either on the Prussian soldiery or on the German leadership." The writings of the British troops involved in the truce bear out this observation. Lloyd-Burch recorded in his diary the belief that the cease-fire was due entirely to the identity of the soldiers opposite: "The Saxon's were in front of my brigade at this time had the Prussians been there no truce would have been held." Holroyd agreed, noting that he would be "greatly surprised if they or we fire a shot tomorrow; whatever Prussian war-lords may do, Bavarian troops are pretty sure not to desecrate Christmas Day." When he discovered that the troops opposite were in fact Saxons rather than Bavarians, he emphasized their communal heritage across the lines, referring to the British and German soldiers collectively as "we and the other Saxons." Edgar Cox also reported in a letter home that all soldiers "except the Prussians" were fraternizing. He even noted that the non-Prussian troops provided a friendly warning to the British, telling them "not to go south of a certain line as there were Prussians there." In fact, Cox claimed, "two of our fellows who disregarded the warning were shot dead." As these examples demonstrate, it is apparent that the British soldiers believed that the impetus for the war originated with the Prussian militaristic influence on the German leadership, and that the Bavarian and Saxon regiments were less responsible for the situation in which the British now found themselves, which made it easier for them to respond to the overtures of friendship offered by these regiments during the Christmas truce.[27]

The British soldiers closed their accounts of the truce with relatively brief summings-up of the event. "It was indeed an ideal Christmas," Brookes noted in his diary, observing that "the spirit of Peace and Goodwill was very striking in comparison with the hatred and death-dealing of the past few months." Ernest Morley lightheartedly characterized his Christmas turn in the trenches as "not so bad as regards weather, it being chiefly frosty and as regards the war was a perfect scream." Pelham-Burn predicted that the enthusiastic fraternization between the soldiers of the opposing sides "was a sight one will never see again," and John Wedderburn-Maxwell called it "the most wonderful thing of the war." Percy Jones summed up the event by noting in his diary that "altogether we had a great day with our enemies, and parted with much hand-shaking and mutual good wishes." Lance Corporal Kenneth Gaunt of the 1/16th Queen's Westminster Rifles did observe that "it seems most weird, talking and laughing with them one minute and killing each other the next," but this was a minority opinion. J. Selby Grigg unconsciously adopted the majority view toward the truce when he wrote that "on the whole, apart from the wet, cold and lack of sleep which one has to get used to, I have quite enjoyed our three days up and wouldn't have missed it for anything." It is clear from the words of the soldiers who participated in the event that the Christmas truce was a memorable episode, but at the same time was considered a temporary and probably unrepeatable one.[28]

In many ways, the letters and diaries of those who participated in the Christmas truce are remarkable more for what was not recorded than what was. While soldiers wrote cheerfully about the opportunities to fraternize with the Germans and move about freely in the trenches without fear of snipers, and less happily about being able to bury the dead lying in No Man's Land, they did not voice any belief that the occurrence of the truce meant the end of the war (although some, heartily fed up with life in the trenches, hoped it would stop soon), or that contact with the Germans removed their rationale for continued fighting. Therefore, at the same time that the men were marveling at what they described as "a very weird Xmas Day" or "an extraordinary state of affairs," they still clearly expected that the war would resume after the brief respite. Claims by British soldiers that the Germans would have prolonged the truce if the British had agreed were made but were infrequent; similarly, observations by soldiers who believed that the truce had any significance beyond that of a brief holiday were also rare.[29]

As the accounts written by the soldiers involved demonstrate, the Christmas truce was not the monolithic event that the current orthodox First World War narrative claims. In spite of Lloyd-Burch observing in his diary that "it seems terrible to think that they were exchanging souvenirs one day and killing one another the next," and Ralph Blewitt writing that he believed that "if it wasn't stopped jolly quick I suppose it would spread all down the line and the armies would cease to fight at all," most participants wrote about "this funny unofficial truce" with "our friends the enemy" as if it were a purely temporary episode. Although many men reported fraternizing with the Germans with unreserved enjoyment, there were other soldiers, such as Wilbert Spencer, who were unable to completely subsume their resentment of the enemy during the holiday cease-fire. In addition, except for the occasional comment about how the truce demonstrated "what a remarkable show this war is," most of those involved in the truce accepted that they would go back to killing Germans as soon as the extraordinary event ended. "It really is a funny war isn't it," Captain Wellesley wrote home rhetorically, without any indication that the truce had caused him to rethink his attitude toward the conflict. Even after the truce ended and bitter fighting resumed, soldiers' attitudes remained unchanged: three months after happily fraternizing with the Germans on Christmas Day, William Chennell wrote to his wife, "I should like the war to finish and yet I should like to see them wiped out, as they thoroughly deserve it," demonstrating that a friendly afternoon spent with the enemy had not changed his mind about the need to defeat them. In spite of claiming that the truce could have spread and caused the armies to cease fighting, Ralph Blewitt noted without surprise that the armistice lasted only through part of Boxing Day, "till some officer came down and said they'd had enough now," at which point "both sides retired to their trenches and started off sniping with increased vigour."[30]

Contrary to the orthodox narrative of the war, the British soldiers involved appear to have had no constraints in writing to their friends and relations at home about singing songs in harmony with the Germans, meeting them in No Man's Land, exchanging food and souvenirs with the enemy, and joining them in joint burial parties. These accounts of the truce, including descriptions of open fraternization and the burial of the frozen and rotting corpses in No Man's Land, arrived home uncensored, which demonstrates that the news of the cease-fire, even in its friendliest or grisliest aspects, was not suppressed or kept from the home front. Additionally, the ease with which these soldiers related stories about their experiences in the truce contradicts the conventional war narrative, which insists civilians had no idea of what life on the Western Front was like. Having, since they had arrived at the Western Front, generally kept their correspondents informed about their attitudes toward the war, the conditions of life in the front lines, their occasional shared jokes with their enemies, their respect for the professionalism of the German soldiers, and the horrors of the war, the British truce participants obviously expected that their friends and relations would view the holiday cease-fire as they did: as a temporary break from fighting but not a reason to stop doing so. The absence of attempts to reassure their correspondents about their unchanged attitudes toward the war or their continued desire to fight demonstrates that the soldiers believed their letters' recipients would enjoy the story of a peaceful Christmas and fraternization between the two armies as much as they had and would view it in the same spirit—as a welcome but transitory holiday from the battle.

It is impossible to detect in these letters and diary entries the disaffected, embittered, and disillusioned soldiers who participate in Murphy's *Truce*. The men fighting in Flanders in 1914 did not need the proximity of the trenches to convince them the German soldiers were not inferior beings or mindless monsters. They already knew that the troops opposite were much like themselves: homesick and tired of rain, cold, and mud. This did not obviate the need to win the war and prevail against German militarism and global ambitions, but it did mean that, for many soldiers along the British front, there was no impediment to celebrating the holiday with the enemy troops that could not be overcome by the Christmas spirit. Although others found that they could not enter into the general holiday mood and therefore spurned the advances of the enemy, this did not necessarily indicate a different attitude toward the war. Frederick A. Brown, who served on the Western Front with the 2nd Monmouths, wrote years later about a company sergeant who responded to overtures from the German trenches on Christmas morning, only to be shot by a sniper. Although in the afternoon many of his fellow soldiers went out to fraternize with the Germans, Brown did not, as he was too upset about the death of a fellow Monmouth. Brown was no more or less enthusiastic a soldier than the rest of his company—in fact, his memoir records a strong level of irritation with petty army rules—but his reaction to the truce was very personal: he could not overlook the treacherous death of his sergeant and therefore declined his opportunity to fraternize with the enemy.[31]

The Christmas truce, for those who did decide to participate in it, was clearly a response by professional soldiers to the holiday season and the unusual proximity with the enemy on the Western Front. Even Brown and Seaton, who desperately want the temporary cease-fire to mean more than just a day off for the war-weary troops, acknowledge that it was prompted "by the dramatic revolution in the style of warfare which took place in 1914 within weeks of the onset of hostilities." Considering that the soldiers on both sides were experiencing an unfamiliar and largely unexpected type of war, with its attendant discomforts and dangers as well as unavoidable close contact with the enemy, the collective truces were probably in retrospect not nearly as surprising as they would be later characterized.

The impromptu cease-fires were entered into by many without hesitation and experienced by most of those who took part in them as a brief but welcome holiday before renewed combat. The absence of any major battles or ongoing engagements during the Christmas season helped provide an opportunity for the soldiers on both sides to take some time out to reinforce their trenches, appreciate the arrival of parcels and letters from home, and, in many but not all cases, celebrate the first Christmas of the war by negotiating a brief cease-fire with their enemies. As the parameters of those individually arranged armistices varied widely, the result was a largely unconnected series of truces, some of which resemble the now-conventional narrative, and some of which diverge sharply from that image. In the current discourse, they have all merged into one "Christmas Truce," in which all soldiers happily fraternized with their new comrades, with whom they joined in defying their hated high-ranking officers, who feared any breach of discipline and wanted to stamp out all signs of friendliness between the two sides. An examination of the British military leaders' reaction to the truce will determine whether they indeed wanted to bring the truce to an immediate end, and if they were successful in doing so.[32]

4

"No War Today"

The Christmas Truce as Reported in Official War Diaries and Regimental Histories

> Although soldiers and officers thought, for a moment, that they could forget the war, the war itself had not forgotten them—and for that reason it punished them.
> —Malcolm Brown, *Meetings in No-Man's-Land: Christmas 1914 and Fraternization in the Great War* (2007)

> After a night entirely free from sniping, a kind of informal truce took place all day. The Germans, who were not allowed near our wire, met our men between the lines on most friendly terms, cigars, cigarettes and news being exchanged freely.
> —11th Brigade, III Corps, Official War Diary entry for 25 December 1914

The Christmas Truce, a 2004 documentary in the BBC *Days That Shook the World* series, features the moment in the First World War "when enemies stopped fighting, and a brief window opened into a world of peace." The dramatization, which claims that the conflict "consumed more than 20,000,000 men, fourteen and a half thousand a day," contrasts the misery of the soldiers in the trenches during December 1914 with the situation of General Horace Smith-Dorrien, leader of the British Army's II Corps, who dines in his quarters in comfort during this time, while confidently announcing that he plans to take Ypres after the holiday. "But this Christmas proves to be an even bigger obstacle than he can imagine," the narrator declares, before the camera cuts to a British soldier in No Man's Land on Christmas Eve hearing carols from the German trenches.[1]

The documentary observes that the truce starts "between lower ranks," and then spreads down the lines. By midday, "nearly half the British frontline army is involved in the truce. They are, in effect, committing mass treason, an offense that can mean the firing squad." After showing some soldiers defying their junior officers' orders and continuing to fraternize with the German troops, the dramatization moves to the headquarters of Field Marshal John French, the leader of the British forces in France. It shows the opulent Christmas lunch to which he has invited both Smith-Dorrien and General Douglas Haig, the leader of I Corps, with whom French intends to discuss restructuring the B.E.F. French, however, is distracted by rumors of a truce in the lines. "British High Command is worried" about these reports, the documentary maintains, "but not nearly worried enough. So far, they have just seen the tip of a very large iceberg."[2]

The BBC program observes that Smith-Dorrien, who had issued orders on 5 December 1914 forbidding instances of friendly contact with the Germans, "has the power to court-martial all those involved." *The Christmas Truce* does concede that no actual punishments were handed down to those who participated in the truce, but the threat of impending doom pervades the entire documentary: ominous background music plays every time military officials learn more about the truce. The documentary makes much of the fact that Smith-Dorrien, who is treated throughout as the commander of half of the British forces in the field, issued an order on 26 December 1914 asking for the names of officers and units that took part in the truce, but it admits this was a "hollow gesture," as there were too many troops involved in the armistice to prosecute, and "the very men he would have to condemn are his best troops."

The focus in the documentary on French's Christmas lunch with Smith-Dorrien and Haig glides over a number of inconvenient facts about the structure of the B.E.F on 25 December 1914 and the battalions that participated in the truce. Although it is true that Haig commanded I Corps and Smith-Dorrien II Corps, the documentary fails to mention that there were three other B.E.F. corps in the front lines in Flanders—III Corps, IV Corps, and the Indian Corps. (See figure 4.) It further ignores the fact that no battalions in I Corps participated in any cease-fires with the Germans, and that, of the twenty-three battalions in II Corps, only seven fraternized with enemy troops. The battalions that made up the III, IV, and Indian Corps, on the other hand, were much more enthusiastic truce participants: in III Corps, under Lieutenant General William Pulteney, twenty-three of twenty-eight battalions joined in the holiday armistice, while the numbers for IV Corps, commanded by Lieutenant General Henry Rawlinson, were twenty-one of twenty-eight, and three of the four battalions in the Indian Corps, headed by Lieutenant General James Willcocks, fraternized with the enemy. The battalions under Smith-Dorrien's command therefore constituted only a small portion of the British fraternizers, and emphasizing his role in issuing orders to end the Christmas truce, as the 2004 documentary does, ignores the much more relaxed attitude toward the event taken by the leadership of III and IV Corps, which commanded over 80 percent of the British troops who took part in the impromptu cease-fire.[3]

Before further analysis of the reactions of the B.E.F.'s leadership to the truce, however, it is worth examining the *Christmas Truce* documentary's contention that junior officers tried to keep their men from joining in the armistices. In fact, the majority of the officers in the front line on 25 December 1914 neither forbade the truces in which their battalions joined nor refused to participate in the episodes themselves. Arthur Pelham-Burn, Frank Black, Ralph Blewitt, H. J. Chappell, John Aiden Liddell, Cecil Lothian Nicholson, Michael Holroyd, R. J. Armes, and John Wedderburn-Maxwell, all quoted in the previous chapter, were frontline officers who had no objection to the negotiated cease-fires, and, in addition, wrote extensive letters home about the truces in which they participated. Captain Arthur Bates of the 1/5th London Rifles of III Corps even wrote to his sister on 24 December 1914 that "my orders to the Co[mpan]y are not to start firing unless the Germans do," indicating that he not only tolerated but even encouraged a Christmas cease-fire in the front lines.[4]

This attitude was shared by other battalion officers. Lieutenant Colonel Laurence Fisher-Rowe, commander of the 1st Grenadier Guards of IV Corps, wrote approvingly to his wife on 25 December that he believed the Germans "want a bit of Peace like us and the Scots Guards I hear have arranged not to have any shooting last night or tonight." In fact, Fisher-Rowe wrote home about the truce daily for a week and not only took no steps to stop the 1st Grenadier Guards from participating in the cease-fire, but was obviously happy for it to continue, at least for the holidays. Additionally, Fisher-Rowe's writings on the subject make it clear he did not believe the truce was either dangerous or bad for discipline, and he certainly did not punish any of his men for their involvement. Although there were a few instances of frontline officers putting an end to individual armistices, they were not

I Corps/General Haig

1st Division/Major-General Haking

1st Brigade	2nd Brigade	3rd Brigade
1st Coldstream Guards	2nd R. Sussex	4th R. Welch Fus.
1st Cameron Highlanders	1st Northamptonshire	2nd R. Munster Fus.
1st Scots Guards	2nd KRRC	1st S. Wales Bord.
1st Black Watch	1st Loyal N. Lancs	1st Gloucestershire
14th London		2nd Welch
		4th Seaforth Highlanders

II Corps/General Smith-Dorrien

3rd Division/Major-General Haldane

7th Brigade	8th Brigade	9th Brigade
1st Wilts	2nd Royal Scots	1st Northum. Fus.
2nd Roy. Irish Rifles	2nd Suffolks	4th Royal Fusiliers
3rd Worcestershires	4th Middlesex	1st Lincolns
1st Hon. Art. Coy.	1st Gordon High.	1st R. Scots Fus.
2nd South Lancs		10th Kings (Liverpool)

III Corps/Lieutenant-General Pulteney

4th Division/Major-General Wilson

10th Brigade	11th Brigade	12th Brigade
2nd Seaforth High.	*1st Hampshires*	*2nd Lancs Fus.*
1st Royal Warwicks	*1st Rifles*	*2nd Essex*
2nd R. Dublin Fus.	*1st Somerset LI*	*2nd Monmouths*
1st R. Irish Fus.	*1st East Lancs*	1st Kings Own
	1/5th London Rifles	2nd Innis. Fus.

IV Corps/Lieutenant-General Rawlinson

7th Division/Major-General Capper

20th Brigade	21st Brigade	22nd Brigade
2nd Borders	*2nd Wilts*	*2nd Queens R.W. Surreys*
2nd Gordon High.	*2nd Bedfords*	*8th Royal Scots*
6th Gordon High.	*2nd Yorks*	2nd Royal Warwicks
2nd Scots Guards	2nd Roy. Scots Fus.	1st Roy. Welch Fusiliers
1st Grenadier Guards		1st South Staffords

Indian Corps/Lieutenant-General Willcocks

Meerut Division

Garhwal Brigade

2/39 Garhwal Rifles	*2/3 Gurkha Rifles*
1/39 Garhwal Rifles	1st Leicesters

Note: Bold italic type indicates unit participated in the Christmas truce.

I Corps/General Haig	
2nd Division/Lieutenant-General Monro	
4th Brigade	6th Brigade
1st Hertfordshire 2nd Coldstream Guards 2nd Grenadier Guards 3rd Coldstream Guards 1st Irish Guards	2nd S. Staffordshire 1st R. Berkshire 1st KRRC 1st Kings (Liverpool)

II Corps/General Smith-Dorrien	
5th Division/Major-General Morland	
14th Brigade	15th Brigade
1st Devons *1st E. Surreys* *2nd Manchesters* 1st D. of Cornwall LI	*1st Bedfords* *6th Cheshires* *1st Cheshires* *1st Norfolks* 1st Dorsets

III Corps/Lieutenant-General Pulteney		
6th Division/Major-General Keir		
16th Brigade	17th Brigade	19th Brigade
1st Leicesters *1st Buffs (E. Kent)* *2nd York and Lancs.* 1st K. Shropshire LI	*2nd Leinsters* *3rd Rifles* *1/16th Q. Westminsters* *1st R. Fusiliers* *1st North Staffs*	*2nd R. Welch Fus.* *2nd A&S Highlanders* *5th Cameronians* 1st Cameronians 1st Middlesex

IV Corps/Lieutenant-General Rawlinson		
8th Division/Major-General Davies		
23rd Brigade	24th Brigade	25th Brigade
2nd Devons *2nd West Yorks* *2nd Cameronians* 2nd Middlesex	*2nd East Lancs* *2nd Northants* *1st Sherwood Foresters* *1st Worcesters* 5th Black Watch	*1/13th London Kens.* *1st Roy. Irish Rifles* 2nd Lincolns *2nd Royal Berks* *2nd Rifles*

Note: Bold italic type indicates unit participated in the Christmas truce.

Figure 4. Structure of British Expeditionary Forces on 25 December 1914, showing which battalions, brigades, divisions, and corps participated in the Christmas truce. (Tables by Dick Gilbreath.)

preventing the truces themselves, but rather bringing specific episodes of fraternization to a close, often at a prearranged time. Chater's letter home about the truce, for example, records that conversation with the opposing troops "continued for about half an hour," after which "most of the men were ordered back to the trenches." Liddell similarly reported that the German officers put an end to the cease-fire, whistling the men "back after about an hour." This action, however, does not appear to have been prompted by any animosity, as Liddell wrote that, while the Germans were leaving, "there was a lot of handshaking and 'Auf wiedersehen,'" which would hardly have been the case if the officers involved had disapproved of the fraternization.[5]

This information about the attitudes of frontline officers toward the Christmas truce appears, it should be noted, in their letters and personal diaries rather than in any authorized record. After all, as Tony Ashworth argues in *Trench Warfare, 1914–1918: The Live and Let Live System,* his work on the ongoing unofficial cease-fires that over the course of the war allowed for a certain level of mutual accommodation in the front lines between the two sides, there would be little point in examining military records for details regarding any sort of defiance of orders or friendly contacts with the enemy, as this is hardly the sort of information that would be recorded in official documents. War diaries, for example, which were kept by officers in the field and chronicled the daily actions of troops in the line, were intended, according to the 1914 *Field Service Pocket Book* issued by the War Office's General Staff, "to furnish an accurate record of the operations from which the history of the war can subsequently be prepared." These accounts, which were sent to divisional headquarters monthly, became the permanent records of the actions of a battalion, brigade, or division. Because they served as the official record of all military activities, and were collected and reviewed by the army leadership, it is reasonable to expect that no news of the truce would be documented in them by participating battalions.[6]

An examination of the diary entries for many battalions that joined in the holiday cease-fire, however, disproves this theory. "A local truce British and Germans intermingled between the trenches," proclaimed the 1st Royal Warwickshires' official record for 25 December 1914. "No shot fired all day." In fact, a review of the war diaries kept by the fifty-four battalions that participated in the truce shows that thirty-five of those battalions—almost two-thirds of those involved—featured the truce in these records.[7] Some of these units went far beyond a

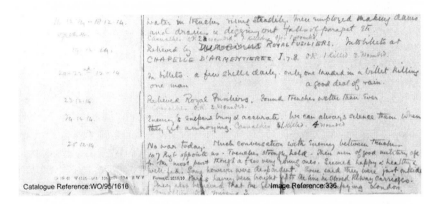

Figure 5. Entry for 25 December 1914, Official War Diary of the 1/16th Queen's Westminster Rifles (detail). (Used by permission of the National Archives, London.)

mere mention of the armistice, recording a surprising level of detail about the cease-fire. The 25 December diary entry for the 1/16th Queen's Westminsters, for example, was particularly forthright: "No war today," it announced boldly. "Much conversation with enemy between trenches." (See figure 5.)

Confounding the theory that those involved in the Christmas truce feared reprisals from their leadership should their participation become known, the diaries of battalions that formed the 25th Brigade of IV Corps recorded the fact that their superior officers were told about the armistices as well as the details of their respective cease-fires. The 1/13th Londons (the Kensingtons), for example, noted not only that they refrained from firing on Christmas Day, but also that the truce was "reported personally by Adjutant to O.C. [officer in charge] 25th Brigade at 9 am," and that the "same conditions" persisted the next day. The 2nd Royal Berkshires recorded that their truce began on Christmas Eve and continued for two days, until they rotated out of the trenches. During that time, "soldiers got up on parapet and advanced half way towards German trenches and in some cases conversed with them." The 2nd Rifles, who relieved the 2nd Royal Berkshires on the evening of 26 December, observed that at that time "an informal truce reigned," and that the "opportunity was taken to do a lot of work in the open and mending wire." When the cease-fire continued through 27 December, "this curious state of affairs" was reported to the brigade headquarters. No adverse reaction from the 25th Brigade leadership was recorded.[8]

The diaries of many brigades, the immediate commanding units for battalions, took much the same relaxed attitude toward the impromptu armistices that sprang up in their ranks. Perhaps because all five of its battalions were involved in the truce, the diary of the 20th Brigade of IV Corps included a vivid description of the event. Drawing heavily on a report about the truce from the 2nd Scots Guards, one of its battalions, the entry mentions the approach by the Germans on Christmas Eve, the agreement not to shoot, the dead soldiers who were located during the cease-fire, the burial party, the information gathered by the soldiers involved, and the continued fraternization on 26 December. On 27 December the 20th Brigade reported that the "Germans tried to come over and enjoy another day's so-called 'armistice' but were informed that they must keep in their trenches," which refusal left them "quite indignant." During the rest of the week, foul weather conditions prevented both sides from focusing on anything except trying to keep dry; the brigade noted the "constant heavy rain," which flooded the trenches and left the Germans, who could "be seen at pumping operations daily," similarly handicapped.[9]

The diary of the 10th Brigade of III Corps also includes detailed information about the truce, noting on 24 December that the 2nd Royal Dublin Fusiliers reported a quiet day, as the "Germans were singing and seemed cheerful," and on the next day that the "Germans appear to think that an armistice exists for Christmas day." It appears that the soldiers of the 10th Brigade, all of whose battalions joined in the truce, thought the same, as an "informal interchange of courtesies took place between troops in the fire trenches of both belligerents." The diary declares that "valuable information was gleaned during the intercourse," but this was limited to a sketch of the enemy's barbed-wire placements and the observation that the Germans looked "cheerful and well fed." Burial of German and British dead also took place, and the diary reports little sniping or shelling over the rest of the week, although actual fraternization was clearly limited to Christmas Day.[10]

On the battalion and brigade level, as these examples demonstrate, the official war diaries of the units involved were often very forthcoming about the truces in which they participated. It was, however, the military leadership at the divisional and corps level that would have been more concerned about the effects of a continuing cease-fire in the lines. I Corps, which was led by General Douglas Haig—whose command of the British Army has become a byword for incompetence and butchery—had two divisions comprising five brigades with a total of twenty-four battalions near or at the front around Christmastime. Although neither Haig nor his subordinates appear to have forbidden fraternization in advance of Christmas, as Smith-Dorrien did, none of the battalions in I Corps participated in the armistice, which directly contradicts the conventional truce narrative of soldiers rebelling against their despised leadership. Additionally, Major General James Aylmer Haldane, the commander of II Corps's 3rd Division, reported in his autobiography that he had also issued orders just before Christmas prohibiting fraternization with the enemy. Haldane's directions appear to have had the desired effect, as the fourteen battalions that made up the three brigades under his command refrained from friendly contact with the enemy, although soldiers in the line just south of them, such as the 6th Cheshires and 2nd Seaforth Highlanders, were fraternizing freely with the Germans. In fact, Haldane, who noted in his memoirs that during September 1914 he "insisted on an aggressive policy—that is to say, no opportunity should be lost for inflicting casualties on our opponent," would, in particular, have made a useful target for the dissatisfaction of soldiers from the 3rd Division, had they been inclined to rebel against army leadership. They did not do so.[11]

Though it is valid to note that the 3rd Division of II Corps was stationed north of the part of the line where the truces occurred, and the battalions constituting I Corps were just south of it, the areas involved were close enough to each other that fraternization could easily have spread throughout these divisions. (See figures 6 and 7.) In fact, the complete lack of participation in the truce by I Corps and the 3rd Division of II Corps demonstrates that a wish to defy their superiors did not form a motivation for soldiers to join in the truce, and that when forbidden outright to do so, soldiers generally obeyed those orders. The restriction on friendly behavior issued to the battalions that formed II Corps is the only example of a corps-wide prohibition found in the official diaries of the British Expeditionary Forces in the time leading up to the truce, and Haldane's self-reported order is the only example of a division-specific one.[12]

In the 5th Division, the other half of II Corps, the situation was more complicated. Reports of occasional amicable relations between

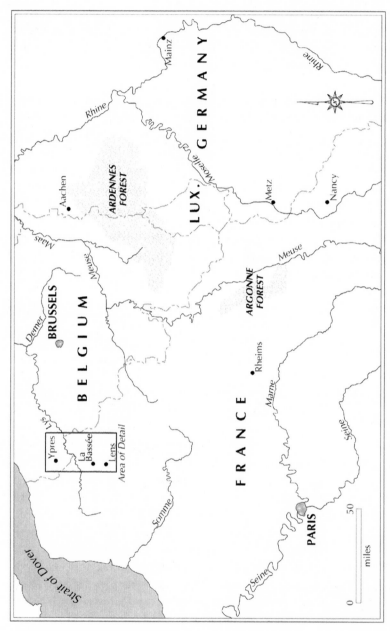

Figure 6. The front and the general area of fighting on the Western Front in December 1914. The area of detail is shown in figure 7. (Map by Dick Gilbreath.)

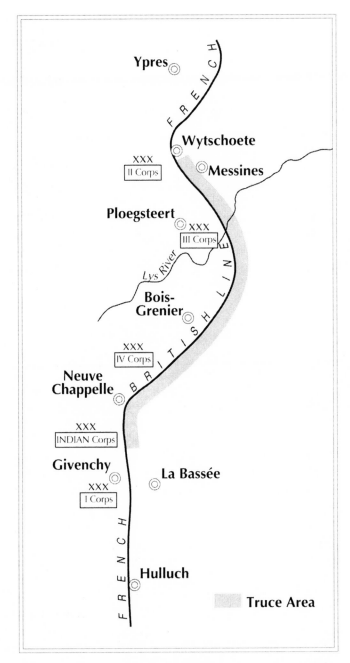

Figure 7. The area of the German-British truce on 25 December 1914. Locations of British corps on the front line are marked. (Map by Dick Gilbreath.)

the British and Germans in the trenches had reached General Smith-Dorrien around the beginning of December 1914. As a result, his chief of staff, George Forestier-Walker, issued a memorandum on 4 December that included a prohibition on "friendly intercourse with the enemy, unofficial armistices (e.g. 'we won't fire if you don't' etc), and the exchange of tobacco and other comforts, however tempting and occasionally amusing they may be." Although this ban on any form of fraternization was only a part of Smith-Dorrien's general injunction to the 3rd and 5th Divisions of II Corps that "Brigade, Battalion and Company Commanders must be enjoined to take every opportunity of carrying out minor enterprises to annoy and intimidate the enemy, and to place him in a state of continual anxiety," it does demonstrate that some localized pre-Christmas cease-fires had attracted the attention of the British military leadership.[13]

This directive forbidding fraternization clearly had some effect, as only seven battalions from the entire 5th Division took part in the truce. In addition, probably as a result of those orders, the diaries of the seven 5th Division battalions that did engage in some form of armistice were fairly taciturn about the subject. The aftermath of the Christmas truce for II Corps was to prove more problematic. The diary of the 15th Brigade of the 5th Division recorded a visit by Smith-Dorrien on 26 December 1914, undertaken for the purposes of assessing the state of the front lines. Later that day, the general issued a confidential memorandum to the "General Officers Commanding Divisions and Brigades, and Officers Commanding Battalions, of the 2nd Corps." In it Smith-Dorrien expressed his displeasure with the large number of shelters in the fire trenches, gaps in the line, lack of support trenches, inadequacy of firing loopholes, and general lethargy of the troops at the front.[14]

After this laundry list of complaints, the general further added that he had just received a report that "on Christmas Day, a friendly gathering had taken place of Germans and British on the neutral ground between the two lines, recounting that many officers had taken part in it." Smith-Dorrien regretted that his previous orders forbidding fraternization had been "useless" in preventing this behavior and instructed commanders to "keep up the fighting spirit and do all we can to discourage friendly intercourse," while requesting the "names of officers and units who took part in this Christmas gathering, with a view to disciplinary action." This communication was forwarded on 28 December to the 14th and 15th Brigades, reminding the commanders of those brigades about the earlier order prohibiting fraternization, and asking for "a fuller investigation of the circumstances . . . and that the names of the officers present, who should have been responsible for preventing the meeting reported, shall be forwarded together with your report as early as possible."[15]

Before receiving this request, Brigadier General Edward Gleichen, commander of the 15th Brigade, had already prepared a brief report about the truce, which stated that "an informal meeting took place yesterday between the lines of trenches of ourselves and the Germans, at which about 200 of our men assisted, and an even larger number of Germans." The account included the names of participating regiments and some minor intelligence details gleaned from the encounters with the enemy. Gleichen's report, which further noted that the Germans said they would not fire between 25 and 27 December, was fairly casual, as befitted a statement about an incident that did not appear to be of great importance but did yield some information about the enemy. After receiving the demand for further information and the names of the officers involved, however, Gleichen prepared a second report. This stated tersely that he had heard of the truce only after it was over, that he understood the armistice had been started by the Germans opposite the 4th Division, and that although "the moving out of a good many men and a few officers was not in accordance with the instructions" provided in the 4 December memo issued by Smith-Dorrien, he believed "that, had they not moved out, the Germans would certainly—though principally with amicable intentions—have come close up to our trenches and quite possibly have come into them in some cases."[16]

Gleichen also included reports from the 1st Norfolks and the 1st and 6th Cheshires that provided brief explanations for the Christmas cease-fire. The Norfolks' account noted rather defensively that the first advances had come from the enemy, and that the only alternative to participating in the cease-fire was to shoot unarmed men. The 1st Cheshires' report stated tactfully that the captain commanding "gave orders that his officers and men were not to go across, but before he quite realized the situation he is inclined to think that individuals did go over," and it further provided the names of the officers in charge. The 6th Cheshires' account was even shorter, describing the armistice as "entirely spontaneous and unexpected" before claiming that the "officers of the 6th Btn. Cheshire Regiment stopped their men from going forward until after some considerable time when they saw that the whole line was out in front." Again, the names of the officers involved were given.[17]

These reports, prepared on the same day that Smith-Dorrien's directive was issued, were immediately forwarded to II Corps Head-quarters. With this information, which acknowledged that at least three of the battalions in the 15th Brigade had participated in the truce, admitted that the officers of those battalions had either permitted or joined in the fraternization, and even provided the names of the officers involved, General Smith-Dorrien was now in a position to take the threatened "disciplinary action" against those officers and battalions. His response was issued two days later, on 30 December 1914, and is worth quoting in full: "The Corps Commander is quite satisfied with the explanation given, and the matter may be considered to be closed." In other words, Smith-Dorrien took only two days to consider the reported fraternizations with the enemy, which had occurred in "direct contravention" of his earlier orders, and in the end decided to do absolutely nothing about them.[18]

The *Christmas Truce* documentary's conclusion that Smith-Dorrien could take no punitive measures against the officers and soldiers involved because there were too many to prosecute, however, shows little understanding of the military mind. Soldiers could be court-martialed to provide an example to others who might have committed or were contemplating the same offenses, and a court-martial could often be as important for promoting military discipline among the ranks as it was for punishing a specific offender. Even if the general had not wanted to lose an experienced officer from the front lines, he could surely have found an inept one to stand in for the others who had also allowed truces. In fact, the famous Smith-Dorrien order asking for the names of officers who joined in the cease-fire that is cited by so many who wish to prove that all truce participants faced, as the *Christmas Truce* documentary alleges, severe punishment for their defiance of orders on 25 December 1914, was addressed to II Corps and therefore applied to only seven of the fifty-four battalions that had participated in truces. Further, Smith-Dorrien's directive did not relate solely to the Christmas truce, but was in fact a much longer critique of the general state of the trenches and the army after the debilitating conditions of the winter campaign.[19]

The III Corps leadership, which saw 60 percent of its frontline troops in the 4th and 6th Divisions participating in the truce, had even less interest in punishing those involved. The 4th Division diary reported the cease-fire without any apparent censure, describing the episode as "a sort of truce," which it admitted was "absolutely unauthorized" but clearly took no action against. The diary further noted that many reports of a quiet day and night had been received, and that a "certain amount of information" had been acquired through contact with the enemy, but it did not report that any brigades or divisions had been ordered to cease truce activities. The 6th Division records noted only that, on 25 December, there was an "unofficial truce" and no firing. The divisional diary entries for the rest of the week reported "no change" in this situation (probably a euphemism for an ongoing cease-fire) and recorded without comment on 1 January 1915 that the "Commander 2nd Army orders that informal understandings with the enemy are not to take place," while acknowledging that general conditions remained "unchanged."[20]

In spite of the superficiality of the information noted about the truce in the 6th Division diaries, however, their records contain further details received from III Corps Headquarters about the armistice. Summaries of information gathered during the armistice were provided by the 4th Division, including reports from the 10th and 12th Brigades, the 1st Royal Warwickshires, the 2nd Essex, and the 2nd Seaforth Highlanders, which identified the German troops opposite them in line and offered details about their attitudes. The presence of these reports, unaccompanied by any apparent censure of the activities, demonstrates that although fraternization was eventually discouraged by III Corps, the truces on Christmas Day appear to have been viewed primarily as intelligence-gathering opportunities by its leadership. The information gleaned on 25 December 1914 by the various battalions and brigades in that corps was then shared among the divisions without any effort to disguise the fact that these details were collected during, for example, the 2nd Seaforth Highlanders' "unofficial armistice" or a "sort of armistice" reported by the 10th Brigade.[21]

The leadership of IV Corps's 7th Division was even more tolerant toward the truces in which its battalions engaged. Of its battalions in the line during Christmas, 75 percent participated in the truce, and the majority of those involved recorded the fact, some in great detail, in their battalion diaries. A review of the diary for the 7th Division, which encompassed the 20th, 21st, and 22nd Brigades, explains why the brigades and battalions involved generally felt able to report their truces so openly. The divisional diary recorded quiet days on 23 and 24 December, and noted that Christmas Day "passed without any hostilities on either side." In fact, "by mutual consent an informal armistice appears to have existed from 9 a.m. till 4 p.m. and parties from both sides went out of the trenches and buried the dead." The 7th Division also reported that, after a quiet night with no firing, another armistice occurred on 26 December "for the purpose of burying the dead," after which "both sides went back to the trenches but very little sniping took place."[22]

In fact, the 7th Division leadership, although it had not directed its battalions to initiate any holiday cease-fire, quickly recognized the use to which the truce could be put: as its diary noted, "Instructions were issued that no further unauthorized communication with the enemy was to take place and that the men were to keep in the trenches: the troops however might refrain from firing unless the enemy fired upon them, in order to allow working parties . . . to continue their work undisturbed." On 27 December the divisional diary did observe that orders had been "received from Corps Head Quarters that nothing in the shape of an armistice was to be arranged without reference to the Corps and that Artillery fire would be continued tomorrow on selected targets, while sniping would be vigorously maintained." These orders, however, were "afterwards modified as regards the sniping, in order that the clearance of the drains in the immediate rear of the firing line might be completed." In any case, as the 7th Division records make clear, the front lines remained quiet for the rest of the week, "probably owing to the attention of both sides being absorbed in drainage operations." The divisional diary continued to record the "lack of aggression" on the part of the Germans, indicating that peaceful conditions persisted in their part of the line for a few weeks after Christmas; no doubt the "modification" of the orders from corps headquarters contributed to the continued cease-fires in the 7th Division's area of the front.[23]

In spite of the disinclination of the 7th Division leadership to punish troops for participating in the truce, its diary demonstrates that it was able to collect more useful information than the 5th Division was able to summon up in response to Smith-Dorrien's ultimatums. A captain with the 2nd Gordon Highlanders provided a detailed report about the soldiers in the German regiment opposite their battalion and the names of British officers whom they had recently taken prisoner, while a German-speaking soldier was able to record the views of the enemy troops in the 69th and 139th Regiments. The commander of the 21st Brigade provided a complete report of the cease-fire on his section of the front, including descriptions of the placement of the German trenches and how strongly they were held. A major with the 22nd Brigade was able to pass on information about recently arrived German reinforcements, and the combined reports enabled the division to produce a map identifying all the German troops facing them in the line. (See figure 8.) By allowing the armistices to continue, the 7th Division was able to collect more intelligence about the Germans, their positions in the line, and the defenses opposite than the 5th Division, which tried to shut its truces down rapidly.

The soldiers in the 8th Division of IV Corps were also enthusiastic

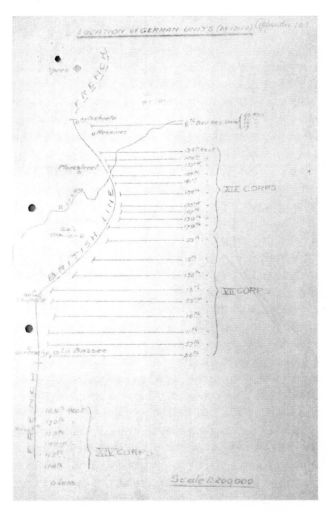

Figure 8. Map drawn by a 7th Division soldier showing the location and identity of German troops along British front lines at Christmas 1914. (Used by permission of the National Archives, London.)

truce participants: nine of its eleven battalions that joined in the armistice recorded the event in their diaries. The 8th Division diary registered the existence of agreements not to fire, arrangements that were clearly sanctioned by the divisional leadership: the entry for 25 December noted that "negotiations took place with Germans at some points along our front regarding burial of dead between the lines," during which it "was mutually agreed to bury the dead and not to fire during the day except in case of necessity." On 26 December the 8th Division noted that "in view of an arrangement made between 7th Div. and Germans to bury dead to-day no firing took place along our front." The division's diary for the rest of the week focused on the wet conditions in the line rather than any fighting.[24]

The Indian Corps's attitude to the truce, in which three of its battalions participated, was clearly more disapproving; as a result, only the 2/39th Garhwals admitted in their diary that during the afternoon the enemy had advanced toward them and offered a truce. The Germans spoke "with officers and men, they gave our men tobacco cigarettes and newspapers, and for about an hour both sides walked about freely outside their trenches and in the open space between the two lines." (See figure 9.) The rest of the night passed quietly, but during the evening orders were received "that such mutual armistices were not to take place in future." The Garhwal Brigade and Meerut Division diaries also both acknowledged the truce, which the divisional diary referred to as "unauthorized," although no punishments were recorded for those who took part.[25]

There can be no doubt that the disapproval that General Smith-Dorrien, the commander of II Corps at the time of the truce, displayed toward any friendly contact between the Germans and the soldiers under his command was at least partially responsible for the relatively low participation of the II Corps battalions in the holiday armistice and the reluctance of the few battalions that did join in the cease-fire to admit to it in their official records. Equally, the relaxed attitudes of the leadership of III and IV Corps toward the episode were reflected in the willingness of the battalions under their command to both engage in an armistice and acknowledge it in their official diaries. Although some battalion or brigade diaries eventually recorded orders forbidding further participation in the truce, most did not refer to any orders issued to cease fraternization or commands to resume shelling or sniping. For example, the diaries of the 1st North Staffordshires and the 2nd Borders, whose cease-fires continued at least until New Year's Day, never

Figure 9. British and German soldiers fighting on Christmas Eve 1914 and fraternizing on Christmas Day 1914. (Drawing by E. R. P. Berryman, 2/39th Garhwal Rifles. Used by permission of Tamsin Baccus.)

noted any injunctions to recommence firing; this was also true for the majority of the battalions participating in the truce. Generally, the diaries of battalions in the line at this time reported that fraternization came to an end by the evening of Christmas or Boxing Day, cease-fires generally persisted for a few days afterward, firing began to pick up again just before or on New Year's Day, and the war was restarted in earnest sometime during January 1915, but they rarely recorded any orders that battalions were to resume fighting.[26]

In addition, the many reports, most of them voluntarily produced, provided by frontline British officers demonstrate that they generally considered the truce an opportunity to increase their knowledge of the German numbers in the line and the layout of the enemy trenches. The intelligence gained during the armistices, including the detailed information about the identity of the troops in the opposite trenches, must surely have been welcomed by the military leadership, even though the knowledge gained benefited both sides. The fact that the divisions and brigades that were most relaxed about the truce were able to collect the best information about the Germans contradicts the current narrative of the truce, which argues that the officers in the front line would have been careful to keep the armistices that they had condoned a secret; instead, the diaries reveal that in fact those officers acknowledged the existence of the truces by providing military intelligence collected during fraternization.

As the official records of the units involved demonstrate, the attitudes of military leadership toward the truce defy the myths that have since been asserted about the event. Of the leaders of the four army corps whose battalions were involved in the armistice, only General Smith-Dorrien of II Corps threatened the officers of those battalions with any punishment for allowing the truce—and he backed down within forty-eight hours of receiving those officers' reports. The commanders of the 7th and 8th Divisions, on the other hand, without necessarily encouraging contact with the enemy, issued orders in response to reports of a general cease-fire at the front that there was to be no firing from the British lines on Christmas Day as long as the Germans did not fire (and, by doing so, obviously turned a blind eye to the extensive fraternization by IV Corps battalions). The leadership of the 4th and 6th Divisions clearly had no serious objection to a temporary truce in the lines and took no steps to censure the frontline officers involved. On the brigade level, there was no unified response to the armistice: some leaders, such as Brigadier General Gleichen of the 15th Brigade, were apparently quite satisfied for the truce to go ahead, whereas the leadership of the 19th Brigade, which ignored the event altogether in its diary, were probably none too pleased to hear about it.[27]

In short, the Christmas truce as reported in the battalion, brigade, and divisional diaries of the B.E.F. bears little resemblance to the episode described in the *Days That Shook the World* episode as "mass treason." The soldiers who took part in the impromptu armistices, and the officers who recorded their participation in their battalions' official military records, clearly did not believe that they were violating military code, but rather celebrating Christmas with a brief armistice for the day, after which, as the 1st Royal Fusiliers' diary noted, "hostilities recommenced!" The acknowledgment by frontline officers of the truce in their battalion diaries constituted a form of notice to army authorities about an event that they were likely to hear about in any case, even without official reports.[28]

The official military reaction to the Christmas truce, therefore, was hardly the unified disapproval accompanied by threats of punishment so central to the conventional narrative of the armistice. Additionally, the more relaxed attitude of "acknowledgement without censure" that most commanders took toward the truce later carried over into the official British military history of the First World War. The 1927 installment of this work, which dealt with the winter campaign of 1914–1915, was written by Brigadier General Sir James E. Edmonds and Captain G. C. Wynne and was surprisingly frank about the grim situation facing the B.E.F. early in the war. The authors admitted that the year following the battles in October and November 1914 "brought little but disillusionment and disappointment," and that Field Marshal French had erred in concurring with the French Commander in Chief Joffre's plans for offensive action during the first months of 1915. In this authorized history, Edmonds and Wynne devoted an entire paragraph to the truce, noting that "there was an informal suspension of arms during daylight on a few parts of the front, and a certain amount of fraternization." They referred to the joint burials of the dead in No Man's Land and added that "in some places there was an exchange of small gifts and a little talk, the Germans expressing themselves confident of early victory."[29]

Edmonds and Wynne further mentioned that "both parties sang Christmas carols and soldier songs"; they concluded with a reference to some minor truces that took place on 25 December of the following year, which they described as "an attempt to repeat this custom of old time warfare on Christmas 1915." More surprising, however, is what the official historians of the war did not report: there is no allusion to any disapproval of either the cease-fire or fraternizations. While it can be argued that one paragraph in a twenty-nine-volume work hardly constitutes excessive notice of an event, the fact that the truce, which cannot be said to have had any effect on the course of the war, received a place at all in the officially authorized history, and that no displeasure on the part of the military leadership was recorded, certainly puts paid to the idea that the holiday cease-fire was the object of censorship from the military leadership both during and after the war.[30]

This is further borne out by the First World War histories of the regiments that served in the conflict, many of which were written by either high-ranking officers or professional military historians. These works served two purposes: they created a cohesive record of the actions of a regiment during the war and acted as a group memoir for those who had served in its ranks. Though the diaries kept daily in the field were the official record of a unit's activities, regimental histories functioned as a tribute to the regiment's achievements, as well as a testimonial to those who had served in one of the regiment's battalions and remembered their service with pride. These histories rarely sold in large quantities; rather, they were intended for a select audience, mainly veterans of the regiments in question whose memories would be reinforced by an account of the battles and campaigns in which the regiment had fought.

For the authors of the chronicles of those regiments who had participated in the Christmas truce, however, the cease-fire posed a certain difficulty: featuring an event of which some military leaders had disapproved might be less than tactful, but ignoring it entirely would mean skipping over an episode that was no doubt remembered fondly by the soldiers involved. For the most part, however, the authors of these histories included the truce in their books, establishing that while a few senior military leaders were probably not delighted to be reminded of the event, the impromptu armistice was not the cause of censure and repression that many have since alleged. The presence of the truce in these works also demonstrates that the soldiers of the regiments involved wanted their memories of the war to be complete; no meaningful episodes were to be expediently ignored.

Information about the impromptu truce available through the regimental histories, however, is often incomplete or misleading, which possibly has contributed to a number of later misconceptions about the event. The majority of these chronicles assert, for example, that the cease-fires lasted only a day or two, when, in fact, as battalion diaries noted, many persisted throughout the holiday week. Foreshadowing the later myth that the truce was brought to an abrupt halt by disapproving officers, these histories often claim that the truces were stopped by orders from military leadership, although this appears to have occurred only in a minority of cases. At the same time, football matches are rarely mentioned in regimental histories, but references to burial of the dead in No Man's Land are much more common. In one sense, however, these histories present the truce accurately: it is credited, variously, to the regiments' professionalism, historical precedent, terrible weather, close contact with the enemy, and the Christmas holidays, but, albeit not surprisingly, never to rebellion against military leadership. The regimental histories of the battalions involved in the cease-fire therefore simultaneously propagated and contradicted the conventional narrative of the truce, while its inclusion by the regimental historians demonstrates that the event was part of the military's overall narrative of the war.[31]

While the discrepancies between the various versions of the truce featured in these regimental histories pose a problem for cohesive military remembrance of the event, an examination of these sources does clarify one point: that the armistice remained a vital memory for the soldiers who had either participated in it or heard about it from their comrades. The Christmas truce is mentioned, whether briefly or at length, in thirty-one histories of forty regiments that contain battalions that participated in it. In addition, a few divisional histories also refer to the truce. These chronicles feature a surprising level of detail about the miseries of the trenches, particularly during the first year of the war, and the tremendous losses suffered by those regiments during this period. The inclusion of these horrific but vital elements of frontline fighting, together with accounts of the truce, demonstrates that these books were designed as remembrances for the veterans of the regiments rather than as glossy public relations exercises meant to please the army leadership. The inclusion of the truce, an episode that was not crucial to the progress of the war, was therefore made clearly on the basis of its interest to those who had participated in it.[32]

The History of the London Rifle Brigade, 1859–1919, written by Major General Sir Frederick Maurice, provides vivid descriptions of the horrible conditions under which its soldiers served in the Flanders trenches, which "generally had two feet or more of icy cold water in them," and posits a connection between those conditions and the truce. Noting that the time in the line at the end of the year was very quiet because both sides were "worn-out," Maurice wrote that a truce was arranged with the Saxons opposite "in order that burying parties might carry out their necessary duties, and this led to meetings in No Man's Land and an exchange of courtesies, which ignorance at that time of German methods and intentions in the matter of poison-gas and other horrors made possible." There were even "rumours of a proposed football match, but the authorities frowned upon ideas of this sort and stopped them," not because of disapproval of fraternization with the enemy, but "quite rightly, because it would have been most unwise to allow the Germans to know how weakly the British trenches were held."[33]

In *Crown and Company: The Historical Records of the 2nd Batt. Royal Dublin Fusiliers,* Colonel H. C. Wylly skirted around the subject of the armistice, noting only that there "was quiet in the front line during the last few days of the first year of the Great War, and the battalion diary under date of December 31st, 1914, contains two words only—'No Sniping!'" In *The Border Regiment in the Great War,* published the following year, however, Wylly not only discussed the event openly but admitted it continued until well into 1915. On Christmas morning, he wrote, the Germans proposed an armistice, which was "arranged until 4 in the afternoon, for the purposes of burying the dead who had been lying between the trenches since the 18th October." A cease-fire to bury fallen comrades was certainly within military tradition, so it would hardly have been surprising if Wylly had left the subject alone after that disclosure, but instead he returned to it later in the history, noting that "the truce which had been mutually and unofficially established during Christmas between the British and the Germans endured, so far as concerned any operations on the front of the 2nd Battalion The Border Regiment, until the end of the first week of the New Year." He further observed that it was not until 8 January that "the troops fired volleys over the German trenches to indicate that fighting was about to recommence, while this somewhat broad hint was accompanied by a message to the same effect which was sent across." The war, with its "usual sniping," then started up again, "and both the Gordon Highlanders and the Border Regiment suffered some few casualties before the men could understand that it was no longer safe to walk about 'on the top.'"[34]

F. Loraine Petre, in *The History of the Norfolk Regiment, 1685–1918,* discussed some of the mild controversy that had surrounded the truce for the 1st Norfolks, which was part of II Corps. "On Christmas Day occurred the famous meeting with the Germans in 'No Man's Land' which drew down the wrath of G.H.Q. and a demand for the names of officers, who, it was held, should have prevented it," Petre wrote, while observing that in the end no punishments were imposed. "The matter was eventually dropped, and no harm was, as a matter of fact, done, seeing that our men managed to have a good look at the German defences, and took good care that the fraternization did not spread over to their own trenches."[35]

The History of the Rifle Brigade in the War of 1914–1918, by Reginald Berkeley, made much of the holiday armistice. As the Rifles had three battalions in the line on Christmas Day, all of whom participated enthusiastically in the event, such notice was hardly surprising. Berkeley even excused the brevity of his three-hundred-word account with the observation that, as "Christmas 1914 and the truce that it brought along the front, with its flavour of the medieval prohibition of fighting on Sunday, have formed the subject of many a writer," there was not much "to add from the experiences of the Rifle Brigade." After describing the Rifles' truces, Berkeley further noted that one of the battalion's diaries recorded that a German juggler entertained both sides in No Man's Land on Christmas Day. "In the dumbfounding unexpectedness of the truce," Berkeley observed, "it would not have surprised anyone very greatly if the German juggler had turned out to be a modern Pied Piper and had led away a hypnotized crowd of friends and enemies into the blue, determining the war for want of troops."[36]

Berkeley's lively account of the truce demonstrates one of the main purposes of a regimental history: to reinforce the memories of those who served in it and who looked back on their service with pride and satisfaction. For the veterans of the Rifle Brigade, as this work establishes, the truce was obviously an important part of their remembrance of the war. In fact, several regiments that had no battalions participating in the truce, such as the Irish Guards and the Royal West Kents, even worked a reference to the armistice into their histories, proving that the event had long since passed into the collective military memory of the war and enjoyed a communal ownership that went far beyond the original members of the B.E.F. who had fraternized with the Germans at Christmas 1914.[37]

As the constant references throughout these regimental histories to the "famous" or "well-known" truce illustrate, the story of the armistice was very much part of the recollections of the war for the soldiers who had been involved in it, and the military historians and officers who wrote these chronicles paid tribute to the memories of the veterans of these regiments by including this vital event in their works. In fact, the lack of censure with which the event was reported in many regimental histories, together with the fact that it was even included in chronicles of units that did not participate in the truce, refutes many of the myths that were later to overtake the holiday armistice.

As the diaries of the battalions, brigades, and divisions involved reveal, there were a few military leaders who opposed the truce, but there were also many who either shrugged it off or tacitly condoned it. What is clear, however, is that although some frontline officers may have had to produce reports explaining their battalions' involvement in the truce, this was the most serious consequence they had to face for their actions: no punishments were handed down for participation in the cease-fire. Contrary to the conventional narrative, the war diaries of the army units involved not only contain a wealth of detail about the event, but also manage to convey some of the delight the soldiers involved experienced during their unexpected holiday in the trenches. This narrative carried over into their regimental histories, which produced surprisingly candid accounts of the holiday armistice. The military world, however, is a relatively small and enclosed one, even during a war. The attitudes of the frontline officers toward the truce, as recorded in their battalion diaries, constituted a form of notice to army authorities about an event that they were likely to hear about in any case, even without official reports. Although the information that was conveyed as part of internal army records proved to be, for a number of regiments and brigades, surprisingly forthright, the censorship prevailing in the British press would certainly influence the way the story of the Christmas truce was presented. An examination of major British newspapers in the weeks following the holiday cease-fire will reveal the way the truce was reported to the British public.

5

"One Day of Peace at the Front"

The Christmas Truce and the British Press

NO CHRISTMAS TRUCE
FIGHTING IN FRANCE AS FIERCE AS EVER
A DETERMINED ADVANCE
(PRESS ASSOCIATION WAR SPECIAL)
At the front Christmas had to be postponed. The materials of
good cheer were there in abundance, but the army was too
engaged with the Germans to be able to enjoy them.
— *Manchester Guardian*, 28 December 1914

A CHRISTMAS TRUCE AT THE FRONT
ENEMIES AT FOOTBALL
GERMAN GETS A FRIENDLY HAIRCUT
That there was an unofficial truce along sections, at least, of the
trenches in France on Christmas Day, and that advantage was
taken of it for some remarkable fraternizing among enemies, is
shown in convincing detail in the following extracts from letters
just arrived from the front. The first was received in Manchester
yesterday from a British officer.
— *Manchester Guardian*, 31 December 1914

In *Death's Men: Soldiers of the Great War*, Denis Winter argues that
during the First World War those on the home front "drew arrows on
maps and talked of battles and campaigns, but what it felt like to be in
the front line or in a base hospital they did not know. Civilians did not
ask and soldiers did not write." Winter credits this reticence to soldiers'
desire to protect their families but also blames the news media for their

failure to communicate the truth about the war. In fact, as he notes in his 1978 work on the conflict, "If newspapers of the first year are a guide, the war was as marginal to people's lives as the Napoleonic wars had been to the generation of Jane Austen." According to Winter, this lack of information, coupled with "rigorous censorship," extended to news of the Christmas truce. Although he claims that the weekly news magazine the *Sphere* "had broken the story of the first Christmas" truce in January 1915, Winter insists that "the censor had intervened" to prevent publication of information about the holiday cease-fire and asserts that the true facts about what happened on the Western Front on 25 December 1914 "only really came out when Captain Chudleigh in the *Telegraph* wrote after the war."[1]

Winter's contention that news of the Christmas truce was suppressed by the British press forms part of his larger argument that the voices of the individuals who fought in the conflict were lost from First World War histories, in which, he notes, the "soldiers' war is at best relegated to a single chapter with colourful accounts of mud and vermin, bully beef and particular deaths in battle." Winter sees the impromptu cease-fires that occurred in the line, whether at Christmas 1914 or other times, as the ultimate expression of the soldiers' respect for their enemies, which "could sometimes turn into an even warmer feeling" resulting in occasional "fraternization, truces, [and] the cessation of violence by mutual consent." By emphasizing the gap between the men serving in the front line and the civilians at home, the solidarity that soldiers felt with their enemies, and the insistence of newspapers on knowingly printing falsehoods about the war and their refusal to publish soldiers' letters after October 1914, Winter endorses the conventional narrative of the Christmas truce and maintains that news of the holiday cease-fire was kept from the home front.[2]

Winter's argument seems reasonable. After all, British newspapers, which generally supported the war and were in the habit of printing whatever stories the government fed them, were likely to be reluctant to broadcast the news of the truce. Although forthright accounts about life in the trenches may have been readily available to the public through publication of soldiers' letters in newspapers (which practice, contrary to Winter's claim, did not stop by November 1914), those reports came from soldiers who believed that fighting the war was necessary, even if they were willing to be candid about its horrors and discomforts. The holiday truce posed an altogether different issue for the British press and presented them with an interesting quandary:

would the news that soldiers had abandoned fighting, albeit temporarily, be subject to censorship? To what extent would newspapers admit to knowledge of the armistice? Would they acknowledge the cease-fire and try to define it as an outlying event, or would they situate it within the larger prowar narrative?

The approach taken toward the existence of the Christmas truce by the mainstream British press reveals a conflicted discourse that simultaneously supports and challenges the conventional narratives of the war and the truce. Many accounts of the cease-fire did appear in the national newspapers and were even featured prominently, but at the same time information about the impromptu holiday truce was confined almost entirely to soldiers' letters. The press dealt with the 1914 armistice, therefore, in the same way as it handled accurate information about the conditions at the front and the attitudes of the British front-line troops: these controversial truths could be safely expressed only by the soldiers themselves. Obviously ambivalent about how to treat an event that so clearly contradicted the contemporaneous narrative of the war and portrayed the Germans as human beings rather than as a faceless enemy, British newspapers limited themselves to presenting the truce through their soldiers' own words and did not report on it in any conventional sense. The length of time the newspapers continued to print letters about the truce—three weeks, which in press terms is an eon—provides a strong indication of the reaction to the cease-fire. If the public response had not been positive, and interest in the cease-fire not overwhelming, British newspapers would surely not have continued to publish letters describing the truce for such a long period.

Although letters featuring the holiday armistice appeared almost daily in the British press from the end of December 1914 through the middle of January 1915, the only articles on the subject that could be characterized as conventional journalism consisted of stories about how the French and German military authorities responded to the truce. In a three-week period, from 31 December 1914 through 20 January 1915, the *Daily Mail, Daily Telegraph, Morning Post, Manchester Guardian,* and *Times* combined published over sixty letters referring to the truce, but only a few articles about any official responses to the event—and those responses concerned only non-British reactions. Additionally, after numerous truce reports had appeared in the *Daily Telegraph* and *Manchester Guardian,* both published editorials that attempted to situate the Christmas truce within the accepted discourse of the war. Aside from those two efforts to reconcile the unofficial armistice with the overarching narrative of the war, coverage of the truce remained under the jurisdiction of the "Letters from the Front" columns and ceased altogether by the end of the third week of January 1915. It should be noted, however, that while letters from soldiers discussing the truce contained ample contradictions to the usual war reporting, both in the details of life at the front they provided and the story of the truce itself, this had no apparent effect on other war news published during this time. In fact, the standard journalistic representations of the conflict continued unabated in British newspapers during the period that personal accounts of the unofficial armistice were featured so prominently in the same publications.[3]

The Christmas truce was not mentioned in the British press until nearly a week after it occurred. As there were no press representatives at the front in the early part of the war, and no official communiqués were ever offered on the subject, the newspapers probably did not even hear of the event until, at a minimum, a few days after Christmas. In the meantime, the reporting of the conflict in the newspapers between Christmas and New Year's Eve consisted of stories that fit comfortably into the contemporaneous narrative of the war, which were fed to journalists through the army's regular press briefings, held far from the front lines in Paris and London. The *Times,* for example, published an article on 26 December entitled "A Carol Sung by Both Sides." This account began with the observation that the correspondent had "always been struck, and never more so than during this Christmastide, with the large-hearted, tolerant attitude our men have unconsciously adopted towards the individual German soldier." As the unnamed journalist—probably embellishing the information received from the army press office—declared, "Malice finds no place at all in the British military equipment, and that is why a season consecrated to goodwill and fellowship finds the hand and heart of the British soldier in sympathy with the Christmas spirit."[4]

To demonstrate the goodness of the generic British soldier's heart, the article noted that carols were sung in the British trenches on Christmas Eve, and that in one case the Germans even sang along. Unfortunately, the harmonizing finished unhappily, as "no sooner had the carol ended than the cynical Teutonic touch was introduced by a shower of bullets from the enemy's trenches." Similarly, the *Daily Mail*'s post-Christmas reporting also started with an account of the stereotypical Hun at his fiendish worst: "Troops Feast While Belgians Fast," read the headline of a 26 December article that discussed how the Germans

celebrated Christmas by "bleeding" the Belgian peasantry of wine
and cigars, noting that "the Belgian people were even asked to make
Christmas cakes for the German soldiers." To further demonize the
enemy, the *Daily Mail* informed its readers that such selfish celebrations were "in obedience to the military order, for notices were issued
several days ago that the troops must do their best to enjoy Yuletide."[5]

On 28 December the *Daily Mail* published an account of the war
purporting to come from a correspondent in Flanders—where in fact
no British journalists were stationed. "Christmas Day," he wrote, "was
a day of strife—in these northern regions at least. The Germans came
down upon the countryside east of Nieuport in a fury of hate. Their
fiercest onslaught of the week they reserved for Christmas Day." The
public, however, was not to worry, as "the whole of the afternoon the
Allies were busy beating them off. The guns thumped, the machine
guns tapped, and rifles cracked. That was the music of Christmas about
Nieuport." The *Daily Telegraph* had similar news on 26 December,
noting that the official communiqué issued in Paris on 25 December reported fighting on the front, and headway having been made in
the form of some slight advances against the enemy. "North of Roye
at Lihu near Lihons," the article claimed, "we also made some progress. These different attacks were carried out with much dash. Everywhere we retained the ground which we had won." As these various
accounts demonstrate, the official reports of the war showed the situation unchanged over the Christmas holiday, and there was no mention of any cease-fires in these articles, which were no doubt based on
official army briefings.[6]

Amid the reports of fierce fighting and German atrocities, the
news of the Christmas truce, when it began trickling through in the
form of rumor and letters from soldiers, must certainly have perplexed
the British-based editors of these papers. There was no communication about the episode from any official source, yet the letters being
passed on to the newspapers from soldiers' friends and families would
have confirmed the existence of the impromptu armistice beyond any
reasonable doubt. Whether by prearrangement or coincidence, British newspapers all took the same approach toward the truce, which
was to offer—verbatim and apparently without censorship—soldiers'
accounts of the armistice rather than conventional articles about it.
The first descriptions of the holiday cease-fire appeared in the press on
31 December 1914, when three newspapers simultaneously published
letters referring to the event.

A typical account in the *Daily Telegraph,* "Christmastide in the Trenches / Greeting the Enemy / Unaccepted Challenges," was credited to a "rifleman in the Queen's Westminsters, writing home on Boxing Day to friends in London," who "describes how certain members of the regiment and the German troops spent a merry Christmas together." The soldier told how his unit shelled the German trenches until it became dark on Christmas Eve, when the British began to sing carols, and the Germans joined in. The British carried on "a sort of 'matey' conversation with the enemy," after which the two sides held "a concert and a dance," followed by a meeting in No Man's Land and an exchange of cigarettes. The rifleman pronounced the Germans "jolly good sports" and was disappointed when a proposed football match on Christmas Day did not come off. He closed the letter by assuring the recipient of its veracity: "I expect you think this a bit of a yarn. In fact, the Regulars, who were in reserve here, would not believe it, and some of them came up to see for themselves."[7]

The *Telegraph* printed two other letters from soldiers in the Queen's Westminster Rifles; one reported that it was the Germans who initiated the carol singing and fire lighting but British troops who shouted, " 'Won't you come half-way and meet us and shake hands?' " When the Germans agreed, "we downed all arms and I went over with —— and met four of them (they weren't taking any risks), and we had a chat, exchanged cigarettes for coffee and sweets, &c." Another rifleman provided a similar description: as the firing died down on Christmas Eve, carols were sung in both lines of trenches, and "compliments of the season" were shouted across. On Christmas Day itself, he continued, the Germans walked about " 'on top,' and some of our fellows went out to meet them, and there, between the two firing lines, the English were shaking hands with the Germans, changing smokes, buttons and hats." As the British troops discovered, many of the Germans spoke English, and a "great number of them had come from London. One man said he had lived in London for ten years, and he was going back. If the Kaiser did not take him he was going back on his own." The day concluded with an arrangement with the Germans "that they would not fire until we did," which held "until five o'clock, when we were relieved by Regulars."[8]

The first soldiers' accounts in the *Manchester Guardian,* which appeared on 31 December, followed a similar pattern. The newspaper quoted a letter from a British officer that told how "at 11 p.m. on 24 December there was absolute peace, bar a little sniping and a few rounds from a machine gun, and then no more. 'The King' was sung, then you heard 'To-morrow is Christmas; if you don't fight, we won't'; and the answer came back 'All right!'" This report contained an account of a football match "with a bully beef tin," and, for a crowning touch of absurdity, "one man went over and cut a German's hair!" The *Morning Post* also published letters about the truce on 31 December, including one from an army captain who noted that the British trenches "in some cases are so near those of the enemy that communication is quite easy" and reported that "an informal compact was arranged—at least at one point of our line, where our people were faced by a Saxon regiment—to the effect that no sniping was to take place for a day." After coming out of their trenches, the English and Germans began, rather domestically, "to hang out their washing and mend their wire entanglements." Unfortunately, the captain wrote, "this happy scene was suddenly upset by the bursting of a big shell, fired from a position many miles in the rear, and everyone scuttled back to his hole in double quick time." The officer reported singing on Christmas evening, courtesy of an "Irish captain with a turn for music," and he closed his account with the observation that it was "a pity the German Press vilify us so much, for here the British soldiers and their adversaries mutually respect each other. And our officers certainly admire the Germans for putting up such a great fight, and this is quite the common opinion."[9]

As the initial accounts published in these three papers indicate, the sole input that the newspapers provided about the Christmas truce, aside from choosing the letters published, was the headlines and very brief explanations prefacing the letters. Except for the short introductions, there was no analysis of the event and no official information provided. In addition, the extent to which these published letters echo the type of information sent privately by soldiers to their friends and families demonstrates that the letters printed were probably not censored in any way by the newspapers. The unexpected overtures for a cease-fire, the mutual respect—qualified by some suspicion—between the two lines, the attribution of enthusiasm for the war to the Prussian regiments, and the pleasure in an unexpected holiday all echo details already noted in soldiers' letters about the truce.

Although by the end of the year the news of the holiday cease-fire was obviously starting to reach the British public, it appears that the press as a whole was unwilling to extrapolate any conclusions from the truce, and it certainly had no intention as yet of committing itself to any approval or interpretation of the event by straightforwardly reporting on it. In addition, the existence of the truce had no discernible effect on the normal newspaper reports about the war. This pattern continued with further letters about the truce that appeared in the next few days. On New Year's Day the British newspapers increased the column space they devoted to the Christmas truce: the *Times, Daily Telegraph, Manchester Guardian,* and *Daily Mail* all published soldiers' accounts of the event, while still refraining from commenting or reporting on it.

The *Times* printed multiple letters about the truce on that day, one of which came from a major in the Royal Field Artillery who reported how, on Christmas Eve, "things went positively dead; there was not a sound. Even our own pet sniper went off duty." After a quiet evening around a fire, at "about 11 o'clock a very excited Infantry officer came along and told us that all fighting was off, and the men were fraternizing in between the trenches." The major then walked up to the front and discovered that "it had been agreed between the soldiers on both sides that there should be no firing until midnight Christmas Day." In fact, the two sides also arranged terms for the cease-fire, agreeing "that if by any mischance a single shot was fired it was not to be taken as an act of war, and an apology would be accepted; also that firing would not be opened without due warning on both sides." The officer further reported that the German desire for an armistice seemed greater than that of the British; the Germans, he claimed, "were all for the truce lasting for 48 hours, but we stuck out for midnight on Christmas."[10]

The *Times* then offered two more accounts of the truce as "interesting corroborative evidence of the letter printed above." One of those letters, from a major in the Leicestershire Regiment, discussed the influence of the event on soldiers' attitudes toward the war. "Even out here," the officer wrote, "there is a time of peace and good will. I've just spent an hour talking to German officers and men, who have drawn a line half-way between our left trenches and theirs and have met all our men and officers there. We exchanged cigars, cigarettes, and papers." The major noted that the German soldiers "are jolly, cheery fellows for the most part," and concluded that, at least for that moment, it seemed "so silly under the circumstances to be fighting them." Another account from a major in the Royal Army Medical Corps reported that a different regiment "actually had a football match with the Saxons, who beat them 3–2!!!" He then offered the less cheerful tale of another regiment that "went out of their trenches just as the others had done, but the enemy—now thought to be Prussians—told them to go back and fired on them before they regained their trenches."[11]

Additionally, the *Times* printed a letter from a member of the London Rifles, who wrote, with fine understatement, that his unit "had rather an interesting time in the trenches on Christmas Eve and Christmas Day." The British and Germans had handled the negotiations before coming out of their trenches, and they agreed on Christmas Eve that "in our part of the firing line . . . there should be no firing and no thought of war on Christmas Day." The two sides visited each other on Christmas Day and exchanged gifts and addresses. Everyone, the writer claimed, "friend and foe, were real good pals. . . . And on Christmas Day a football match was played between them and us in front of the trench." The letter related how the enemy troops "even allowed us to bury all our dead lying in front, and some of them, with hats in hand, brought in one of our dead officers from behind their trench, so that we could bury him decently." Because of this, the author confided, "I now have a very different opinion of the Germans." By the time the letter was written, however, the rifleman reported that "both sides have already started the firing, and are already enemies again. Strange it all seems, doesn't it?"[12]

As more soldiers' accounts of the event appeared, the letters the newspapers published from truce participants recounting their experiences, as well as the themes expressed in those letters, continued to resemble those already presented as private correspondence. The proximity of the trenches, the individual arrangements for cease-fires, the meetings between trenches and exchanges of gifts, the joint burial parties, and even the occasional football match were all common truce elements that continued to be printed alongside the more customary reporting about the war. The *Daily Mail*, for example, published two letters about the Christmas truce on 1 January 1915, but the paper unwittingly demonstrated the dichotomy between the reports of the truce and the standard war narrative by choosing first to summarize, in an editorial entitled "The New Year," the reasons that the British had gone to war. The editorial asserted Britain was fighting to maintain its liberty, restore Belgian sovereignty, preserve French independence, and prevent Germany from "plotting and preparing our destruction." The *Daily Mail* declared, however, that there was still more at stake: "Let Germany win, and the whole gospel of despotism, based on the anarchic doctrine that nothing counts in this world except the sheer mass of organized strength, receives a new and indefinite lease." If the Allies prevailed, on the other hand, "liberty steps into the sun once more, and there will at length be a chance not only of striking off the burden of armaments but also of redrawing the map along the lasting lines of race, nationality and justice." It was therefore, the editorial concluded, Britain's "glorious privilege to-day, as it has been many times in the past, to turn the scale against a jack-booted Colossus seeking to stamp out the liberties of Europe."[13]

After clearly stating Britain's war aims and pointing out the differences between the two sides, the *Daily Mail* may have felt more at ease about printing its first accounts of the impromptu armistice. Under the banner headline "One Day of Peace at the Front," the *Mail* provided a version of the truce that focused mainly on a joint funeral service. The account began with the burial of a Scottish soldier, during which troops from both sides began venturing out of their respective trenches. The British chaplain had just gone forward to meet with the German commander when a rabbit suddenly appeared. The Germans and British both ran out into No Man's Land, "and a marvelous thing happened. It was like a football match, the hare being the football, and gray tunicked Germans the one side, and the kilted 'Jocks' the other. The game was won by the Germans, who captured the prize."[14]

As a result of the chase, the officer wrote, "a sudden friendship had been struck up, the truce of God had been called, and for the rest of Christmas Day not a shot was fired along our section." The two sides proceeded to remove the dead soldiers lying out in No Man's Land, as "over the sixty yards separating the trenches were scores and scores of dead soldiers, and soon spades were flung up by comrades on guard in both trenches, and by instinct each side set to to dig graves for their dead." The British padre reached an agreement with the German commander to have a truce for the day, accompanied by a joint burial service. The officer noted that the "whole German staff showed a fine spirit of respect during the service for the dead." Prayers were said by both sides, first by the chaplain in English, then translated by a German divinity student, and the officer observed that "it was a memorable sight to see officers and men who had been fighting and as I write are fighting against one another as fiercely as ever, bareheaded, reverent, and keeping sacred truce as they did homage to the memory of the dead on Christmas Day, 1914."[15]

Whether the *Daily Mail* felt that an editorial reminding its readers of the reasons that Britain was fighting the war nullified the reports of the apparent lack of enmity on the Western Front, or whether it saw relatively little harm in recounting events that all the other papers were featuring, stories about the armistice certainly ran counter to its normal reports of the war. The *Daily Telegraph* and the *Manchester Guardian* also printed soldiers' accounts of the truce on 1 January 1915, although the letters that ran in those papers introduced some elements that were new to the public truce narrative. The *Telegraph*, for example, featured an account from a soldier in the Queen's Westminster Rifles who noted the possible risks of the cease-fire when he reported that, while his unit was fraternizing in No Man's Land, "two of our men went too far, and went into their trenches, and haven't since returned, so I suppose they are prisoners."[16] Another letter discussed a twenty-four-hour truce arranged by an infantryman who went into the German trenches to negotiate it, the first time a British soldier was reported to have been invited into a German trench. The soldier noted that the cease-fires "happened along most of the British front except where the Prussians opposed them." The next day, however, "all was changed, and where they had been at peace they were again at war, with the guns roaring and the rifles firing." The *Telegraph*'s coverage of the event clearly underlined the expectation that the truce was to be for a specific period only and not the precursor to a more enduring cease-fire. This last point was borne out by the headlines in the *Telegraph* on that same day reporting the "real" news of the war: "German Atrocities in Belgium / Maltreatment of Wounded / Firing on the Red Cross."[17]

The *Manchester Guardian* also continued to provide letters about the truce, including one from a Manchester soldier who wrote to his wife that the Germans had displayed lit Christmas trees on their parapets before beckoning the British out into No Man's Land. Champagne was drunk by the officers, and they were then joined by the men. The Germans, "having occupied a brewery," presented the British with two barrels of beer. The truce lasted only twenty-four hours, according to the soldier, after which "they are at it again this morning." He also reported that the Germans had told the British that "their officers fire on them if they don't fire on us every time they see an English soldier." Another letter, from Private Lydall of the London Rifle Brigade, noted that "some understanding was arrived at with the Germans and not a shot was fired," after which the two sides met in No Man's Land, "exchanged souvenirs and chatted." Looking back on the experience, the private remarked that the Germans "weren't a half bad lot, really.

You would never think we were flying at one another's throats a few hours previously."[18]

During the week following New Year's Day, the Christmas truce continued to be featured in the major British papers, although none of the newspapers printed letters about the event on a daily basis. As noted in relation to letters received privately, the soldiers' accounts published by the British press continued not only to challenge the contemporaneous narrative of the war, but also to provide details that contest the modern conventions of the armistice. A letter published in the *Daily Telegraph* on 2 January, for example, demonstrated that higher-ranking officers did not always oppose the truce. A colonel of an infantry regiment who went up the trenches on Christmas Day to wish his soldiers a happy Christmas observed that as he was leaving, "there was a sudden hurrah and rush, and our men and the Germans both started running to one another, and met half-way and shook hands." The colonel expressed some reservations, ordering his men back, but he "was told they wanted a truce for the day to bury their dead, so I agreed to that."

Leaving half the men in the trenches to "keep a smart look-out," the colonel went forward and "joined the crowd." An obliging Saxon interpreted for the officer while he spoke to the German soldiers. Catching the Christmas spirit, the colonel agreed that "if they would have an armistice on New Year's Day we would play them at football between our lines." After noting the details of a joint burial service, the colonel observed, in closing, that the Germans seemed keen on the idea of playing the British at football, which might now be practicable, as "there won't be any obstacles like dead Germans lying about unless they try another attack before then." The *Telegraph* also printed a letter from a soldier in the 3rd Rifles that discussed the truce and closed with the rifleman reporting his belief that the cease-fire was a one-off experience; as he remarked resignedly, "I don't expect we shall shake hands with the enemy again for a long time to come."[19]

Demonstrating that the published accounts of the event encompassed the holiday armistice in all its diverse manifestations, the *Morning Post* produced an instance of official interference in the truce, printing a letter from an officer who noted that the British and German soldiers had arranged "to have a two hours' interval on Boxing Day from 2 p.m. to 4 p.m. for a football match. This, however, was prevented by our superiors at Headquarters." The author accepted this restriction philosophically while at the same time reflecting that "it is terrible to think that on one day we can be at such peace, with such good feeling, and on the others we must occupy our minds inventing diabolical methods of destroying one another." Ironically, in light of this account, an editorial published in the *Morning Post* on the same day argued that "war in itself is a thing indifferent, being either good or bad, according to its use and services. In the present case," the editorial continued, "peace for this country would have been a far greater evil than war, not only because it would have meant an evil day only deferred, but because it would have been enjoyed at the expense of a national moral surrender." With its customary disregard of any dissonance engendered by the continued information on the truce and the stance that the newspaper was taking toward the war, coverage in the *Morning Post* epitomized the contradictions inherent in the simultaneous reports of the holiday cease-fire and the ongoing conflict.[20]

Continued firsthand accounts of the Christmas truce in the *Times* in early January 1915 show that the cease-fire took as many forms as the soldiers who participated in it. A letter from an officer in a Highland regiment, for example, demonstrated his increasing frustration with the German troops who refused to fight on Christmas. The officer described himself as initially "horrified at discovering that some of our men actually had gone out, imbued more with the idea of seeing the German trenches than anything else; they met half-way, and there ensued the giving of cigarettes and receiving of cigars, and they arranged (the private soldiers of one army and the private soldiers of the other) a 48 hours' armistice." At this point, however, the officer recalled the lessons of history, and while noting that "it was all most irregular," he consoled himself with the reflection that "the Peninsular and other wars will furnish many such examples; eventually both sides were induced to return to their respective trenches, but the enemy sang all night."[21]

The officer's irritation recurred the next day, when once again "out came those Germans to wish us 'A Happy Day.'" He told the Germans that "we were at war with them, and that really they must play the game and pretend to fight; they went back, but again attempted to come towards us." Tiring of appeals to their enemies' sporting instincts, the British troops "fired over their heads, they fired a shot back to show they understood, and the rest of the day passed quietly in this part of the line, but in others a great deal of fraternizing went on." In spite of his impatience with the Germans' refusal to "play the game" and fight on Christmas Day, the officer finished his account with the reflection that it was "a great hope for future peace when two great nations, hating each other as foes have seldom hated, one side vowing eternal hate and vengeance and setting their venom to music, should on Christmas Day, and for all that the word implies, lay down their arms, exchange smokes, and wish each other happiness!" It is clear from some of the letters published in the press that it was not just the editors of the newspapers who found the truce difficult to reconcile with their attitudes toward the war: evidently some soldiers were also perplexed by the contradictions inherent in the event.[22]

Another hesitant truce participant was a junior officer in a rifle brigade who observed lit Christmas trees on the German parapets on Christmas Eve. The officer, who noted that "no truce had been proclaimed," was strongly against "allowing the blighters to enjoy themselves, especially as they had killed one of our men that afternoon." His less experienced captain "(who hadn't seen our wounded going mad and slowly dying outside the German trenches on the Aisne) wouldn't let me shoot; however, I soon had an excuse, as one of the Germans fired at us, so I quickly lined up my platoon and had those Christmastrees down and out." The officer later heard that two officers from another trench met two German officers in No Man's Land, which he thought "an awfully stupid thing to do, as it might easily have had different results; but our captains are new and, not having seen the Germans in their true light yet, apparently won't believe the stories of their treachery and brutality."[23]

On Christmas, however, the two sides had a "sort of mutual truce; nothing on paper or even in words, but a sort of mutual understanding." The officer reported that some of his suspicions were allayed when he saw that the Germans opposite were Saxons, "because they're good fellows on the whole and play the game as far as they know it." The German dead lying between the lines were buried, and the Germans told the British that they would not shoot at them for now but warned them that, when their eastern army returned on 1 January, "they were going to wipe us off the face of the earth." In response, the officer wrote that the British "roared with laughter, but [the Germans] were quite serious about it and evidently believed it all." In the evening the officer "took good care to double my sentries, as I trust these fellows devil an inch," but in spite of his caution, he still thought it possible that the "politicians will be wrong now, and that the war will come to an end because every one will get fed up and refuse to go on shooting."[24]

This officer's letter demonstrates once again that the newspapers found horrific details about service in the front lines acceptable to print when they came directly from British soldiers: reports of wounded "going mad and slowly dying" were certainly not featured in any of the conventional newspaper reports on the war, and neither was speculation that soldiers might just quit fighting if they felt "fed up" with the war. The *Times* also printed a letter from a Belgian soldier describing a truce that appeared much tamer than those experienced by the British: he reported singing from both trenches, a brief meeting in No Man's Land, and Christmas passing without hearing one shot fired the whole day. These letters in the *Times*, including the first report from a truce participant who was neither British nor German, added a layer of complexity to the information previously provided about the truce, and the continued coverage of the holiday cease-fire demonstrated how popular the story had proved to be with British readers.[25]

During the first week of January 1915, the participants' printed accounts of the truce expanded to include reports that demonstrated its intermittent nature, showing just how different soldiers' experiences in the front line on Christmas Day could be. Two letters in the *Manchester Guardian* on 6 January from different companies of the 2nd East Lancashires provide an example of this: in the first, from a private in B Company, the German troops requested a cease-fire for the British to collect and bury two bodies of British soldiers that were near the German trenches. "Not a shot was fired between us after that up to the time of our relief on Christmas night," the soldier wrote. "The scene was very dramatic, and I don't suppose will be witnessed again on a battlefield." It certainly was not witnessed by members of the same battalion's D Company, who heard the Germans singing but did not participate in a truce. "Oh, by the way, they have a novel way of wishing one a happy Christmas—namely, shouting out 'A happy Christmas to you!' and then firing a number of shots at us, only they couldn't hit us, as we were out of sight of them," a soldier in that company reported. "Of course we returned the salute with interest."[26]

The *Guardian* also published an account from a subaltern at the front who joined in a truce that was arranged with the Germans for the purposes of burying both the British and German dead "who had been lying out in the open since the fierce night-fighting a week earlier." The subaltern, arriving at the site, found the bodies already laid out in rows, and he "went along those dreadful ranks and scanned the faces, fearing at every step to recognize one I knew. It was a ghastly sight. They lay stiffly in contorted attitudes, dirty with frozen mud and powdered with rime." Two common graves were dug, but because the burials could not be completed on Christmas Day, the truce was extended to 26 December. As a result, the Germans "left us alone that night to enjoy a peaceful Christmas." The next day a service was read over the graves, and the subaltern confessed himself moved by the occasion, writing that it "was one of the most impressive things I have ever witnessed. Friend and foe stood side by side, bare-headed, watching the tall, grave figure of the padre outlined against the frosty landscape as he blessed the poor broken bodies at his feet. Then, with more formal salutes, we turned and made our way back to our respective ruts." In spite of the cheerful tone of most of the letters published about the holiday cease-fire, they nevertheless contained reminders of the horrors of war and the "poor broken bodies" of dead comrades.[27]

As the first week of January 1915 drew to a close, the number of letters referring to the Christmas truce published in the newspapers began to dwindle. The papers also began to feature accounts by soldiers in the front line at times other than Christmas, or by soldiers who were in the front line at Christmas but did not participate in a truce, reminding their readers that the armistice had not been a universal experience. The *Daily Mail*, for example, printed a letter from a gunner in the Royal Field Artillery who described going into the trenches on Christmas morning. "We got into action about eleven o'clock on Christmas morning by the side of a road," he wrote, "and after we had got the guns into position and covered them with trees we had about half an hour's football." After this interlude, they "got the order 'Eyes front' (which means every man to his post), and then we started sending the 'Germs' over Christmas boxes which went into their trenches, so I guess there are a few there who would not have any Christmas pudding."[28]

While the quantity of letters about the truce tapered off, the newspapers began to produce short articles about the responses of the French and German military authorities to the unofficial cease-fire. On 6 January the *Manchester Guardian* featured an article headlined "A Sequel to the Truce / French and Germans Refuse to Fight Afterwards," which was purportedly based on a conversation that a journalist had with a French soldier in a Parisian hospital. The soldier related that "on the night of December 24 the French and Germans at a particular place came out of their respective trenches and met half-way between them." The sequel to this episode, the reporter wrote, "was more interesting than the event itself," for the "French and German soldiers who had thus fraternized subsequently refused to fire on one another, and had to be removed from the trenches and replaced by other men." The *Guardian* featured another article on 14 January, discussing truces between the French and Germans that "alarmed" the French government leaders, who had since "forbidden the French papers to publish them, and have even suppressed stories of fraternization between English and German soldiers in an English paper published in Paris." The paper also reported disapproving reactions to the truce from the German government. The appearance of these articles could be credited either to public interest in the truce generally or to the desire to show the Germans had no taste for further fighting, which was certainly a moral that some British soldiers had deduced from the cease-fire.[29]

The *Times* also featured a similar article, sent by a correspondent in Amsterdam, entitled "The Christmas Truce / Stringent German Army Order." It noted that the German newspapers had "recently published numerous descriptions of attempted friendly overtures between the trenches of the Germans and the French." The article quoted the German paper *Tägliche Rundschau*, which observed that " 'every one will recognize that this fraternizing has its serious side, for war is no sport, and one must affirm with regret that those who made or countenanced these overtures evidently mistook the seriousness of the situation.' " As a result, the newspaper reported, an army order had been issued on 29 December forbidding fraternization and warning the troops that "every approach to the enemy . . . will be punished as treason." On 9 January the *Daily Mail* also picked up this article for its own pages, which illustrates the newspapers' willingness to discuss official reaction to the holiday armistice—as long as it wasn't British official reaction.[30]

The *Illustrated London News,* a weekly journal that turned the news of the day into simple stories accompanied by photographs and drawings, featured the Christmas truce on the front page of its 9 January edition, under the headline "The Light of Peace in the Trenches on Christmas Eve: A German Soldier Opens the Spontaneous Truce by Approaching the British Lines with a Small Christmas Tree." The journal clearly assumed its readers would be already familiar with the event, and the brief caption for the drawing contained the information that in some sections of the front the Germans, on Christmas Eve, "decorated their trenches with Christmas-trees and paper lanterns, and invited our troops to stop shooting and come over to smoke and have a palaver."

Both sides, the journal reported, continued the cessation of hostilities the next day, and "spent a happy Christmas."[31]

Charles Lowe, a columnist for the *Illustrated London News*, poetically noted in the same edition that "Christmastide brought with it to our trenches in Flanders a sort of 'truce of God' by mutual consent, accompanied by such fraternizing between opposing foes as had never been seen, perhaps, since Peninsular days or the siege of Sebastopol." Of course, he observed, "afterwards the fighting went on as briskly as ever—with results on the whole, as unfavourable to the 'Boches' in Belgium as it has been to them in South-West Africa, where we have re-occupied Walfinch Bay." The journal contained further drawings representing different aspects of the truce, with titles such as "British and German Soldiers Arm-in-Arm and Exchanging Headgear" and "Saxons and Anglo-Saxons Fraternizing on the Field of Battle." The captions under these drawings described the truce as "informal and spontaneous" and noted that there was " 'peace on earth and goodwill towards men' among those who a few hours before had been seeking each other's blood, and were bound to do so again after the truce was over." The journal reminded its readers that the German troops participating in the truce were, of course, Saxons, while in other areas of the front, "where Prussian troops were said to be stationed, there was a certain amount of fighting." The paper described some fairly standard elements of the truce, including the exchange of cigarettes, and noted that "some of the British, it is said, visited the German trenches, and an Anglo-German football match was even played." The Christmas truce, it appears, was considered an acceptable subject for coverage by different categories of the British press, as long as it was made clear that the armistice was both spontaneous and temporary and would shortly be followed by renewed combat.[32]

Until this time, the British newspapers had refrained from either reporting or providing substantial comments on the truce. Now, more than two weeks after the event, and a week after coverage of it had begun to appear in the press, the *Daily Telegraph* apparently felt ready—or perhaps compelled—to tackle the subject. In an editorial published on 7 January 1915, it acknowledged that "probably no news since the war began has made a greater sensation, and certainly none has made better reading than the accounts which have come through from the trenches of the unofficial armistice established between certain sections of the German line and our own on Christmas Eve and Christmas Day." The newspaper noted that the stories of the truce seemed incredible "in view of the ferocity of the combatants during months past and of the authenticated tales of German atrocities and trickery." The *Telegraph* obviously feared that the news about the truce might lead the British public to believe that the German soldier, once "outside the influence of the Prussian military machine," was a "good-hearted peace loving individual."[33]

This interpretation of the event was inaccurate, the editorial asserted. Truces were traditional, had always occurred between troops facing one another in war, and arose "from a growing feeling of respect for your adversary" with whom soldiers shared "common hardships and common dangers." In those circumstances, "the national feeling gives way before the fellow-feeling for the man opposite, who, after all, is not responsible for the war and is only obeying orders." Having established that, as it had preached all along, the German leadership and not the unfortunately deluded common German soldier bore the blame for the conflict, the *Daily Telegraph* then tried to put the best face possible on the truce. Since it could not ignore the cease-fire, it instead enjoined its readers to remember that it was the kaiser who had started the war and that, on Christmas Day, "the brave Bavarians and Saxons exchanged greetings and gifts and the dead whilst the author of all Europe's miseries was publically announcing 'that to the enemy I send bullets and bayonets.'" Although the *Telegraph* editorial tried to situate the truce within its assumed war narrative by reminding its readers that a day of goodwill on the part of the troops did not absolve the kaiser of responsibility for starting the war, most of the other newspapers made no similar effort, confining themselves to further letters about the truce and articles on the effects of fraternization in the German and French armies.[34]

In its own attempt to reconcile the inconsistencies between the Christmas truce and the continuing fighting on the Western Front, the *Manchester Guardian* featured an editorial about the event in its 9 January edition. In an endeavor to position the truce in the overall context of the war, the *Guardian* tried to characterize the armistice as proof that, though battles might destroy the bodies of soldiers, their souls would survive intact. The editorial noted that the message of the truce, which some wanted to explain as "a truce of God," was in fact something altogether more complex. The *Guardian* presented the cease-fire as "the simple and unexamined impulse of human souls, drawn together in face of a common and desperate plight." To the skeptics who observed that the soldiers involved went immediately back to the business of killing each other, the *Guardian* pointed out that the reasons for the war still existed—that Belgium still had to be liberated and the Germans "taught that Culture cannot be carried by the sword," and that the Allied soldiers, therefore, had good reasons to continue fighting.[35]

The editorial argued that the real lesson to be gained from the truce was that the British soldier, though capable, both physically and morally, of defeating the Germans (with their "insufficient insight into the better way"), would return from the war neither brutalized nor scarred by his experiences. The fact that the British troops were able to put aside their arms for one day, the *Guardian* theorized, proved that "the soul of man" was greater than the guns that the armies used, and that the British soldier had been briefly granted a vision of an ideal "that things seen can have no power at all over the things which are not seen." While this editorial contained some contradictory elements, it was at least an attempt to reconcile the armistice with the public's perception of the war by providing a reasoned argument (although skewed in favor of the superior moral character of the British) about the motivations of the soldiers involved, in contrast to the *Daily Telegraph* editorial that was satisfied with continuing to blame the kaiser for the conflict.[36]

These editorials, which appeared more than two weeks after the truce took place, constituted the only contemporaneous journalistic attempts to explain the event and find a place for it within the narrative of the war. The approaches that were taken by the *Daily Telegraph* and *Guardian* differed greatly: whereas the *Daily Telegraph* merely maintained its pre-truce stance, the *Guardian* attempted to assign greater meaning to the event within the context of the eventual end of the war and the emotional effects of the conflict on the men involved. After the publication of these two editorials, coverage of the truce tapered off dramatically; most newspapers printed only the occasional letter on the subject until about the third week in January 1915, when accounts of the truce disappeared from British newspaper columns altogether.

The Christmas truce, as presented in the pages of the British press, resembled in complexity the event as viewed by individual soldiers in their private letters, demonstrating that the newspapers did not make any effort to shape the narrative by either including or ignoring letters that presented a specific view of the holiday armistice. During the three weeks that the Christmas truce was featured prominently in the British newspapers, however, the ambivalence of the press toward the event was apparent. While it was obvious that the story of the truce was tremendously popular—after all, twenty-one days would be far too long to feature an episode that bored the public—it was equally clear that British newspaper editors were unwilling to commit themselves to an opinion on the subject. By confining the reports of the truce to the "Letters from the Front" columns, the British press segregated the event from the rest of its war coverage, thereby protecting its normal representations of the conflict, which remained unaltered by the news of the unofficial cease-fire. The only attempts at reporting on the truce covered French and German sanctions toward it, and British official reaction to the episode was not recorded in any newspaper.[37]

In addition, the rather feeble attempt on the part of the *Daily Telegraph* and the more robust opinion from the *Manchester Guardian,* both attempting to "explain" the truce within the context of the overarching war narrative, shows how the temporary armistice and the soldiers' attitudes toward the conflict and their enemies confounded the newspapers' endeavors to present the First World War as a seamless narrative of triumphant good against easily vanquished evil. In spite of this ambivalence toward the event, however, the story of the truce in all its complexity was openly published, and the British public as a whole was therefore able to understand the event and the emotions of the soldiers involved through their own words, which the papers printed without apparent censorship. In addition, the popularity of the story shows that, whatever reservations the British press may have had about the truce, the British public was able to absorb and accept it without loss of faith in its soldiers or the cause for which the nation fought. In fact, it probably comforted many civilians to know that their soldiers had enjoyed, if only for its novelty value, their unusual Christmas in the trenches. It now remains to be seen whether the knowledge of the Christmas truce would sink without a trace during the remaining years of war, or whether, having received so much attention, it would continue to remain part of the collective memory of the conflict.

6

"That Unique and Weird Christmas"

The Christmas Truce during the War

And then, to all intents, the story was forgotten. It disappeared
under the gas clouds of Ypres and the colossal casualty lists of
the Somme and Passchendaele.
> —Malcolm Brown, "When Peace Broke Out,"
> *Manchester Guardian,* 23 December 2001

The fraternizing of the British and Germans at their first
Christmas under arms, in 1914, will, perhaps, always be
accounted as the most curious episode of the war.
> —Stephen Stapleton, "The Relations between
> the Trenches," *Contemporary Review,* 1917

"One of the strangest and most significant events of the war" was how
George Perris described the Christmas truce in *The Campaign of 1914
in France and Belgium,* his 1915 book about the initial months of
fighting. In this work, which tried to present an evenhanded view of
the war and the events leading up to the conflict, Perris, a journalist and political writer, predicted that as the great wave of violence
would only slow Europe's progress toward the goal of a more civilized
and morally advanced world, no nation could actually "win" the war.
At the same time, he envisaged the possibility of a hopeful ending to
the conflict: if it resulted in a "real European partnership," then "the
blood offering of the great war will not have been all in vain." It was
within this more optimistic view of the conflict that Perris situated
the truce. He described the scene on Christmas Eve, when the British troops faced their Saxon counterparts across No Man's Land, and
observed that when carol singing came from the German trenches, the
British snipers simply ceased shooting. Thereafter fraternization began

in earnest, including an agreement for the truce to continue until midnight on Christmas Day.[1]

Perris included joint burial services and a football match, as well as officers who came out "to see 'the fun,'" in his account of the truce. From these scenes he drew a hopeful lesson, that "such acts, such men, give us back our faith in the virtue of life and the common human heart." As the temporary cease-fire had not been sanctioned by the countries' leaders or suggested to the troops by any idealists, but rather came from the hearts of the men involved, it was a vision "of reconciliation" that would sustain the soldiers "when many a day of dear-bought but necessary victory has sunk into oblivion. The men who went back to their guns, if they survive, will recall it as the day when Christmas became real for them." Perris took the 1914 armistice as a sign that there was still hope for a better world to rise from the ashes of the battlefield, seeing the episode as proof that "our sons' ways will not be as ours. They will make a new Europe." Perris believed that the truce reflected the possibility that the war could engender a better world than the one Europe had left behind on 4 August 1914, and his attempts to shape the cease-fire into a myth that underlined the general themes of his work illustrates how little time it took for the holiday armistice to be pressed into the service of a more overreaching discourse.[2]

The inclusion of the Christmas truce in Perris's history also contradicts one of the most persistent myths of the truce: the belief that, once it was over, the cease-fire disappeared immediately from the British public's consciousness. Malcolm Brown is one of the most fervent advocates of this theory; in *Meetings in No Man's Land*, for example, he notes that long before 1916, subsequent events "had almost wiped the story from the collective memory. To all intents and purposes, it was forgotten." This is far from the only inaccurate idea that is now firmly embedded in the truce's modern narrative, which has proved to be stubbornly resistant to the available evidence. As befitted an event that, even for those involved, had a slight air of unreality about it, the end of the Christmas truce proved to be only the beginning of the myths that would eventually be constructed around it. A headline for the "Letters from the Front" column in the *Daily Mail* on 1 January 1915, "One Day of Peace at the Front," illustrates one of the main beliefs about the truce: that the cease-fire lasted for only Christmas Day (after which, according to the conventional narrative, it was ruthlessly suppressed by the authorities). Another subsequent truce myth, the theory that soldiers who participated in the holiday armistice later had to be transferred to other parts of the line because they then refused to fight the enemies whom they had befriended, which can be traced back to newspaper accounts published shortly after the truce, was further propagated by soldiers in the line.[3]

An additional misconception that remains part of the conventional narrative of the truce is that there were no further holiday cease-fires in any of the subsequent years of the war, a "fact" underlined in the 2004 *Days That Shook the World* documentary, which stated that, although on Christmas 1914 "half of the British army took part in the greatest act of spontaneous peace in any war," on 25 December 1915, "there will be no repeat," owing to the war's breaking of the "common bond of soldiers," as well as "threats to court-martial fraternizers and shoot deserters." Interestingly, another legend about the truce—which, while contradicting the idea that no further cease-fires occurred, appears to run concurrently with it—concerns Iain Colquhoun, a captain with the Scots Guards, who participated in a 1915 truce and, according to numerous sources, was court-martialed and severely punished for disobeying orders.[4]

Demonstrating that cease-fires (if not actual truces) continued on the Western Front after Christmas or even, in a few cases, New Year's Day, war diaries for a number of regiments continued to report peaceful spells in the line and a lack of aggression from both sides well into January 1915. The diary of the 2nd Lancashire Fusiliers for 2 through 5 January, for example, recorded the frontline situation as "very quiet practically no sniping." The 2nd Yorks noted on 3 January 1915 that the battalion "got on well with improvements to the trenches as there was no firing." The 1st Rifles' diary reflects diminished activity over the course of January 1915, beginning with the observation on 1 January that the front remained "very quiet, very little sniping or shelling by either side." Thereafter, the line continued "fairly quiet but began slowly to increase in activity as regards sniping," and the battalion closed out January's entries with the sly observation that "this has been a very quiet month and we have got through a lot of work owing to the enemy's disinclination to annoy us." Other war diaries, including those of the 2nd Borders and the 2nd Rifles, also reported continuing cease-fires or extremely inactive fronts during this time.[5]

The 1st Somerset Light Infantry went even further in reporting a continued truce, albeit without fraternization, throughout the first week of January and noted the implicit knowledge about this cease-fire by the military leadership. On 1 January its diary recorded that "peaceable conditions still continue," and good progress was subsequently made on all frontline construction. The battalion's 2 January entry is even more unambiguous, noting that the "unofficial truce still continues," and that on 3 January there were only a few shell exchanges. The next day the diary reported that conditions were, "as usual, very quiet," and that "the General" had come up to the lines to inspect the new construction. Similar entries continued for another six days, during which time various senior leaders, including "Lt. Colonel Prowse" and "Gen. Hunter Weston," visited the battalion's front lines and must have detected, without apparent censure, the lack of fighting on this part of the front. The 1st Somersets seem, throughout this time, to have been quite content not to disturb the equilibrium at the front, particularly in view of the persistent rain that constantly undermined their efforts to construct new breastworks. On 11 January, however, their diary recorded that the "truce came to an abrupt end today and sniping started again in earnest."[6]

The willingness of the military leadership to condone continued inactivity in the front line, as evidenced by the lack of reserve with which some units reported prolonged periods of quiet during January 1915, stands in sharp contrast to the conventional narrative of the cease-fire, which suggests that army leaders ordered an immediate resumption of the war shortly after the (one-day) Christmas truce ended. Instead, the presence of senior officers in the 1st Somerset trenches in early January, during a time when a truce not only remained in effect but was written about openly in the battalion diary, indicates that frontline officers did not fear reprisals for reporting ongoing armistices, and that under the right circumstances, such as horrific weather preventing any chance of successful aggression against the enemy, high-ranking leaders were certainly prepared to overlook continuing peaceful conditions in the trenches.

Even after it ended, the holiday armistice continued to be featured in diary entries and letters written home from the Western Front, which demonstrates that the episode had certainly not been forgotten by the soldiers who had taken part in it. Although after Christmas most truce participants quickly reverted to discussing the war in the same manner as they had before the cease-fire, as the memory of the armistice was presumably overridden by new events, a few continued to refer to the episode in their letters home. These soldiers even discussed the theory, which would later be accepted as fact, that troops would be moved to different places in the line in order to reinvigorate the war.

On 27 December 1914 Harold Atkins told his father that his battalion hoped "to have another truce on New Years' Day, and have fixed up a footer match." Wondering how "this business will end," Atkins speculated that "perhaps they will change the battalions." Captain Dillon wrote home on 17 January that this in fact had happened, noting that the German authorities were "very angry" about the Christmas fraternization, and as a result "changed the Saxon Regt. for a Prussian Jaeger Regt. and we fight them continuously."[7]

W. A. F. Foxx-Pitt, a junior officer with the 2nd Cheshires, which rotated into the trenches right after Christmas, wrote to his mother at the end of December that his time in the line was very quiet: "Luckily we have got a very peaceful lot of Germans in front of us and we have come to a sort of agreement that if one side doesn't shoot the other won't so we walk about fairly safely, but you never know who will start shooting. You can see them walking about the top of their trenches." These tales of continued calm periods in the front lines even appeared in some newspapers; the *Manchester Guardian* published a letter on 22 January 1915 from a corporal who noted that his battalion was serving opposite some Bavarians, who since Christmas "have been turning friendly and speaking to the British from the trenches." Another letter printed on the same day reported renewed firing "just before the New Year came in," but when it stopped "one of the Germans started to sing over to our trenches, and when he'd finished his song he shouted, 'Good night boys. We're going to bed, and I wish you all a happy New Year.' "[8]

Although these brief allusions to the Christmas armistice and further friendliness from the enemy were not as common as the initial reports of the truce itself, the fact that these anecdotes were published in the British press demonstrates that censorship remained relaxed even after the cease-fire and did not prevent soldiers referring to the event in their letters. In fact, when writing home on 7 January 1915, Cuthbert Lawson, an officer with the 3rd Royal Horse Artillery, made light of the military leadership's reaction to the truce. "I suppose you saw in the papers about the English and Germans fraternizing on Christmas day—most of it is quite true," he told his mother, adding that "Sir John French has sent round an awful stinker saying how reprehensible it is, or words to that effect, and expressing his great surprise that such a thing should have happened! Rather amusing isn't it?" French's disapproval of the event obviously did not carry a great deal of weight with at least one soldier in the front lines.[9]

Although it is true that no truce on the same scale as the 1914 one took place the following year, smaller armistices did occur in parts of the line on Christmas in 1915, and news of these cease-fires got around quickly. Second Lieutenant H. Ridsdale of the Royal Engineers recorded in his diary on 25 December 1915 that, although the artillery did not participate in a truce, "the Scots and Coldstreams appear to have met the Germans halfway between the lines." W. Tate, with the 2nd Coldstream Guards, pronounced his first Christmas in the lines "very good indeed," as early on "Dec. 25th (Xmas Day) the German Infantry (14th Prussians) came out of their trenches and walked towards our line. We did not fire on them, as they had no equipment or arms of any sort; some of our fellows went over to meet them. They shook hands and exchanged greetings, they also exchanged money and cigarettes, etc." Although specific orders against fraternization over the holiday period were issued in 1915 by British military leaders, they do not appear to have prevented at least a few small truces. No doubt there were also some cases of cease-fires (without fraternization) in the lines on that day, although the troops involved probably made no efforts to publicize them.[10]

The most famous case of fraternization in 1915 took place on 25 December between the 1st Scots Guards and the Germans stationed in the trenches opposite them. Captain Iain Colquhoun, a company commander, wrote extensively about the episode in his diary, in which he noted that on Christmas morning, at about 9 A.M., the Germans advanced into No Man's Land, and he went out to meet a German officer, who asked for a truce for Christmas. Colquhoun "replied that this was impossible. [The German officer] then asked for ¾ hr. to bury his dead. I agreed." The two sides took half an hour to bury their respective dead and spent the remaining fifteen minutes talking and exchanging cigars and cigarettes. "When the time was up, I blew a whistle, and both sides returned to their trenches," Colquhoun wrote. "For the rest of the day the Germans walked about and sat on their parapets. Our men did much the same, but remained in their trenches. Not a shot was fired." That night, the Germans lit up their trenches with lights, which, together with the full moon, caused Colquhoun to declare it was "the prettiest sight I have ever seen." After that, the shelling resumed.[11]

The next day, Colquhoun was called to "explain to Court of Inquiry my conduct on Christmas Day." He reported that the brigadier "doesn't mind a bit," but that Major General Cavan (Rudolph

Lambart, Earl of Cavan) was "furious about it." The 2nd Scots Guards and the Coldstream Guards were "also implicated." On 30 December Colquhoun wrote that "the row about the Xmas truce is still going on"—presumably the irate major general was not prepared to let the matter go—and that he "had to write my account of the thing about 8 times." On 4 January 1916 Colquhoun "received [a] note from the Colonel telling me that I was under close arrest for my share in the Xmas Day truce, also Miles Barne. The others implicated are not being prosecuted against." His status was then changed to open arrest, and on 5 January he was "ordered to attend a 'Summary of Evidence' at H.Q." Evidence was given on that day against Colquhoun and Barne, and they were both charged.[12]

On the same day as the Summary of Evidence, Colquhoun received word that his wife had gone into labor. Although under arrest, he was granted leave to go back to England for the birth of his child. He returned to France afterward and attended the court-martial, which was held on 17 January. The two officers were represented at these proceedings by Raymond Asquith, a noted barrister and the son of the prime minister. Barne's case went first; he was tried for "conduct to the prejudice of good order and military discipline for not giving definite enough orders for the procedure on Christmas day when in Command of the Batt." Barne's trial ended at 2:00 P.M., and a verdict of not guilty was given at 2:10, leaving him "exonerated from all blame," a judgment Asquith had predicted in a 12 January letter to his wife. Colquhoun's trial then commenced. He faced a charge of "Conduct to the Prejudice of good order and military discipline in that on the 25th Dec. [he] (1) agreed to a truce with the enemy [and] (2) permitted a cessation of hostilities." Colquhoun was questioned by Raymond Asquith "with the object of proving that when I went up to the trenches on Xmas morning, I found a very advanced situation which I did my best to regularize by having a definite agreement as to how long the situation was to last." After others presented evidence, character witnesses for Colquhoun, among them a brigadier general and a colonel, were called, and then speeches for both the prosecution and accused were given.[13]

After five hours of deliberation, the court found Colquhoun guilty and "then closed to consider its sentence." Three days later Colquhoun heard that the sentence, a reprimand, was "quashed by G.H.Q.," which really, Colquhoun wrote, "means that the whole thing is washed out." Brown and Seaton report that General Haig himself remitted the sentence because of Colquhoun's "distinguished record in the field." As Asquith observed, "There was no doubt that he committed a technical offense, but in reality he showed a good deal of decision and common sense, and his military character is so first rate that they ought to take a lenient view of the case," which is apparently how Haig also viewed the matter.[14]

At first glance, these two courts-martial, which represented the only times officers were prosecuted during the First World War for allowing fraternization at Christmastime, appear to fit the standard narrative of both the truce and the war. In reality, however, not only was one officer entirely exonerated—a decision that the court took just ten minutes to reach—but the second officer charged, who was represented by the son of the prime minister, had his sentence quashed by General Haig within three days of the verdict's being handed down. This episode involving Captain Colquhoun, which ended with the judicial equivalent of a whimper rather than a bang, is nevertheless one that has recently been blown out of all proportion. In their work on the truce, Brown and Seaton, for example, call the reaction to the fraternization "a considerable fracas," noting that it became "a minor scandal." Weintraub characterizes Colquhoun's court-martial as the predictable reaction of a callous leadership, insisting that "from the command standpoint, conspicuous examples had to be made"—however big a stretch it may be to call a quashed reprimand a "conspicuous example." Until recently, the Colquhoun clan's website even contained the information that the "late chief, Sir Iain Colquhoun 31st of Luss . . . was condemned to death by a court martial but pardoned by King George V for fraternising on Christmas Day with the Germans in No Man's Land."[15]

In the end, however, this was really quite a simple affair. Two officers were charged with conduct prejudicial to good order; one was found not guilty and the other had his very mild sentence quashed. Had the military leadership wished to make an example of these two officers for daring to allow their troops to fraternize with the enemy, it would have ensured that they were punished, and punished severely, for their actions. Instead, the British Army's commander in chief took the time and trouble to make sure the sentence was entirely dismissed, and as Colquhoun later wrote, the "whole Guards division and everyone who knows the facts of the case all say it was a monstrous thing that the Court martial even took place." In addition, it should be noted that Colquhoun, who remained in service throughout the war, eventually rose to the rank of brigadier general, demonstrating that the episode did nothing to impede his career. There is no report that any officers from other battalions were prosecuted for allowing holiday cease-fires, even though Tate's diary entry verifies that the 2nd Coldstream Guards also participated in a truce, as did the 1st Scots Guards, and Ridsdale's diary makes it clear that these armistices were well known throughout the front lines. Once again, the evidence from Christmas 1915 confirms that, contrary to the conventional narrative of the truce, the military leadership really had no serious interest in punishing soldiers for permitting brief cease-fires in the front lines, and in spite of having caught some officers in the act of allowing their men to fraternize after orders were explicitly issued to prevent it, were prepared to overlook the matter even after a court-martial and a guilty verdict.[16]

As references in battalion diaries to the lack of a Christmas truce on the Western Front in subsequent years illustrate, the 1914 armistice remained part of the general military memory of the war. The lack of further information in the newspapers about the truce after January 1915, however, did not prevent the home front from also remembering the 1914 cease-fire long after it had ended. It remained a vital presence in books written about the war and in the soldiers' memoirs that began to appear in 1915, which shows how, aided by the memories of those who had participated in the event, the "wonderful Christmas outburst" had become part of the general narrative of the war. The truce was featured, for example, in a number of multivolume accounts about the war that were written between 1915 and 1919. In these serials, such as *The Times History of the War*, published in a weekly journal format, and *Nelson's History of the War*, which was written by John Buchan in twenty-four volumes over the course of the conflict, the war was parceled up and presented to the British home front as a coherent narrative, and the truce found its place as part of the general chronicle in these accounts. In addition, authors such as Arthur Conan Doyle and George Perris tried to write about the war more reflectively, endeavoring to examine its overall meaning rather than its day-to-day events; here, too, the Christmas cease-fire had a role in the overall discourse. During this period the armistice was also featured in posthumously published collections of letters from frontline officers and memoirs written by soldiers invalided home, including the autobiographical account of Bruce Bairnsfather, the famous cartoonist of trench life, who provided one of the most memorable descriptions of the event. Additionally, the guns had barely stopped firing when Field Marshal French, who headed the B.E.F in the first year of the war, rushed into print with the self-justifying volume *1914*, in which he reconsidered his disapproval of the unofficial cease-fire. From 1915 through 1919, the truce remained an accepted part of the narrative of the war, kept alive in the public memory through works written about the conflict.[17]

Nelson's History of the War was later criticized for not being nearly hard enough on the British military and political leadership, but John Buchan's serial was not strictly propaganda; he was forthright, for example, about such matters as the conditions under which the soldiers served. To write, at that time, about "the misery of standing for hours up to the waist in icy water, of having every pore of the skin impregnated with mud, of finding the walls of a trench dissolving in slimy torrents, while rifles jammed, clothes rotted, and feet were frostbitten" may not, in light of information from soldiers already published in the British press, have been particularly novel, but certainly Buchan pulled no punches when it came to letting the public know what their troops had to endure. Buchan's attitude toward the Christmas truce similarly refused to romanticize the episode, even if his view of the average Tommy was somewhat rose-colored. Introducing the holiday cease-fire with the observation that the British soldier, "nothing if not a good sportsman," exhibited "none of that childish venom of hate which seems to have been officially regarded in Germany as the proper spirit in which to fight battles," Buchan attributed the willingness of the British to participate in the truce to their professionalism, although of course he did not give the German soldiers similar credit. He also observed that the truce had historical precedents, as "outposts have always fraternized to some extent,—they did it in the Peninsula and in the Crimea," and he noted that propinquity also played a part in the armistice, observing that "the close contact of the lines led to the extraordinary truce of Christmas Day." Additional confirmation of Buchan's realistic attitude toward the cease-fire is demonstrated by his admission that the episode was probably "connived at by the commanders on both sides, for some of our trenches were nearly flooded out, and the Germans had much timbering to do." In Buchan's view, the truce was a very natural event: grounded in historical precedent and British good sportsmanship, abetted by bad weather and the need to relieve boredom, and providing an opportunity to carry out repairs to trenches, it appeared to him neither surprising nor a symptom of rebellion by fed-up troops.[18]

Part 45 of *The Times History of the War*, published in the same year, took a rather more moralistic tone toward the truce, although it did generally get its facts right. In the 29 June 1915 edition of the series, entitled "The Winter Campaign in France," the *Times* noted that Christmas Eve was "an appropriate time for the slackening of hostile activities," but it admitted that "no one was prepared for the extraordinary outbursts of good-will and good feelings towards enemies which actually took place on this strange Christmas Day." The *Times* credited the truce to "the psychology exhibited by soldiers facing each other in combat on the field, and engaged for months past in constant fighting," who commenced fraternization "on this great anniversary simply on account of its Christian significance." It then described the episode as "the most interesting, certainly the most moving, feature of this winter campaign," and noted that although the British public approved of the event, the German leadership certainly did not, which highlighted the tolerance of the British in contrast to the Prussian rigidity of their enemy.[19]

With some slight variations on these themes, the *Times* provided a fairly straightforward account of the events leading up and contributing to the truce, including the terrible conditions in Flanders, the exhaustion of the troops after the fall campaign, and the familiarity of the soldiers on both sides of the line with each other, and it further acknowledged that the home front had been fully aware of—and enjoyed—the news of the cease-fire. The report went on to remark on the extent of the truce, which took place "over a very considerable part of the line," and observed, most surprisingly, "that it is worth remarking that in the British lines orders were received on Christmas morning not to shoot unless it was absolutely necessary." This, incidentally, was the first time that such orders had been acknowledged in print; Buchan's belief that "commanders on both sides" had "connived" at the truce because it was convenient to have a breathing space in which to effect trench repairs was as far as anyone had gone previously in implicating senior leadership in the cease-fire's continuance. The *Times*'s account went on to relate many already familiar truce elements while acknowledging the approval of fraternization from "higher ups," such as the report that "the Colonel of a British Infantry regiment met enemy officers (again apparently Saxons) and told them that if they would have an armistice on New Year's Day the British would play them at football." The *Times* also observed that there were "traces of suspicion" on each side, wrote about a burial service for some German dead, and noted requests from Germans who had lived in London to forward letters and photos to friends in England.[20]

So far, so relatively realistic, but the *Times* had now decided to impose a narrative on the holiday cease-fire. Noting that the truce was "a text from which many morals may be preached," the *Times* could not resist pointing out its favorite one. The account observed that "from the German side, this exhibition of goodwill consorted badly with the enemy's avowed policy of 'frightfulness,'" and it therefore received, "as may easily be imagined, no support from the German Higher Command," which in fact issued orders prohibiting further fraternization. The *Times* then went on to remind its readers that fraternization had taken place during the Peninsular Wars, and that such impromptu truces were more likely to result from the proximity of the two opposing sides than from war-weariness—at least as far as the British were concerned. The truce, however, might induce German soldiers, who "had been led to expect a short and glorious campaign," to believe that "the fury of the war had spent itself." Of course, there was no fear expressed that British soldiers, who never had "any real hate of the Germans" and who could therefore forget enmity and respond to the "exhibition of German sentiment" during the Christmas season, would believe that the truce betokened the end of the war. For the *Times*, therefore, the truce proved that the Germans were in fact completely fed up with the war and simultaneously demonstrated that the British soldier was a true sportsman who just wanted to celebrate Christmas.[21]

The report, now turned editorial, incorrectly noted that all truces had taken place against Saxon troops and reminded readers that the "frightful" Prussian behavior that had caused the war also required its continuation, in spite of the generous feelings that the Christmas season and German "sentiment" aroused in the equable, sporting, and always fair British soldier. The *Times,* apparently, had saved its polemic on the truce for a less transient medium than its daily newspaper but had no trouble reaching the same conclusion as the *Daily Telegraph* had months earlier: truces may be traditional, and this one therefore understandable, particularly in light of the well-known British sense of fair play, but no matter what had happened on Christmas 1914, the frightful Prussian-influenced German state still had to be defeated. The only surprising part of the account was the admission that British soldiers had been instructed not to fire on the Germans unless they fired first, but this fact had been buried, without comment, in the long passage devoted to the truce. Although the *Times* got many of the details about the armistice correct, its decision to cast the episode in these dramatic terms imposed a moral on the narrative of the cease-fire that had not been drawn by those who had participated in it.[22]

Bruce Bairnsfather, the famous war cartoonist who served with the 1st Royal Warwicks from 1914 to 1915, before he was invalided home with hearing damage and shell shock, provided a less didactic take on the truce in his 1916 memoir of life in the trenches, *Bullets and Billets*. Interspersed with many of the drawings for which he was famous, the memoir tried to give an accurate and sardonic account of life in the front lines. His war cartoons were well appreciated by other soldiers; as Cyril Falls, the military historian who also served in the trenches, said of Bairnsfather's work, "He did as much as most people to help us to endure what we had to endure." Early in the memoir, Bairnsfather advised his audience to try a small experiment to gain an understanding of what life in the trenches was like: "Select a flat ten-acre ploughed field, so sited that all the surface water of the surrounding country drains into it. Now cut a zig-zag slot about four feet deep and three feet wide diagonally across, dam off as much water as you can so as to leave about a hundred yards of squelchy mud; delve out a hole at one side of the slot, then endeavour to live there for a month on bully beef and damp biscuits, whilst a friend has instructions to fire at you with his Winchester every time you put your head above the surface."[23]

Bairnsfather wrote about his initial disappointment at finding his battalion assigned to the trenches on Christmas Day but conceded that "looking back on it all, I wouldn't have missed that unique and weird Christmas for anything." He recalled how the Germans began singing on Christmas Eve, then called out to the British, who sent an emissary across No Man's Land in the form of a sergeant (at first suspicious and reluctant), who returned with a gift of German cigars. This episode, Bairnsfather noted, although it "did not lessen our ardour or determination," came as "a welcome relief to the daily monotony of antagonism." The next morning, German soldiers appeared in No Man's Land and the British also started to show themselves, which led to a day of fraternization. In spite of the friendly relations, however, Bairnsfather claimed that he and his fellow soldiers could not forget that the Germans, "these sausage-eating wretches, who had elected to start this infernal European fracas, and in so doing had brought us all into the same muddy pickle as themselves," were the enemy. He reported that the British soldiers, "superior, broadminded, more frank, and lovable beings," regarded "these faded, unimaginative products of perverted kulture as a set of objectionable but amusing lunatics whose heads had *got* to be eventually smacked."

Bairnsfather's Christmas day ended peacefully with a photograph being taken of the two sides which, he imagined, would repose "on some Hun mantelpieces, showing clearly and unmistakably to admiring strafers how a group of perfidious English surrendered unconditionally on Christmas Day to the brave Deutschers." (See figure 10.) After the photo session, the two groups "began to disperse," as a general "feeling that the authorities on both sides were not very enthusiastic about this fraternizing seemed to creep across the gathering," although "there was a distinct and friendly understanding that Christmas Day would be left to finish in tranquillity." Bairnsfather summed up the episode by noting that although "there was not an atom of hate on either side that day; and yet, on our side, not for a moment was the will to war and the will to beat them relaxed." Absent the sermonizing that seemed to accompany other references to the Christmas cease-fire during this period, Bairnsfather's retrospective view of the event mirrored that of truce participants who wrote home about the cease-fire: he saw it as a welcome break from the monotony of life in the trenches in a war that had to be won.

In the same year that Bairnsfather's memoir was issued, Arthur Conan Doyle published the first installment of his six-volume series, *The British Campaign in France and Flanders*. In it Doyle analyzed the causes of the war, fixing the blame firmly on Germany. "Looking at the matter from the German point of view, there were some root-causes out of which this monstrous growth had come, and it is only fair that these should be acknowledged and recorded," Doyle wrote. His fairness, however, stopped abruptly at the edge of the English Channel: "These causes can all be traced to the fact that Britain stood between Germany and that world-empire of which she dreamed." Having placed the British firmly on the side of the angels, Doyle was prepared to look charitably on the truce, when "Christmas brought about something like fraternization" between the two armies. But this "amazing spectacle"—and here Doyle arrived at the moral of his lesson—"must arouse bitter thoughts concerning those high-born conspirators against the peace of the world, who in their mad ambition

Figure 10. "Look at this bloke's buttons, 'Arry. I should reckon 'e 'as a maid to dress 'im." German and British soldiers fraternizing on Christmas Day 1914. (Cartoon by Bruce Bairnsfather.)

had hounded those men on to take each other by the throat rather than by the hand." The truce, which remained "one human episode amid all the atrocities which have stained the memory of the war," had to end, as the Germans, bent on world domination, resumed their aggression. For Doyle, therefore, the armistice proved to be merely a brief Christmas celebration and a respite from battle before the effort to beat the "frightful" Germans was renewed.[24]

The letters to his mother written from the Western Front by Edward Hulse, an officer with the 2nd Scots Guards who participated in the 1914 truce, which were published privately in 1916, include one of the most thorough contemporaneous accounts of the truce available. Sir Edward, who had enlisted well before the war, displayed many of the characteristics of the professional British officer class: he despised liberals, thought all Germans greatly inferior creatures, and appears to have swallowed whole any propaganda he encountered. He spoke, in his letters home, about "bagging" Germans and hoped that "some strong unscrupulous fellow with an iron hand to run things" would take over in Britain, observing that everything would work much better "if we could put the whole country under martial law, Government included."[25]

Considering his views, it may seem surprising that Hulse was willing to participate in the truce, but his letter about the cease-fire shows that he had no trouble fitting the event into his general outlook on the war and the enemy. He reported that, on Christmas morning, four unarmed Germans came out of the trenches and advanced toward the British lines, and Hulse and another British soldier went out to meet them. Cigarettes and cigars were exchanged, and Hulse instructed the Germans not to come out past the halfway line between the trenches. He then went to headquarters to report the incident. When he returned to the front line, the British and German troops were out in No Man's Land, happily fraternizing. Hulse called for the German officers and arranged the parameters of the armistice with them: no soldiers should advance more than halfway between the trenches, everyone should be unarmed, and neither side would fire unless the other did. The fraternization continued, souvenirs and addresses were exchanged, and both sides sang boisterously.[26]

At this point, Captain George Paynter, also of the 2nd Scots Guards, arrived at the front lines (presumably from headquarters) and produced a large bottle of rum, which was shared with the Germans. Both sides then repaired to their respective trenches to eat their Christmas meal but in the afternoon returned to No Man's Land for continued fraternization. Even after the armistice ended by mutual agreement at 4:30, the Germans continued to protest that they would not fire, and, as Hulse noted, since Captain Paynter "had told us not to, unless they did, we prepared for a quiet night, but warned all sentries to be doubly on the alert." The next day the 2nd Scots Guards participated in a ceremony at which twenty-nine British dead were buried, which Hulse referred to in a second letter as "the sadder side of Xmas Day," while noting that "it was a great thing being able to collect them, and their relations, to whom of course they had been reported missing, will be put out of suspense and hoping that they are prisoners."[27]

The general cease-fire continued throughout Boxing Day, and the Scots Guards used the time to build up their barbed-wire defenses; Hulse noted that the Germans "came out and sat on their parapet, and watched us doing it, although we had informed them that the truce was ended." Hulse wrote, however, that he still "had instructions not to fire till the enemy did." After the 2nd Scots Guards had returned to the trenches on New Year's Eve, Hulse reiterated that "the 158th German regiment have not yet fired a shot since Christmas," which he believed proved that they "are genuinely sick of the whole thing." Hulse, not surprisingly, saw the Christmas truce as confirmation of the enemy's lack of enthusiasm for the war on the Western Front rather than a symptom of rebellion on the part of the British. In fact, rather than inspiring Hulse with goodwill toward the enemy, the truce only confirmed his poor opinion of the Germans and provided his battalion with a good opportunity to shore up its defenses.[28]

Hulse's letter has, in the years since it was published, been featured in a number of accounts of the truce. The BBC's *Days That Shook the World: The Christmas Truce*, for example, based much of its dramatization of the holiday armistice on Hulse's description of the experiences of the 2nd Scots Guards on 25 December 1914. The documentary, however, consolidates Hulse's two trips into No Man's Land into one and leaves out the crucial facts that he reported the German offer of a truce back to headquarters after the first meeting and that he obviously received permission to continue the cease-fire. "Taking the most pragmatic course, Hulse decides that his men deserve a day off," the documentary reports. "He chooses to ignore the fact that they're sharing it with the enemy—until his commanding officer arrives. Captain George Paynter is the last word in authority for Hulse and his men—and the last chance to call a halt before word reaches HQ. But instead of stopping the party, he fuels it with Fortnum and Mason's rum." Not only does the episode avoid revealing that Paynter was hardly the "last chance" to stop the truce before "word reaches HQ"—impossible because Hulse has already told headquarters himself, and Paynter arrived from there bearing his bottle of celebratory spirits—but it also omits any mention of Paynter's orders not to fire on the enemy. The *Christmas Truce* documentary is far from the only occasion that this account of the truce has been employed to emphasize a disingenuous narrative of the event, but at the time it was published, Hulse's report was considered merely an excellent description of what the introduction to the volume of his letters described as "the most extraordinary event of the war—the Christmas Truce of 1914."[29]

Another view of the holiday armistice was provided by Brigadier General Edward Gleichen, who on 28 December 1914 supplied one of the responses to Smith-Dorrien's demand for reports on the truce. In 1917 Gleichen published an account of the "doings" of the 15th Brigade, which was based on "a very scrappy diary" he had kept in France from 1914 through 1915. The work contains the usual frank descriptions of life in the trenches; in fact, Gleichen proved particularly effusive on the subject of Belgian mud. "O that mud!" he wrote. "We have heard lots about Flanders mud, but the reality transcends imagination, especially in winter. Greasy, slippery, holding clay, over your toes in most places and over your ankles in all the rest—where it is not over your knees,—it is the most horrible 'going' I know anywhere." The book also includes a reference to the truce, in which three of the brigade's five battalions participated. Gleichen wrote that the Germans came out of their trenches unarmed, "with boxes of cigars and seasonable remarks." In the face of these overtures, Gleichen asked rhetorically, What were the British to do? "Shoot? You could not shoot unarmed men. Let them come? You could not let them come into your trenches; so the only thing feasible at the moment was done—and some of our men met them halfway and began talking to them." While noting that the brigade "got into trouble for doing it," he justified the fraternization with the observation that it was "difficult to see what we could otherwise have done," and besides, the officers involved got "excellent close views of the German trenches." Although obviously annoyed, even two years later, by Smith-Dorrien's orders regarding the incident, Gleichen still had no hesitation about discussing his brigade's part in the truce in a memoir published during the war.[30]

In a 1917 *Contemporary Review* article, "The Relations between the Trenches," Stephen Stapleton examined the "common brotherhood of man" that existed between the opposing sides. While asserting that the British thought the German soldiers were "treacherous fighters," he still admitted that the historical practice of fraternizing between even bitter enemies (Stapleton mentioned the customary armistices between the Greeks and Trojans and French and British truces during the Napoleonic Wars) had been followed during the first year of fighting. He credited the truce to "a common feeling of inquisitiveness," claiming that the two sides were just curious about their enemy. In spite of the exchange of souvenirs, however, Stapleton maintained that, once in No Man's Land, "for the most part, British and Germans stood with arms folded across their breasts and stared at each other with a kind of dread fascination." He believed that the truce was never repeated not because the British high command gave orders preventing a recurrence, but rather because of the introduction into the conflict by the Germans "of the barbaric elements of 'frightfulness,' hitherto confined to savage tribes at war; their use of such devilish inventions as poison gas and liquid fire; [and] their belief only in brute strength." The British troops, according to Stapleton, felt no personal rancor toward the Germans during the first part of the war; in fact, he argued that "British feeling is extraordinarily devoid of the vindictiveness that springs from revenge," as proven by the generous way the British treated German prisoners. Once more, the Christmas truce, in which both sides participated equally and which was generally initiated by the Germans, was used to prove the lack of vindictiveness on the part of the British, while Stapleton blamed the fact that it never recurred on German "frightfulness."[31]

Later, in 1917, the 2nd Seaforth Highlanders, who were apparently still nostalgic about the 1914 truce, noted in their war diary that "it was Xmas Day, but there was no fraternizing." As this was the last Christmas of the war, there would be no opportunity for another holiday armistice, but it is clear that at least some battalions continued to mourn its absence. Field Marshal John French also reflected on the truce a few years after the event, writing in his 1919 memoir of the first year of the war, *1914*, that, upon hearing about the holiday cease-fire, he had issued "immediate orders to prevent any recurrence of such conduct," adding that his response to the news was to call "the local commanders to strict account, which resulted in a good deal of trouble." This single sentence from his memoir has been quoted in many descriptions of the Christmas truce and cited as proof of the "severe" military reaction to it, but as has already been noted, there was neither much accounting nor any real trouble. In fact, the cease-fires continued happily and without interference in many parts of the line well beyond Christmas Day. Clearly, French believed (or at least pretended to believe) that his displeasure had prompted definitive action and that all truces had therefore been stopped immediately.[32]

In retrospect, however, French was "not sure that, had the question of the agreement upon an armistice for the day been submitted to me, I should have dissented from it." After all, he had "always attached the utmost importance to the maintenance of that chivalry in war which has almost invariably characterized every campaign of modern times in which this country has been engaged," an attitude that was not held by the Germans, who had "glaringly and wantonly set all such sentiments at defiance by their ruthless conduct of the present war; even from its very commencement." French then recalled a similar circumstance in the Boer War, when a cease-fire for the purposes of burying the dead had been proposed on Christmas, and he had sent a box of cigars and a bottle of whiskey to his counterpart in the South African army to seal the deal, after which the South African general obligingly freed two British prisoners.[33]

"Soldiers should have no politics," French declared in conclusion, "but should cultivate a free-masonry of their own and, emulating the knights of old, should honour a brave enemy only second to a comrade, and like them rejoice to split a friendly lance to-day and ride boot to boot in the charge to-morrow." This change of heart on French's part is, unsurprisingly, not included in the many accounts of the truce that prominently feature his "immediate orders" to prevent the fraternization. Murphy, in *Truce,* equates the displeasure expressed in French's memoir, five years after the 1914 armistice, with Smith-Dorrien's directive issued on 26 December 1914, implying that both date from immediately after the truce and were direct orders. "Because Smith-Dorrien had also heard that some officers were actually encouraging the truce, he issued an ominous warning. . . . The commander of all British troops, Field Marshall John French, was just as angry," Murphy writes, before quoting from *1914* about French's "immediate" orders. In fact, if French issued any written orders regarding the truce, they have never come to light, so it can be safely assumed that French in fact confined himself to reprimands of the senior leadership, which resulted in precisely one order not to fraternize, issued by Smith-Dorrien.[34]

Having thus proven that he was on the soldiers' side all along, French spent most of the rest of his book criticizing the War Office for undermining his efforts by "failing to speed up the manufacture of munitions of war and . . . the derailment of troops and war material to the Dardanelles," which "was undoubtedly the chief cause" of the "lack of success of our endeavours." By establishing that he could not be held responsible for the failure of the British army to defeat the Germans in the first winter of the war, and claiming that, had he been asked in advance, he might well have approved of the still very popular truce, French's memoir, which Brian Bond characterizes as "a belt of ammunition fired at French's enemies in general," presumably helped him wash his hands of the entire 1914–1915 debacle.[35]

As French's retrospective approval of the event illustrates, the Christmas truce was firmly entrenched in the British collective memory by the end of the war, and frequent references to it from 1915 through 1919 demonstrate that it was an accepted part of the narrative of the conflict. The fact that it continued to be mentioned in soldiers' letters and war diaries shows that the supposed censure of the event from the military leadership did little to prevent the soldiers who joined in from reporting their participation. In fact, the rather mocking tone taken by one officer toward French's purported orders bringing the truce to a halt, as well as the continued cease-fires in the lines in the beginning of January 1915 and the willingness to report them in the diaries of the battalions involved, reveal that soldiers certainly felt free to speak about the episodes. Although a brief truce the following year did attract some unwelcome attention from an unhappy major general, the results of the ensuing court-martial show how little interest the leadership had in disciplining those involved. In addition, histories, memoirs, and serial accounts of the war published throughout the conflict frequently featured the truce, and although some writers could not resist turning the event into a morality tale that highlighted their view of the war and the enemy, the basic facts of the cease-fire continued to be reported relatively realistically during this period.

With the arrival of peace, however, views on the war would begin to undergo a metamorphosis, and the truce, now part of the general narrative of the conflict, would also experience a certain amount of revisionist treatment as the soldiers involved, and those writing about the war more generally, began to reconsider the conflict in light of the peace that followed it.

7

"The Curious Christmas Truce"

The First World War and the Christmas Truce, 1920–1959

The earliest fraternizations, at Christmas 1914, could also be seen as such a formless outcry, but they carried a very different message. Essentially, they were a way to stop thinking about the war, to humanize it for these few moments when enemies met each other as brothers.

    —Marc Ferro, *Meetings in No Man's Land* (2007)

I did not leave the trench myself, feeling too sick at what had happened to Collins, and thinking some of us had better be ready in case of any other treacherous act. One short bearded German N.C.O. approached near to our wire, and upon being warned away, spat and snarled "English swine—wait until tonight."

    —F. A. Brown, 2nd Monmouthshires, 1939 memoir

On 31 March 1930 Parliament considered the issue of whether the Labour government should overturn a 1920 undertaking that prevented the years that conscientious objectors had remained in the civil service during the war being counted toward their pensions and proscribed their promotion over war veterans. The question aroused strong feelings on both sides of the House; the Conservatives bitterly opposed the action on the grounds that "the man who has served his country deserves more consideration than the man who has refused to do so," while the government argued that since conscientious objectors were allowed by law to refuse service in the armed forces, even if conscripted, it could not "punish people for doing something which the State has said they have a right to do." The parliamentary debate on this issue encompassed widely diverse views about the First World War, particularly from members of Parliament (M.P.s) who had served in the conflict. Kingsley Griffith, a Liberal, noted that he "was in the front-line trenches, in 1914" and "that we had a feeling of irritation against the conscientious objectors." The Conservative Bertie Leighton admitted that he could "understand a man disliking war and I can understand men doing all that they can to prevent war, but I cannot understand men who, when the country is in danger, refuse to lift one finger to help it." George Benson, a Labour M.P., announced that he spoke "as one who was a conscientious objector during the War, and I only hope that hon. Members opposite are as proud of their War record as I am of mine."[1]

In the midst of this controversy, one M.P. argued that dying in battle was the "greatest and most glorious service" a man could give to his country. Benson vehemently pointed out "that men were not sent into the Army for the definite purpose of dying, but to kill," and that he "was not prepared to admit that killing another man was the highest form of service to one's country." At this point, Major McKenzie Wood, a Liberal who had served with the Gordon Highlanders during the war, joined the debate, passionately asserting that when he had volunteered for service, he did so not to kill, but "to prevent killing," and further stating that "during the whole time I was in the Army, or during the whole of the War, I can honestly say that I never had the slightest degree of animosity against anyone, even against those who were opposed to us in the War."[2]

To emphasize the nature of his convictions, Major Wood declared that "at Christmas, 1914, I was in the front trenches, and took part in what was well known at the time as a truce," when his unit "went over in front of the trenches, and shook hands with many of our German enemies." He observed that a "great number of people think we did something that was degrading," but that as a result of that experience, "I then came to the conclusion that I have held very firmly ever since, that if we had been left to ourselves there would never have been another shot fired." Major Wood argued that "the fact that we were being controlled by others . . . made it necessary for us to start trying to shoot one another again," and that it was only because "we were all in the grip of a political system which was bad" that the war had continued. This view, he noted, had prompted his entry into politics and certainly influenced his belief that "it required, in many cases at any rate, an extraordinary amount of moral courage to be a conscientious objector during the War, and, for my part, I think we ought to see that people who had that strong moral courage to do what they did ought not to be penalised further."[3]

Since in 1930 there were 148,000 First World War veterans in the Civil Service and only 230 conscientious objectors, the fervor aroused by a subject that would affect so few men reveals not only that the British still felt passionately about the war twelve years after it had ended, but also that their attitudes toward it continued to vary widely. There was certainly no political consensus on the conflict at this time: Benson, a conscientious objector, had been elected to Parliament, but so had Captain Austin Hudson, who declared in the same debate that if conscientious objectors "would not undertake the unpleasant part of their obligation of citizenship, they should not later on participate in the advantages which would accrue to them from being citizens." Though by 1930, according to the conventional narrative of the war, those who had refused to fight in it out of moral conviction should have received credit for their resistance to a senseless and futile war, this parliamentary debate illustrates how that belief was just one view of the conflict, and that support for those who fought in what was still perceived by many as a worthy cause also held its own among public opinion.[4]

For Major Woods, memories of the truce provided an inspiration that guided his postwar behavior and prompted him to argue that the British soldiers had been in the grip of a "bad" political system that had involved them in a senseless war. A year earlier, Charles Edmund Carrington, also a veteran of the conflict, strongly opposed the idea that veterans looked back on the war with abhorrence. "A legend has grown up, propagated not by soldiers but by journalists," Carrington declared in his 1929 memoir, A Subaltern's War, "that these men who went gaily to fight in the mood of Rupert Brooke and Julian Grenfell, lost their faith amid the horrors of the trenches and returned in a mood of anger and despair." According to Carrington, these attitudes did not reflect the feelings of the vast majority of the soldiers who fought in the war, who never became "'disenchanted,' for war had never offered them an enchanting prospect." The average British soldier, he maintained, "had not wanted war, but he had engaged in it; he liked it even less than he expected, but he proposed to see it through; and if, which God forbid, similar circumstances arose in 1929, he would do the same again."[5]

The current popular discourse of the First World War, which stresses the supposed bitterness of veterans of the conflict as well as the failure of the peace that followed it, identifies general disillusionment as the dominant narrative of the war during the 1920s and 1930s. As Ludovic Kennedy wrote in the introduction to Alan Lloyd's *The War in the Trenches,* "For many of England's young men the outbreak of the 1914 war seemed a romantic adventure, an opportunity for winning honour and glory—'as swimmers,' Rupert Brooke saw them, 'into cleanness leaping.' Four years later, after millions of young Englishmen, Frenchmen and Germans had perished on the muddy battlefields of the Somme and the Aisne and Passchendaele, the war was recognized for what it was: one of the bloodiest and most futile conflicts in history." Kennedy's 1976 assumption that, in 1919, everyone thought the war had been completely pointless was far from accurate. During the interwar years, as journalists and historians picked over the carcass of the conflict, writers produced fictional accounts of the war, and soldiers began to write their memoirs, many views about the First World War competed for ascendancy in British public discourse. What various works produced from 1920 through 1939 mainly demonstrate is the multiplicity of narratives presented during those two decades. Some minor unifying themes do emerge from these diverse books, among them the idealization of the soldiers who fought in the conflict and the surprisingly stark depiction of conditions on the Western Front, but a consensus on the war itself was notably absent. Throughout the interwar period, the Christmas truce was not forgotten but continued to be an accepted part of the history of the First World War even as it was increasingly employed by writers in pursuit of a cohesive narrative to impose on the conflict.[6]

In contrast to the soldier-poets who wrote of their embitterment long before the war ended and then later made it a central theme of their memoirs, there were many veterans, such as Carrington, who continued to view their service on the Western Front and their part in helping to defeat the Central Powers as worthwhile. There were historians and journalists who reviewed the conflict and concluded that, on balance, the rationale on which the war had been fought was valid, and that while its results, including the peace treaty, may not have been ideal, they were overall as satisfactory as could be expected under difficult circumstances. There were others who reached the opposite conclusion and, upon reconsidering the conflict, saw nothing but waste and horror. This diversity of views produced a fragmented discourse of the war during the first two decades after it ended, and the Christmas truce remained part of that narrative battleground, credited with meanings as varied as the attitudes of those who wrote about it.

Disillusionment with the war was well represented long before the famous memoirs of Graves, Sassoon, and Edmund Blunden appeared in the late 1920s. This theme was thoroughly explored by Philip Gibbs, a war correspondent for the *Daily Telegraph*, in his 1920 memoir, *Realities of War.* Planting himself firmly on the futile-and-wasteful side of the argument, Gibbs used this work to vent his frustrations with four years of "official briefings" from the army. *Realities of War* therefore served as a fierce polemic against the War Office, Kitchener, the generals and officers ("who had the brains of canaries"), the politicians, other journalists, and British civilians—against everyone, in fact, except British soldiers serving in the front lines, whom Gibbs romanticized beyond all reality. Although protesting that, as he was "not a soldier nor a military expert," he had no right to blame Field Marshal French for his actions, Gibbs's mock-innocent assertion that "our High Command had to learn by mistakes, by ghastly mistakes, repeated often, until they became visible to the military mind, and were paid for again by the slaughter of British youth" demonstrated that his sympathies lay entirely with the "other ranks."[7]

British soldiers, Gibbs claimed, were motivated to fight largely by an unspoken love of their country and not "because they hated the Germans, because, after a few turns in the trenches, they had a fellow-feeling for the poor devils over the way." The Christmas truce, for Gibbs, was proof of this sense of camaraderie: British troops at the front "but for stringent regulations . . . would have fraternized with the enemy at the slightest excuse, and did so in the winter of 1914, to the great scandal of G.H.Q." Although he blamed Germany for starting the war, Gibbs declared that the troops on both sides of the line had "no real quarrel with each other." In *Realities of War,* he praised the goodwill and simple hearts of the frontline soldiers, who in the postwar period were still "inspired by the humble belief that humanity may be cured of its cruelty and stupidity," and he claimed that the truce exemplified their sense of brotherhood with their enemies.[8]

C. E. Montague, who enlisted in the war in 1914 despite the fact that he was well over the age limit, was similarly forthright about his attitude toward the conflict, as is clear from the title of his 1922 work. When the war broke out, he wrote in *Disenchantment*, "all the air was ringing with rousing assurances. France to be saved, Belgium righted, freedom and civilization re-won, a sour, soiled, crooked old world to be rid of bullies and crooks and reclaimed for straightness, decency, good-nature, the ways of common men dealing with common men. What a chance!" Montague, like Gibbs, idealized British soldiers, whom he believed were "simply and happily friendly, trustful, and keen."[9] Unfortunately, Montague maintained, these men imagined that those who led them were of equal goodwill, and "that was the paradise that the bottom fell out of." Montague contended that these soldiers had joined up for honorable reasons, but the war had debased their souls, which were annihilated by the conflict even when their bodies survived. The Christmas truce, he maintained, was proof that the soldiers had started the war with good principles. "Even on the dull earth it takes time and pains to get a clean-run boy or young man into a mean frame of mind," Montague argued, providing as an example a "fine N.C.O. of the Grenadier Guards [who] was killed near Laventie—no one knows how—while going over to shake hands with the Germans on Christmas morning. 'What! not shake hands on Christmas Day?' He would have thought it poor, sulky fighting."[10]

Disenchantment features a "typical" truce that began when two British officers approached the German trenches (lit with Christmas trees) on Christmas Eve and proposed a cease-fire to the surprised inhabitants. As a result, "on Christmas Day the two sides exchanged cigarettes and played football together. The English intended the truce to end with the day, as agreed, but decided not to shoot next day till the enemy did." Since the Germans remained peaceful, the British did as well, even sending a subaltern across to explain away a rifle shot off by accident while cleaning, which the enemy excused, although one German who was not so forgiving shot the unlucky messenger in the knee. The British sportingly "took it that some German sentry had misunderstood our fluke shot. They did not impute dishonour." This, Montague claimed, was because the soldiers at this point of the war still retained their "trustful" and "friendly" prewar values. For Gibbs the truce demonstrated the goodwill and camaraderie that British soldiers felt toward their German counterparts, whereas for Montague the cease-fire symbolized the principles in which British soldiers believed before they were betrayed by the callous actions of their politicians and generals. For both men, however, the 1914 armistice had become a symbol rather than an event, a moment of truth in a hated war and one that had little to do with the motivations of the men who had actually participated in it.[11]

These books, written soon after the end of the war, foreshadowed the emergence in the late 1920s of the many fictional and autobiographical works that were to recast the narrative of the war for the next eighty-five years, including R. C. Sherriff's *Journey's End*, Blunden's *Undertones of War*, and the opening volume of Sassoon's *Sherston Trilogy*, *Memoirs of a Fox-Hunting Gentleman*. What the authors of all these works had in common was their service in the trenches on the Western Front and their collective view of the war as futile and unnecessary. Regarding the publication of *All Quiet on the Western Front*, in 1929, Hew Strachan observes, "There had been many interpretations of the war; thereafter one increasingly dominated over the others." Also contributing to the shift of the war's narrative was Lord Arthur Ponsonby's *Falsehood in War-Time*, which was published during the same period. Ponsonby's work, which purported to debunk anti-German propaganda, also promoted the belief that the war had been instigated by both sides equally. Lessening German responsibility for the war also removed its justification, and this, combined with the endorsement of the idea that "the war had been an identical and equally disastrous experience for all soldiers and all armies," contributed to the changing attitude toward the conflict that began to take effect at the end of this decade, one that shared the blame for the war among all the combatant countries.[12]

Even within this narrative of disillusionment, however, the implicit view of the Christmas truce as the soldiers' rebellion against a hated war received some surprising resistance. In *Good-bye to All That*, Robert Graves, who because of his opposition to the 1914–1918 conflict might have been expected to take the attitude that the Christmas truce was an act of defiance on the part of the soldiers involved, demonstrated instead his loyalty to his regiment and admiration for their professionalism by describing the 2nd Royal Welch Fusiliers' 1914 armistice with the enemy as no "emotional hiatus" but rather "a commonplace of military tradition—an exchange of courtesies between officers of opposing armies." As is clear from this example, even by the end of the 1920s the war's discourse had not yet hardened into the set parameters that would define it much later in the century.[13]

In addition, while the school of disillusionment had many supporters, it was a simple task to find as many dissenters. Although the quintessential antiwar novel, *All Quiet on the Western Front*, was issued in Britain in 1929, the previous year saw the publication of H. W. Wilson's *The War Guilt*, which advanced the theory that the Allies had no choice but to form a coalition against the Central Powers, because when "a preponderant state arises and shows aggressive purposes by its armaments or its actions, other states will be forced to group themselves into ententes or alliances against it, as the alternative to surrendering their liberty and submitting to injustice."[14] In his 1927 work, *Lions Led by Donkeys*, P. A. Thompson attributed the cause of the conflict to Germany's "fatal error," which was "that they did not 'play the game,'" and he complained that "in forcing the actual outbreak of war, and in their conduct of the war itself, they transgressed every law of civilization and humanity." Thompson believed that once Germany had conquered Europe, it would then turn its attention to England, which "must soon have dropped to second place." He therefore criticized British military leaders not for their incompetence, as Alan Clark was later to do in a similarly titled history, but rather for their willingness to undertake offensives on the Western Front in the early part of the war to please the French, when it would have been better for the British to wait until their numbers increased before commencing large battles.[15]

In his work Thompson described the horrors of the front line, where the men "lived in bitter, biting cold, soaked to the skin; with mud in their nails, their hair, their eyes—mud everywhere," but he noted that in spite of the terrible conditions of the war, British soldiers felt "no personal animosity for the fellows in the trench on the other side, fifty yards away." This led him to the subject of the truce, "the only time during the War when both sides fraternized." He wrote about the singing in the trenches on Christmas Eve and how the two sides met in No Man's Land the next day, when the British were surprised to see "that 'Jerry' was spic and span, well shaven, and possessing an abundance of cigars and champagne." Thompson noted that the cease-fire "prevailed for some days afterwards," with a spirit of cooperation between the two sides, exemplified by a British engineer who, while "putting up barbed wire borrowed a mallet from a neighbouring 'Jerry' who was similarly employed." For Thompson, however, the truce served as a distraction from his main theme: Germany's sole responsibility for the war and Britain's delay in giving that country the beating it deserved by allowing political motivations to influence battlefield strategies.[16]

In the introduction to their survey of the conflict, the authors of *An Outline History of the Great War* declared that understanding "what the war felt like is even more important than to know its events in outline." To this end, G. V. Carey and H. S. Scott noted that "the false glamour which is apt to be shed on war, when viewed from a distance, finds no place in this narrative." To assert in 1928 that a history of the First World War must avoid idealizing the conflict certainly contradicts current ideas about the war's orthodox narrative, which suggests that by the end of the 1920s, the war was generally seen as an exercise in senseless destruction. In spite of their determination not to romanticize the war, however, Carey and Scott still venerated the British soldiers, who opposed "the splendid bravery of the Germans" with "the patient and stubborn resistance of perfect fitness and great skill." It is in this vein that Carey and Scott acknowledged the Christmas truce, but with a twist: it was because of their inability to "reach the Channel ports and Paris," and their distractions in Poland, "that, when Christmas came, the German troops fraternized freely with their enemies wherever they could." In this account, which emphasized the bravery of the B.E.F., the cease-fire was a sign that the Germans were disheartened by their lack of success in the war, while the British, referred to only as "their enemies," were reduced to passive actors, relieved of their responsibility for the truce.[17]

It is impossible to review these varied pre-1930 books, treatises, and histories and find any universal attitudes denoting a consensus about the war. Some condemned it while others defended it, and few common themes can be found, aside from the emphasis on the patience, fortitude, and goodwill of the British soldier—whether those qualities had been, alternatively, drawn on to fight a war worth winning or manipulated and betrayed in order to prevail in a senseless conflict. The following decade saw little change in this dichotomy of opinion, as disillusionment with the 1914–1918 conflict continued to compete with the view that it had been a worthwhile war, and the truce was still used to support both sides equally. In 1930, the year that Major Woods was declaring in Parliament that the holiday cease-fire would have signaled the end of fighting if the soldiers had been left to themselves, the historian Liddell Hart, who had also served in the trenches of Flanders, drew a rather different conclusion from the impromptu armistice.

Liddell Hart's survey of the war presented a more evenhanded approach to the conflict than many written during the previous decade, and although he laid the largest responsibility for the war on the kaiser, whose "bellicose utterances and attitude . . . filled Europe with gunpowder," he also believed that, in the summer of 1914, the "rush to the abyss" had been "driven by the motor of 'military necessity.'" In *The Real War,* Liddell Hart promoted the concept of inevitability, that is, the idea that the war had happened because no one knew how to stop it, which later became an important element in the conflict's orthodox narrative. He further observed that Europe welcomed the war with "an immeasurable sigh of relief," as "a revolt of the spirit against the monotony and triviality of the everyday round." This initial enthusiasm, Liddell Hart argued, was followed by passion, "the natural ferocity of war." As the war continued past its first months, he identified a third phase, the "momentary growth of a spirit of tolerance, symbolized by the fraternization which took place on Christmas Day," although "this in turn was to wane as the strain of the war became felt and the reality of the struggle for existence came home to the warring sides."[18]

For Liddell Hart the truce was a stage in the frontline soldiers' eventual acceptance of the lengthy deadlock on the Western Front. Absent a quick victory, neither side could maintain its early enthusiasm for the war or sustain the passion that succeeded its initial emotions. The cease-fire, according to Liddell Hart, was a symptom of the process through which both sides accustomed themselves to the idea of trench warfare, an acceptance that was eventually replaced by the determined resignation that characterized soldiers' attitudes for the rest of the war. The holiday armistice, in other words, was merely one step in the progression toward the attitudes eventually adopted by the British Army that enabled it to win a war that neither side had known how to prevent.

The contradictions inherent in the 1914 armistice's being cited in the same year by one veteran as proof of the soldiers' rebellion against the war, and by another as evidence of the troops' acceptance of the long and necessary battle ahead of them, demonstrate how little consensus could be found, even twelve years after the First World War had ended, on either its meaning or that of the Christmas truce. Additionally, Major Wood and Liddell Hart were not the only veterans who used the cease-fire to illustrate their assumptions about the war during the 1930s. Like Carrington, Lieutenant Colonel Graham Seton Hutchinson, who served with the 2nd Argyll and Sutherland Highlanders, obviously intended his memoir to counter the waste-and-futility narrative expressed in certain antiwar works. "The reader has been led to believe," Hutchinson asserted in 1932's *Warrior*, "unless indeed he knew the whole or half the truth before, that every attack was a costly failure, that assault followed assault until each man and every man died, his body hideously torn and mangled." The war, Hutchinson admitted, was terrible, but it also "raised the qualities of honour, patriotism, and devotion to an ideal, to an eminence never previously attained in all the history of mankind."[19]

Having staked out his position on the "purity of motive" with which the British had entered the war, Hutchinson then turned to the continuing cease-fire in his battalion's part of the line in early January 1915. Admitting that "the fires of patriotism were soon damped by the unequal struggle with the elements," he described the conditions that led to an ongoing armistice, when the troops "were so preoccupied with the task of keeping the water at a sufficiently low level . . . that a rifle was seldom fired from our line." Not only was fighting impossible under these circumstances, but the shared misery resulted in intermittent fraternizing that was part of "an unwritten armistice covering a front of some miles." The two sides occasionally met while crossing No Man's Land, exchanged the odd souvenir, and even shared working tools; as Hutchinson observed, "Hammers and mallets became mutual property."[20]

Hutchinson then noted that plans were on for a joint football match when the "High Command" issued orders, "about which there could be no equivocation, that warlike measures against the enemy must be adopted forthwith." The Argyll and Sutherland Highlanders bowed to the inevitable but first warned the Germans that the war would resume the next day. The enemy, however, continued to send out working parties, which placed the British in a quandary, as it "went wholly against tradition to open fire on apparently peaceful, and certainly unarmed German soldiers." Eventually a small bomb was thrown and wounded a German in the leg; the enemy quickly retaliated (proving that their previous peaceful attitude had been merely a "ruse to test the British aggressive intentions"), and the two sides returned to "the warfare of sniping, bombing, patrols, and walking in a crouched position."[21]

Hutchinson's version of the cease-fire, which continued on certain parts of the front during early January, not only conforms to the reports of truces in the diaries of various battalions, but was also an event that the self-proclaimed "warrior" had no problem fitting into his view of his fellow soldiers, which was that they were sportsmen who would lay down their arms to allow both sides to cope undisturbed with the terrible conditions at the front. His belief that these views on the war were shared by all veterans, however, was contradicted by Frank Richards's book, *Old Soldiers Never Die*, which was published a year later. Richards, who served with the 2nd Royal Welch Fusiliers, reportedly received assistance from Robert Graves when writing his memoir, which is unsurprising: Richards was the sort of cheerful professional soldier, impervious to discipline and with a healthy scepticism about army leadership, whom Graves admired. On Christmas morning, Richards reported, both sides stuck up boards that said "Merry Christmas" and a few soldiers ventured out in No Man's Land, where they were soon followed by the rest of the troops.[22]

A Welch Fusiliers officer, who according to Richards was already generally unpopular, tried to stop the exodus, "but he was too late: the whole of the Company was now out, and so were the Germans. He had to accept the situation, so soon he and the other company officers climbed out, too." The two sides "mucked in all day with one another," exchanged complaints about how "fed up" they all were with the war, and drank the beer the Germans offered. "The officers came to an understanding that the unofficial truce would end at midnight," but the British soldiers, who returned to their trenches at dusk, decided not to start shooting before the Germans did, and the cease-fire lasted through Boxing Day. That evening, the Welch Fusiliers were "surprised" to find themselves relieved by another battalion, who told them that the truce had been general in the front line. Apart from Richards's broad hint that the relief of the 2nd Welch Fusiliers was unexpected and therefore somehow related to the truce, an assertion not borne out by the battalion's war diary, his account is fairly routine, giving a quick wink to the soldiers' defiance of a particularly disliked officer whose orders to return to the trenches were ignored.[23]

On the other hand, Captain J. C. Dunn, also of the 2nd Royal Welch Fusiliers, believed that the truce displayed his regiment to advantage. In *The War the Infantry Knew: 1914–1919*, Dunn obviously felt obliged to counter some of the antiwar literature so prevalent in the decade before 1938, the year this memoir was published.[24] Explaining his divergence with the First World War's school of disillusionment, Dunn observed that most of the enormous number of books written about the war "have come from writers whose emotions have been quickened by the penitential mood that follows all great wars." For Dunn, in spite of remembering the conflict as "a time of trench warfare with eruptions of great violence, of waning morale, of increasing vexation and heartache," the memories of the war that remained with him were encapsulated in "the gay self-sacrifice of junior officers and of non-commissioned officers; by the resource and cheerfulness in discomfort of the men of our Old Army, and their prompt answer to every call, confident in themselves and in each other: beside them the Territorial and New Army personnel had the native virtues common to all, good nature and endurance." Although the reports of the Christmas truce that appear in *The War the Infantry Knew* were drawn from accounts provided by members of the battalion, making it unclear whether Dunn participated in the event, the selections chosen underline his themes of the professionalism and good humor of the B.E.F., although both versions minimized any fraternization between the two sides.[25]

In the first account, a screen with "Merry Christmas" painted on it was put up in the morning, and both sides walked about in the open behind their lines. Later, the Germans came into No Man's Land, but the British, who "were forbidden to leave" their trenches, threw them "tins of food with plenty of sympathy in the shape of, 'Here you are, you poor hungry bastards,' and other such-like endearments." A Welch Fusiliers' captain went out to meet the Germans when they rolled over two barrels of beer, and the officers "agreed to recall all men to the trenches and have no more fraternizing." A cease-fire was negotiated, and "the Germans were allowed to bury their dead." The second account, written by the captain who met with the Germans, maintained that "strict orders had been issued that there was to be no fraternizing on Christmas Day" and reported that he told the German officers that they should get their men back behind the parapets, as it was dangerous for them to be "running about in the open like this," in case someone fired. A mutual cease-fire was agreed on, and the Germans, the officer recorded, "played the game, not a shot all night." The truce ended when the two captains appeared on their respective parapets: "Both bowed and saluted and got down into our respective trenches . . . and the War was on again." For Dunn, as for Robert Graves of the same regiment, the truce demonstrated that the professionalism of the Royal Welch Fusiliers overrode the personal animosities of war, and that, as long as the Germans "played the game," the regiment could be counted on to do the same.[26]

Later during the same decade, the truce appeared again in a history from another veteran of the conflict, who was not concerned "with its causes remote or immediate, nor with the so-called settlement which followed," but instead focused on the conduct of the war itself. In *A History of the Great War*, Charles Cruttwell advanced the theory, later embraced by A. J. P. Taylor, that the combat plans of the countries involved, which focused on the offensive, made mobilization the equivalent of war. As "any improvisation, except in detail" was rendered impossible by the complexity of those plans, the order to mobilize was essentially a declaration of war. Cruttwell's argument that "universal insecurity" made every country nervous, and therefore more inclined to fight, spread the responsibility for the conflict among all the "continental belligerents," except Britain, which "entered the war in defense of her treaty obligations toward Belgium and not under the terms of any general alliance."[27]

After arguing that Britain's hands were relatively clean of blame for the general debacle, Cruttwell then examined the 1914 fighting closely. He pointed out that although trenches served to protect the men within them, they had their psychological pitfalls: "Stationary warfare," he observed, bred "a sense of isolation and of disproportionate risk between the troops in the line and the staff." The French approach to trench fighting, which was to remain relatively inactive unless an attack was expected, enabled them to hold their front line with few men, whereas the "British were very thick on the ground, and the troops were enjoined to harass the enemy by every possible pinprick, such as fighting patrols, and burst of fire on his nightly working parties." In spite of this, Cruttwell observed, "it was the British and not the French soldiers who were the actors in the curious 'Christmas Truce' of 1914, when fraternizing between the lines, even games of football and mutual trench visits were common, and in some sectors lasted for nearly a week."[28]

Toward the end of the 1930s, with Britain on the brink of another war against Germany, many veterans throughout the country must have reflected on their service in the last one. Frederick Brown, who fought with the 2nd Monmouthshires on the Western Front during the first year of the war, and later served in Mesopotamia, began his 1939 unpublished memoir by declaring that he never imagined "after the Great War of 1914–1918, that our country would be called upon to once again fight the battle 'for civilization' during my lifetime." As "the impossible" had happened, however, he wanted "to place on record as far as my memory will permit" an account of his experiences in the previous war.[29]

Brown, a corporal in the 2nd Monmouths at the start of the conflict, embarked for France on 5 November. The Monmouths were in the trenches for Christmas 1914, and Brown recalled the bitter cold of Christmas Eve and waking at dawn. He contrasted the thoughts of home with "our bleak surroundings," looking at "where a German soldier had been buried, and his foot had actually been sticking out in our trench until we covered it up with earth." Then, "a strange happening occurred, which is generally not accepted, but well known to those who were present in this part of the line." A rumor began to spread that there would be an armistice for Christmas so the Germans could bury their dead. Brown then described how "German heads appeared" over the parapets of the trenches opposite, which were only thirty-five yards away, and a Monmouths sergeant looked over the top of the British trench, waving a box of cigarettes. However, "a shot rang out, and the poor Sergt. staggered back into the trench, shot through the chest. I can still hear his cries 'Oh my God, they have shot me,' and he died immediately."[30]

After that, Brown wrote, the Monmouths got back in their trenches, "with very bitter feelings on our part." Fraternization did occur later that afternoon, although Brown explained that the British soldiers went out "mostly to collect souvenirs in the shape of helmets etc." The Germans apologized for the shooting of the sergeant, but Brown remained in his trench throughout the day, still angry about the killing of the unarmed soldier. "After this," he noted, "all fraternizing was strictly forbidden." Although he later received wounds in Mesopotamia that left him permanently disabled and forced him to relinquish his chosen career, Brown did not seem to feel either the anger toward the war that prompted many veterans to write memoirs condemning it, or the defensiveness that pervaded aggressively militaristic memoirs such as Hutchinson's *Warrior*. Instead, Brown accepted the necessity of the war in which he had fought and been so severely wounded, just as he was resigned to the thought of the next one, which he also recognized as a battle "for civilization."

From Gibbs's overwrought *Realities of War* through Brown's matter-of-fact account of the same conflict nearly twenty years later, the narrative of the First World War in the interwar years embraced a multiplicity of viewpoints. The two decades saw a great deal written about the truce from soldiers who had participated in it and writers who wished to make use of it to underline their view of the conflict, such as Montague, who used the truce to demonstrate his disillusionment with the war, or Liddell Hart, who employed it to illustrate his theories about the attitudes of the combatant countries during the early stages of the conflict. On the basis of an overview of books written about the war during the 1920s and 1930s, it can certainly be argued that Carey and Scott were correct in their assertion that it would be "foolish to pretend that the war had no redeeming features." Though some veterans could not, even years after it ended, forget the horrors of the war, for many the victory they had won in the field and "the recollection of a comfortable billet, a cheerful mess, the smoke-laden atmosphere of an estaminet, the unexpected encounter of a friend," or the Christmas Day they fraternized with the Germans, remained as strong a reality as the "months of stagnation and sordid horror."[31]

In addition, it is worth noting that the most famous antiwar work of the interwar years, *All Quiet on the Western Front,* ignored the truce entirely, and that some disillusioned veterans who, like Graves, characterized the conflict as "wicked nonsense," did not cite the 1914 cease-fire in support of their views. During this time, the truce, whether recalled fondly in a memoir or used as a moral in an antiwar treatise, remained both a well-remembered event and an accepted feature within the narrative of the war. Competing strands of the war's narrative, including vivid descriptions of the horrors of the front line and the remembrance of the camaraderie found in the trenches, were characteristic of the diverse views of the conflict held during this period. The attitudes expressed in various works written during the first two decades after the war's end demonstrate that no all-encompassing view of the conflict dominated either its discourse or that of the Christmas truce. After memories of the old world war were, at least temporarily, subsumed during the new global conflict, however, the post–Second World War narrative of the First World War would begin to undergo a decided shift in perspective—and drag the truce along behind it.[32]

Two works about the First World War, originally published in 1938 and 1940 and revised during the Second World War and afterward, exemplify the continued varied discourse of the conflict that struggled to take into account the new and even larger war that had overtaken the world. The titles of these histories, Ephraim Lipson's *Europe, 1914–1939* and *A Sketch-Map History of the Great War and After, 1914–1935,* by I. Richards, J. B. Goodson, and J. A. Morris, illustrate an increasing awareness that the interwar years formed as much a part of the narrative as the war itself. Defending the Treaty of Versailles, for example, against charges that it had caused the German sense of grievance that prompted the rise of Nazism and the onset of the Second World War, Lipson maintained that, while it had become fashionable to condemn it "as a bad treaty," and assert that if the Allies had been more lenient, Germany would have "reconciled herself more readily," this could not be certain. "It is at least doubtful whether the military caste, shorn of its prestige and smarting under the stigma of defeat," Lipson argued, "would not have repudiated even a lenient treaty, and endeavoured sooner or later to recover for Germany the dominant position she had formerly enjoyed in Europe." Characterizing Germany, in 1944, as "the country which alone could have averted the conflagration," Lipson assigned to it the major responsibility for the war. Richards, Goodson, and Morris similarly contended that German attitudes and actions, particularly its demand for " 'a place in the sun' " and its rivalry with France, Russia, and Britain, had been the main impetus for the First World War, demonstrating that, even in the 1940s, many historians continued to support this view of the conflict.[33]

Aylmer Haldane, the general in charge of the 3rd Division in 1914, also concurred with this analysis. In his autobiography, *A Soldier's Saga,* published in 1948, he maintained that Germany, by doing nothing "to prevent what must inevitably lead to a general conflagration in Europe," and instead encouraging the conflict for its own ends, bore responsibility for the war. In his chronicle of the war, Haldane included his orders to the 3rd Division forbidding a truce at Christmas 1914 and noted that, while his division did not participate in an armistice, in other commands "advances made by the Germans were not repelled, and in consequence certain commanders got into hot water with higher authority." Haldane also repeated a quite astonishing and uncredited tale about how in one section "the enemy tried to repeat a truce—unauthorized, of course—which had taken place earlier and was warned what would happen. One of the German officers then came forward and asked that the gun-fire might be opened on his men between the lines, on which they sat down close to our parapets and some time elapsed before they could be made to return to their own defences." It is very difficult to believe that a German officer would have asked the British to fire on his own men to get them to stop fraternizing, but Haldane apparently found this story sufficiently plausible to include in his work as further evidence that officers on both sides were willing to punish soldiers who participated in the truce.[34]

Haldane's endorsement of the myth that retribution followed the 1914 truce was part of the continuing alteration that the narrative of the armistice underwent in the postwar period. Whereas previously the idea that soldiers involved suffered reprisals from their commanders for their participation in the armistice had been a minority view, at this time it began to creep into the dominant discourse of the truce. Mary Renault's 1953 novel, *The Charioteer,* also featured a new interpretation of the cease-fire. In the book, which was set during the Second

World War, Laurie O'Dell, the main character, discusses the moral implications of the war with a conscientious objector who is performing alternative service at the home where O'Dell is convalescing. The C.O. explains that, while he believes that there may be times when it is right to kill, he is not prepared to be commanded to do so, as he could not surrender "my moral choice to men I'd never met, about whose moral standards I knew nothing whatever." O'Dell responds that there is no way to defeat Nazi Germany, except by fighting the Germans: " 'In Napoleon's day if you wanted to cross the Channel in the middle of the war and talk sensibly to the enemy there was almost nothing to stop you. Even in 1914 they had the Christmas Truce and it very nearly worked. Nowadays we're all sealed off in airtight cans and there's nothing between war and surrender. You can't convert a propaganda machine.' " In the view presented in Renault's novel, therefore, the truce had been transformed from an unexpected holiday for the soldiers involved into something that had "very nearly worked," that is, had almost ended the war. The accounts of the truce, one factual and one fictional, put forward by Haldane and Renault forty years after it occurred, are two sides of the same coin, underlining the myth that the armistice was frowned on by the authorities, who saw it as a threat to the fighting spirit of the troops, but was initiated by frontline soldiers out of a desire to stop a senseless war.[35]

In *A Fox under My Cloak*, a semiautobiographical account of his wartime experiences in the "London Highlanders," Henry Williamson, the author of the well-known children's book *Tarka the Otter,* also discussed the holiday armistice. For Williamson, who joined the 1/5th London Rifles in January 1914 and was with the battalion on the Western Front on the first Christmas of the war, the truce, during which he realized "that war was created by greed, misplaced zeal and bigotry," greatly influenced his postwar views. These attitudes are reflected in his fictionalized account of the 1914 armistice, which was published forty years after the event had taken place. In Williamson's version, Phillip Maddison, his alter ego, takes advantage of the peaceful conditions on 25 December 1914 to visit his cousin Willie in the London Rifles. Arriving at their trenches, Maddison locates his relative, who is "full of the strangeness of Christmas Day" and excitedly tells Phillip that " 'it's most extraordinary, but the Germans think exactly about the war as we do! They can't lose, they say, because God is on their side. And they say they are fighting for civilization, just as we are! Surely, if all the Germans and all the English knew this, at home, then this ghastly war would end. If we started to walk back, and they did, too, it would be over!'" The only reason the war continues, Willie argues, is that "'the people at home do not know the whole truth,'" and that, if the British public realized that the Germans were "'just the same'" and "'fighting with identical ideas to drive them on,'" they would see that the whole conflict was pointless, and it would end immediately. In the novel, the truce lasts until New Year's Eve, when the Saxons send over a note stating "that a staff-inspection was taking place at midnight along the Corps front; the 'automatic pistolen' would be fired in accordance with orders; but they would be fired high." The Germans keep their word, and the truce ends, according to Williamson, only when the "Saxon Corps left; Prussians took over the front," and sniping and shelling resumes.[36]

In Williamson's account, the truce ended by German instigation, when Prussians were put in the line and the enemy was ordered to fire, rather than by orders from the British generals, but otherwise this version of events presaged the story of the truce that would later dominate the antiwar narrative in the 1960s and afterward. Oddly, Williamson, who in the 1930s became a passionate fascist who believed that "Hitler was essentially a good man who wanted only to build a new and better Germany," and in 1969 described the Second World War as "a war of the moneylenders' revenge," has been accepted as reliable on the subject of the Christmas truce and the senselessness of the war, and his version of events has been assumed, in the years since *A Fox under My Cloak* was published, to embody a representative view.[37]

The truce described in Arthur Cook's *A Soldier's War*, which appeared two years after the Williamson account, is one that would be much more recognizable to the men involved. Cook, who was an N.C.O. with the 1st Somerset Light Infantry during the war, kept a diary, which was published shortly after his death. While Cook's unit appears to have been out of the line on Christmas Day itself, his entry for 28 December indicates that, when relieving another company at the front on that day, they discovered that "during the last few days our men and the enemy have been fraternizing and exchanging souvenirs," and that socializing with the Germans continued. The Somersets, Cook wrote, were "making the most of this fantastic situation while it lasts, for it enables us to bring in our dead who have been lying about since December 19 and give them a proper burial." As Cook made very clear in his diary, the truce was never expected to be anything but temporary, as demonstrated by his observation that the Somersets were "making the most" of the armistice while they could.[38]

Echoing Cook's general attitudes toward the conflict, two histories of the First World War, also published during the 1950s, reveal that for many historians the interpretations of the interwar years still persisted. Arthur Booth, in *The True Book about the First World War,* placed the blame for the war firmly on the Germans, particularly the kaiser, whom he characterized as a cowardly bully. Booth believed that the Germans had hoped the French would reject their prewar conditions, as "France's abject compliance with the demand would have been the last thing the German generals wanted; what they really wanted was war," and he defended the British decision to go to war over the violation of Belgian neutrality. A year later, in *The Great War,* Cyril Falls scornfully dismissed the German theory "that their superior skill, endurance, and bravery" had been overcome only by the exceptional equipment and arms of the Allied Forces, "as if there were something unfair, even treacherous and contemptible, in waging a war of material." In fact, he maintained, it was the "easy armistice terms" that had largely contributed to the myth that the German army was never defeated. The war, Falls claimed, although "looked on with particular abhorrence by many people because it seems to them to have been waged with unexampled clumsiness and to stand for a picture of slaughter and misery," was, in his opinion, the inspiration for "an enthusiasm for ideals, of determination and bravery in face of death and suffering, of generosity of spirit."[39]

As these examples demonstrate, even in the late 1950s, when fictional representations of the truce underscored an altered narrative of the war, some historians still argued that the First World War had been justified and defended the generals who had led the fight and the treaty that had ended it. This narrative tide was about to turn, however: whereas previously the argument that the war had been futile and senseless had been left mainly to novelists, poets, journalists, and polemicists, it was now about to be taken up wholesale by historians.

An examination of memoirs, fiction, histories, and polemics published between 1920 and 1959 reveals that no single view dominated the narrative of the First World War. Veterans and nonveterans alike maintained varied opinions on the conflict, and works published during this four-decade period are notable mainly for the way they contributed to the fragmentation of the public discourse of the war. The 1960s, however, would soon put an end to this diversity and establish a narrative of the war that would drive out the dissenting voices that had contributed to and enriched the debate from the end of the conflict through its fiftieth anniversary.

8

"The Famous Christmas Truce"

The First World War and the Christmas Truce, 1960–1969

> And after that the story went underground for many years.
> The play and film *Oh! What A Lovely War* revived it—to some
> disbelief—in the 60s.
> —Malcolm Brown, "When Peace Broke Out" (2001)

> The whole world knew that on Christmas Day, 1914, there was
> some fraternizing at one part of the line, and even an attempt at
> a game of football.
> —George Coppard, *With a Machine Gun to Cambrai:*
> *The Tale of a Young Tommy in Kitchener's Army,*
> *1914–1918* (1969)

"Prisoners of national pride, shackled together by treaty obligations," was how the warring powers were described in 1964's *The Great War*, a twenty-six-part documentary created by the BBC to mark the occasion of the fiftieth anniversary of the start of the First World War. Described by Emma Hanna, author of *The Great War on the Small Screen*, as "a televised monument to the dead of 1914–18," the program reinforced many now-familiar elements of the conflict's discourse: the "accidental" war, the mud, the horror, the shell-shocked soldiers, and the ignorant home front. The producers of the series were not above manipulating images—and the audience—in an attempt to increase the impact of their interpretation of the conflict: the photograph of a war-weary soldier, sitting among a pile of corpses the viewer assumes he will soon join, which was used during the opening credits for every episode, was in fact a composite of two photographs, one of the soldier and another of dead bodies in a trench. The series argued that in 1914 the nations of Europe, while all fearful of war, were also suffering from the tensions of various internal and external conflicts, including class war at home, mistrust between nations, competition for colonies, and resentment over previous wars. The assassinations at Sarajevo were the spark that ignited this volatile mix, and with the deaths of Franz Ferdinand and his wife, the "peace of Europe died with them."[1]

The title of the second episode, "For such a stupid reason, too," sums up the series' approach toward the entire war. The documentary seized on the theme of the conflict's inevitability, an increasingly prevalent historiographical theory, noting that France, Germany, and Russia had been ensnared in war by their respective mobilization plans. By establishing that all the combatant nations could now be considered victims of the strategies of their own hidebound military leadership, the series furthered the idea that Europe inadvertently became entangled in a conflict that none of those involved had wanted. The third episode, for example, asserted that the "invasion of Belgium was demanded by the Schlieffen plan" but failed to observe that the strategy had been endorsed and set into motion by German leaders who had chosen to follow it, instead presenting the offensive against Belgium as a course of action that the passive (and presumably unwilling) Germans had no choice but to follow. The fifth installment in the series, entitled "This business may last a long time," which dealt with the winter of 1914 and the stalemate on the Western Front, featured the Christmas armistice at the end of the episode. The truce participant selected to discuss the event was Henry Williamson, whose 1955 novel, *A Fox under My Cloak,* had contained such a long and detailed description of the cease-fire.[2]

The 1964 interview with Williamson, from which documentary footage was chosen, repeated many of the elements that he earlier featured in his fictional work, but on this occasion it was Williamson himself, rather than his fictitious cousin Willie, who made the supposedly momentous discovery that the Germans also believed that their cause was sacred. When the dead soldiers between the lines were buried on Christmas Day, Williamson professed to be astonished that the Germans wrote the words "für Vaterland und Freiheit" (for fatherland and freedom) on the crosses marking the graves of their comrades. "I said to a German," Williamson recalled, "excuse me, but how can you be fighting for freedom, you started the war, and *we* are fighting for freedom. And he said, excuse me, English comrade, but we are fighting for freedom, for our country." Williamson claimed that he followed this exchange by asking how the German could write "Here rest in God" on the grave of a dead soldier, and the German replied, "Oh, yes, God is on our side," which Williamson stated he countered with the assertion that "he is on our side." Williamson maintained that the declaration made by the German "was a tremendous shock, to think that these chaps, who were like ourselves, whom we liked and who felt about the war as we did," actually believed, as did the British, that God supported their cause. He further claimed that, following this exchange, the German genially said, "Well, English comrade, do not let us quarrel on Christmas Day," ending a frankly incredible account of the truce with a final note of absurdity.

The 1964 documentary featured Williamson as the only veteran discussing the Christmas cease-fire and thus tacitly endorsed his account of it, but in fact Williamson's version of the event was contradicted by a letter he wrote home to his mother on 26 December 1914, which was printed in the *Daily Express* shortly afterward. In it he briefly described the truce, noting that it took place in a limited area, "only for about a mile or two on either side of us (so far as we know)," which demonstrates that the event Williamson would later claim exposed the universal feelings of both sides he perceived at the time to be quite limited in scope. Williamson had also recorded the reluctance of both sides to venture forth into No Man's Land, noting that, despite the German and British soldiers calling to each other to come out, everyone stayed put "for some time, neither fully trusting the other, until, after much promising to 'play the game' a bold Tommy crept out & stood between the trenches, & immediately a Saxon came to meet him." Fraternization then ensued, and cigars and cigarettes were exchanged and smoked. Williamson then wrote that there was a joint burial service, "over the dead Germans who perished in the 'last attack that was repulsed' against us. The Germans put 'For Fatherland & Freedom' on the cross. They obviously think their cause is a just one." Williamson's contemporaneous account illustrates that he was making an assumption about the enemy troops' motives rather than reporting their statements, and it makes it unlikely that Williamson engaged in the conversation with a German soldier that he would describe fifty years later at such length in *A Fox under My Cloak* and the interview for *The Great War*. In fact, J. Selby Grigg, from the same battalion as Williamson, also reported in a letter home the burial of a German soldier on 25 December 1914 in No Man's Land, but without

Williamson's embellishments, instead noting that a German officer read a short prayer service over the unknown soldier's grave before the Germans "stuck a bit of wood over the grave—no name on it only 'Fur Vaterland and Freheit' [sic] (for Fatherland and Freedom)." Grigg's version of events makes it even less probable that Williamson would have, under those solemn circumstances, started an argument with a German soldier about their respective motivations for fighting the war. It seems likely, therefore, that Williamson invented these details long after the fact to underscore his contention that the Christmas truce had been a turning point in his attitude toward the First World War. As his daughter-in-law Anne dutifully observed years later in *A Patriot's Progress: Henry Williamson and the First World War*, the "fraternization over Christmas 1914 made a deep and lasting impression" on Williamson, who "could never forget what he learned that day—that the German soldiers thought as deeply and sincerely as the English that they were fighting for God and their country."[3]

If Williamson had indeed had the epiphany on 25 December 1914 that he later described, even without the benefit of a conversation with a genial German soldier, it had no immediate influence on his view of the war. On 10 January 1915, for example, he wrote to his father that though it would take a long time to "drive [the Germans] across Belgium," he hoped that "when the floods and ooze had subsided somewhat, we can, by superior numbers, drive their flanks right back and so force their whole line to withdraw." Williamson added more optimistically, however, that while the British line was temporarily stalemated, "the French are doing splendidly in Alsace"—hardly the views of someone who, two weeks earlier, had suddenly seen the war as a farce and an exercise in futility.

This attitude was not confined to the immediate post-truce period. On 19 May 1917, Williamson, by that time a transport officer and safely out of the front line, wrote to his mother: "They say our dead out there are being stripped by him [the enemy], he wants the clothes for making paper!!! Still when we do finally get in those trenches—we will call it even!!" In fact, the only reference he made in later correspondence to the eye-opening events of 25 December was in a 9 January 1915 letter, again to his mother, when he noted that "my letter of Xmas Day has appeared in the Daily Express" and suggested that another letter about the war that he was sending, of "general" rather than "personal" interest, be instead submitted to the *Daily Mail,* which Williamson thought "a better paper." Additionally, although Williamson credited the fraternization itself with enabling the two sides to understand that the soldiers opposite them were men like themselves, with the same feelings for their country and as little enjoyment of mud, cold, rats, and trenches as they had, this opinion ran counter to the attitudes of many of the other soldiers involved in the truce, who cited this realization as a reason for fraternization rather than a result of it.[4]

A letter written by Williamson in 1969 to a fellow veteran reveals his attitude toward the truce in an even more troubling context. "I was also in the Xmas Day truce," Williamson observed, "and spoke to many Germans, marveling (I was only a little older than you) that they believed in the righteousness of their cause, that God was on their side, and they could not lose the war." In fact, Williamson added that he had always found the Germans to be "chivalrous opponents," who helped the British wounded on the Somme and at Passchendaele, "while the lying papers and Home Front Fireside Lancers kept up the hatred," even through to "the wicked Treaty of Versailles, and War 2." Apparently, in Williamson's view, the Second World War could also be credited to anti-German propaganda, whereas the truce revealed the true feelings of the soldiers on both sides.[5]

Williamson's memories, being strongly informed by both his fascist ideology and his later opposition to the conflict, made the inclusion of his solitary and unchallenged version of the truce troubling in the context of a series purporting to be the definitive word on the First World War. At the same time, as his 1969 letter to a fellow soldier illustrates, Williamson made no secret of his support for fascism and the influence this had on his opinion of the war. The producers of *The Great War* should have been aware of this and, at minimum, balanced his account of the truce with that of a veteran who had no particular axe to grind, but Williamson's version of the armistice doubtless proved too useful at underlining the series' main theme, that of the pointlessness of the war. The final episode in the series, "And we were young," ended with images of young, happy soldiers marching off to war and crowds cheering them on, ironically contrasted with photographs of piles of dead bodies and blighted landscapes. *The Great War* helped establish, as Todman later notes, "the myth that it had been a uniquely horrific experience for those who had fought it," a contention that was underlined by Henry Williamson's embellished version of the truce, which sought to demonstrate that the soldiers from both sides had the same motivations and had been trapped into the conflict by their uncaring governments.[6]

It was through such distortions, errors, and inventions—many of them well-meaning, as there is no doubt that Williamson later developed a hatred of the war that influenced his views retrospectively, but others, such as the juxtaposed photograph, which deliberately encouraged false conclusions—that the series promoted a certain narrative of the First World War. *The Great War,* however, did not invent this view of the conflict, which until the approach of the fiftieth anniversary of 1914 had been just one strand in a diverse discourse encompassing a spectrum of opinions about the war, from disillusionment through full-throated patriotic support. The five years before the documentary aired had seen a dramatic shift in the discourse of the First World War, which included the imposition of a single narrative that exaggerated contemporaneous disenchantment with the conflict and, even more damningly, blamed it for causing the Second World War. With the trauma of the later war still fresh in the mind of the British public—rationing, for example, ended only in 1954, and the rubble of damaged and destroyed buildings remained in many large cities, serving as a reminder of the extensive German bombing campaigns—the First World War was, in retrospect, available to serve as a handy scapegoat. During the 1960s the diminishment in the numbers of First World War veterans helped contribute to an altered narrative; as Todman observes, as the conflict "receded into history and personal contact with it has been lost, it has become increasingly easy to judge the war as futile." The effect of this phenomenon would be exacerbated by the fact that the least likely survivors, fifty years on, would be those who had already been serving in the army at the time that war was declared, the professional soldiers who were the vast majority of the British fighting force in Flanders during 1914 through 1915, and who fought in the war because it was their job to do so. These troops had, as Janet Watson would later describe, "an attitude of work, rather than service," which made their outlook on the war very different from that of those who volunteered after war was declared, and their proportionately larger loss from the body of veterans who were now solicited for their views on the war surely helped contribute to this more monolithic narrative.[7]

In the early 1960s, however, this altered discourse was driven primarily by historians reevaluating the First World War. James Cameron, whose work *1914* appeared in 1959, anticipated the very different view of the conflict that was to prevail in the 1960s. Enlarging on Liddell Hart's notion of inevitability, Cameron discussed the "machine" of war, which "seemed to be grinding irresistibly on" and which "nothing could stop." Cameron further explored many of the themes that were later to dominate the conflict's discourse, including the censorship that made truths about the war "contraband," and the gulf between the home front and the war-weary soldier. Most soldiers, he claimed, endured trench warfare mutely; only a few were able to express "their personal trauma . . . in writing and verse," trying to purge "something of the horror by expressing it horribly, defining with irony the pain of fear and despair."[8]

Cameron ended his history with the story of the Christmas truce, the better to emphasize its role as a counterpoint to the senseless slaughter that had not only preceded it, but also was to follow it for four long years afterward. He described the "curious phenomenon" of lit Christmas trees on the German trenches and the sound of the Germans singing hymns. Cameron accurately noted that French as well as British soldiers "saw the Germans climb one by one from their trenches, singing and signalling as they sang," and then they also "climbed out, leaving their rifles behind them." The enemies, "many hundreds of men, many thousands of men," met in No Man's Land, "exchanging gifts and sharing cigarettes." This, Cameron proclaimed, "was the Christmas truce that the Commands had refused; it was the subject of many disciplinary measures and was never to happen again." Although he placed the main fraternization on Christmas Eve, Cameron's version of the truce was generally accurate, and it even included French soldiers, which was a rare acknowledgment at the time. The context in which he situated the cease-fire, as an ironic challenge to the war itself, and his report of the "many disciplinary measures" that followed it, however, established the narrative elements that were soon to overtake the story of the truce and become increasingly accepted as hard facts.[9]

Alan Clark, who, according to his biographer Ion Trewin, worried that Cameron's *1914* would narrow the market for his own work, need not have been concerned: *The Donkeys,* his famous 1961 critique of the blundering British First World War generals who destroyed "the old professional army of the United Kingdom that always won the last battle," saw an unparalleled success that enshrined in the public's mind the belief in the British military leadership's general incompetence, previously only hinted at in histories by Liddell Hart and Cruttwell. In this work Alan Clark paid tribute to the members of the original B.E.F., who, he claimed, "have no memorial" in print. Because of the ineptitude of their military leadership, Clark argued, these soldiers were repeatedly "called upon to do the impossible, and in the end they were all killed. It was as simple as that." It was certainly not as simple as that: though the British Army was asked to undertake battle campaigns in 1914 and 1915 that turned out very badly indeed, the histories, memoirs, and fiction written by ex-soldiers such as Montague, Sassoon, Liddell Hart, Cruttwell, Wylly, and Julian Henriques demonstrate that numerous veterans of the first year of the war survived the conflict and, what is more, published many memorials to their fallen comrades. Clark, however, was never one to let facts stand in the way of a good story, and his account of the 1915 campaigns suffers from a number of easily disproven and rather dubious assertions, all in pursuit of a predetermined moral.[10]

Clark's discussion of the Christmas truce provided a fairly correct summary of the armistice itself, but his assertions about its aftermath echoed the statements presented by Cameron. He first noted that, on 25 December, "there had been no firing, and in many sectors the troops had climbed out of their trenches and, meeting in No-Man's-Land, had talked and exchanged gifts," but he then stated categorically that the cease-fire "met with the strongest disapproval at G.H.Q. and the officers responsible were punished." As a result, the truce "did not happen again." Clark's account, which cited Field Marshal French's memoir, *1914*, as his only source for this information, interpreted the B.E.F. leader's claim that, after hearing about the truce, he "called the local commanders to strict account, which resulted in a great deal of trouble," to mean that those who participated in the truce were disciplined and therefore suffered for their actions. This supposition, advanced by Clark as fact, underlines his contention that the "lion" soldiers, the "flower of the richest, most powerful, nation on earth," who brought to the trenches "decency, regularity, a Christian upbringing, a concept of chivalry; over-riding faith in the inevitable triumph of right over wrong," were betrayed by their idiotic leadership, who punished them for displaying civility toward their enemies.[11]

Although the complementary opinions of Cameron and Clark on the war and the 1914 cease-fire echo some of the judgments offered about both events during the previous four decades, the difference in their influence on the prevailing narrative can be attributed, at least in part, to the lack of prominent opposing viewpoints. During the interwar years, the characterization of the conflict as senseless and futile, an interpretation promoted by Graves, Sassoon, Gibbs, and Montague, had been offset by the histories written by Carey and Scott, Liddell

Hart, and Cruttwell, all of whom, while they had specific criticisms of the way it had been fought, believed that the war had been a necessary evil. In the 1960s, however, Clark's interpretation of the war, as exemplified by his main theme, that of the idiotic leadership sacrificing its brave soldiers in a useless cause, went largely unchallenged. As a result, in the aftermath of the more worthwhile Second World War, the First World War became in retrospect the "bad" war, a chronicle of stupidity, horror, and waste, fought for no good reason, prosecuted incompetently, and worthy of remembrance only as a lesson in how the old-fashioned British values of patriotism and loyalty had betrayed an entire generation, who had been slaughtered in the service of beliefs that were now exposed as naive.

Within the new growing consensus, the First World War, now blamed for causing the Second World War, became retrospectively established as a futile and senseless conflict—an interpretation that was widely assumed to date back to 1918 and the end of the war. As a result of this narrative shift, the truce was pressed into the service of the new view of the war and suddenly became transformed from its previous place as a minor curiosity in the history of the war, evidence of the lack of rancor on the part of British troops toward their enemies, and a cherished memory for the soldiers involved. The new "Christmas Truce," repurposed to serve as proof that on 25 December 1914 the troops who fought in the First World War had rebelled not only against the politicians and generals who were sacrificing their lives for nothing, but also against the war itself, would have been largely unrecognizable to those who had participated in it. As a result, the voices of the few soldiers left who had actually joined in the holiday armistice were now either drowned out in the clamor of the truce's reimagined story or swayed by the new analysis of the war, leaving their memories vulnerable to a viewpoint that had greater narrative appeal.

The power of the new discourse of the war to drive out previous interpretations can be demonstrated by Cameron's contention that the armistice "was the subject of many disciplinary measures" and Clark's insistence that the officers who allowed their men to participate in the Christmas truce suffered for it. In spite of the statement made by Field Marshal French in his memoir (which never specified that the officers involved were disciplined), the myth that soldiers who joined in the truce were punished for their actions was noticeably absent from the majority of works written between 1920 and 1960 that discussed the impromptu armistice. Although there were a few exceptions to this rule, including Haldane's 1948 autobiography, the accounts, memoirs, and regimental histories published during the First World War and in the first four decades after it ended did not mention any penalties imposed after the truce. In the 1960s, however, the idea that strict and immediate disciplinary action was taken against those who joined in the armistice became a standard feature of the Christmas truce narrative, asserted without proof and accepted without question. Similarly, the myth that the First World War had been an exercise in futility, as presented in the new popular histories by Clark, A. J. P Taylor, and Barbara Tuchman, was reinforced through the media of television and film, which offered similar conclusions about the war. As a result, historians who advanced what had previously been more mainstream positions on the conflict, such as John Terraine or Llewellyn Woodward, found their works sidelined in the rush to pass judgment on the now ironically titled "lovely war" of Joan Littlewood and Richard Attenborough.

The main mythmaker of the First World War was the acclaimed historian A. J. P. Taylor, described by his biographer Chris Wrigley as "respected by much of the academic history profession as well as appealing to a wide readership beyond the bounds of higher education."[12] His works on both the First and Second World Wars gained an especially large readership in Britain, and his influence on the public discourse of the war cannot be overestimated. His 1961 publication, *The Origins of the Second World War*, pronounced a fatal judgment on the earlier conflict, noting that "the first war explains the second and, in fact, caused it, in so far as one event causes another." The Germans, Taylor went on to explain, "fought specifically in the second war to reverse the verdict of the first and destroy the settlement which followed it," but the subtleties of this argument were lost in the easier-to-grasp concept that the First World War and, more specifically, the war-guilt clause and reparations imposed on Germany through the Treaty of Versailles were to blame for the Second World War. This was a charge from which the reputation of the 1914–1918 war never recovered, and the following year, Barbara Tuchman's equally successful *The Guns of August* endorsed these theories by wildly inflating the human cost of the conflict. "Sucking up lives at a rate of 5,000 and sometimes 50,000 a day," Tuchman wrote, "absorbing munitions, energy, money, brains, and trained men, the Western Front ate up Allied war resources and predetermined the failure of back-door efforts like that of the Dardanelles which might otherwise have shortened the war." It is the horrifying—and inaccurate—figure of 5,000 to 50,000 killed each day (which, even at the minimal rate, would have meant 8,250,000 killed on the Western Front alone between 1914 and 1918—and Tuchman's figures apply just to Allied casualties) that is remembered from this work, rather than her point that the focus on that front doomed other efforts that might have ended the conflict earlier.[13]

The timing of these histories raises another factor that contributed to the formation of the narrative of the First World War during the early 1960s, which was the post-1945 development of a state of hostility and permanent warlike footing that dominated relations between the Soviet bloc and the West. As Gary Sheffield notes, A. J. P. Taylor's history of the First World War was "coloured by contemporary concerns about the Cold War," and the popularity of such anti–nuclear weapons organizations as the Campaign for Nuclear Disarmament (CND), of which Taylor was one of the most famous founding members, was part of the impetus behind the shift in attitude toward the 1914–1918 conflict, which was seen by many as emblematic of the way minor tensions between countries could easily escalate and result in horrendous unintentional consequences. If it was difficult in the 1960s to justify involvement in the First World War, or even understand why it had started, what guarantee was there that another, even deadlier war could be prevented? In the frigid depths of the Cold War, as the 1962 Cuban Missile Crisis underlined the ease with which the world could slip into a third global conflict, it became harder for those defending involvement in the First World War to be heard above the voices appealing for an end to all wars before those wars could doom humanity to extinction.[14]

Taylor's *History of the First World War,* published the year after the standoff between Soviet Russia and the United States and described by Niall Ferguson as "the most successful of all books on the subject," presented a narrative of both the war and the armistice that was clearly informed by Taylor's political beliefs. In this history Taylor enlarged on his earlier work, advancing his famous theory that the war had begun because no one knew how to stop it. "Nowhere," he declared, "was there conscious determination to provoke a war." The European powers, all of whom were committed to a belief in attack as "the only effective means of modern war," had enormous armies that, once set in motion, could not be stopped. "The plans for mobilizing these millions rested on railways; and railway timetables cannot be improvised," Taylor argued. "Once started, the wagons and carriages must roll remorselessly and inevitably forward to their predestined goal." As a result, the First World War was "imposed on the statesmen of Europe by railway timetables." This argument, so appealing in its simplicity, must be read carefully in line with Taylor's political beliefs and ideas that, as expressed in his book on the origins of the Second World War, "human blunders . . . usually do more to shape history than human wickedness." His fears that "human blunders" might lead to the destruction of the world in the 1960s through the inadvertent triggering of nuclear war surely influenced his attempt to recast the First World War as an accident of history.[15]

Taylor, in an effort to underline the futility of the conflict, also emphasized the lack of articulated aims of First World War combatants, contending that "no one asked what the war was about. The Germans had started the war in order to win; the Allies fought so as not to lose." As countless histories of the period have noted, the Germans had a definite aim in promulgating war: their goal was to dominate central and western Europe, both economically and militarily. Although Taylor may have dismissed it in 1963 as an unworthy motivation, the Allies' fight "not to lose" was indeed a valid war aim, since against German aggression it was either fight or capitulate, which would leave Belgium, northern France, and parts of central and eastern Europe under German control, and the victor no doubt eyeing Britain hungrily across the Channel.[16]

As a result of his attitude toward the war, Taylor's take on the truce opted for full-out irony: he claimed that on Christmas Day 1914, while those at home in Britain and Germany were beseeching the Almighty to destroy their respective enemies, those "enemies" were at the same time cheerfully "exchanging cigarettes" and displaying a complete lack of rancor toward each other in No Man's Land. A similar view of both the war and the truce was promoted by the Theatre Workshop's *Oh, What a Lovely War*, which premiered at the Royal Theatre Stratford East in 1963. The drama enlarged on many of the themes already introduced by Cameron, Taylor, and Clark, singling out for particular censure the ignorant home front and the shockingly inept generals. Although the play's script and direction are credited to the Theatre Workshop as a whole, Joan Littlewood is generally recognized as the guiding spirit behind its production. Littlewood saw the theater as a vehicle for social awareness, with a focus on class struggle. This outlook is very apparent in the play, where the uncaring, upper-class commanders of the British military are presented as being concerned more with their own standing in society and their personal reputations than with the safety and security of their men. *Oh, What a Lovely War* portrays the common soldiers as working-class puppets ("Pierrots") enticed unknowingly into the War Game and thereafter at the mercy of the insensitive monsters who send them off to be "senselessly killed." The new narrative of the Christmas truce fit seamlessly into this version of the war, and its "pathos," according to the plot notes, "comes through the way in which the two sides of the conflict are depicted as vulnerable human beings. Despite the carnage around them, the German and British soldiers are able to share their cultural differences and basic similarities through the singing of their songs and the exchange of gifts." Unfortunately, the relevant scene, in keeping with the Theatre Workshop's emphasis on improvisation, contained little information that would promote this idea of the truce and consisted mostly of "Tommies" and "Jerries" shouting inanities at each other in working-class dialects: "Right, Jerry, 'ere's your Christmas box" is a representative sample of dialogue.[17]

Although the public was very much taken with the Theatre Workshop's view of the war, as the play's transferring to London's West End later in 1963 demonstrates, the *Times*'s theater critic was somewhat less impressed, dismissing its "familiar view of the 1914–18 War as a criminally wasteful adventure in which the stoic courage of the common soldiers was equaled only by the sanctimonious incompetence of their commanders and the blind jingoism of the civilians." The influence of the works of Clark, Taylor, and Tuchman can be deduced from this offhand criticism, which assumed that the British public was not only well acquainted with this view of the war, but by 1963 found it hardly earth-shattering. The review, however, did praise the production for its "presentation of the men at the front," noting that it took "an unusually well-developed sense of truth to stage a scene like the Christmas night fraternization in no-man's-land without becoming mawkish." This quite casual mention of the holiday armistice, tossed in at the end of the review, demonstrates just how well known the event was to the British public in 1963: the *Times*'s theater reviewer, without even using the word *truce* or mentioning the year 1914, assumed that the newspaper's readers needed no explanation to understand this reference. The myth propagated by Brown and Seaton that the Christmas truce was "brought to general notice" by its inclusion in *Oh, What a Lovely War* is contradicted by this review, which appeared the day after the play premiered and certainly assumed the *Times*'s readers' general familiarity with the event.[18]

Fifty years after it had begun, the battle lines of the First World War narrative were clearly drawn: historians had to either try to defend a conflict increasingly seen as senseless and futile or line up on the side of Clark, Taylor, and Tuchman, opponents of a war that had served no purpose except to create another one while becoming a byword for unparalleled horror and misery. The reinforcement of this monolithic discourse through such popular works as *The Great War* or *Oh, What a Lovely War* gave the impression that no other interpretation of the conflict was permissible, or even possible. In this atmosphere, a sensible history such as Llewellyn Woodward's 1967 work, *Great Britain and the War of 1914–1918*, was unlikely to garner much attention. Woodward himself explained why, noting the recent popularity of what he called " 'donkey' studies," which reduced the war to a few simplified facts: that "the armies were badly led; the officers were unsuited to their tasks; [and] they ordered the maiming and killing of hundreds of thousands of innocent soldiers in unnecessary military combat."[19]

Woodward, in fact, agreed that many "commanders just did not know how to set about their task of winning the war," for which he blamed the British, "who had allowed this dangerous state of affairs" and therefore "could not complain of the consequences when they had left the fate of a generation in the hands of a custom-bound clique." At the same time, he took exception to many of the elements of the recent war narrative, noting that it was erroneous to state that "the war broke out accidentally, and that given more time and greater skill in negotiation it would have been avoided," as the Germans, "if they had been willing to do so, could have called off the war before it was too late." Similarly, John Terraine's 1964 defense of Haig's leadership in *The Western Front, 1914–1918*, and his complementary argument that there had been no alternative to the terrible losses on the Western Front made no dent on the now overriding narrative of the war, which had overtaken the words of those who still disagreed with this viewpoint.[20]

Surprisingly, a very different take on both the First World War and the holiday armistice was presented by a man famous for his disillusionment with the 1914–1918 conflict. In Robert Graves's work of fiction "Christmas Truce," which was published in 1962, a soldier's grandson tries to persuade his grandfather to join him in a protest march against nuclear weapons, citing the 1914 armistice, in which the veteran had participated, as proof that it was possible for enemies to see reason and get along with each other. " 'And *you* didn't hate the Germans even when you were fighting them—in spite of the newspapers,'" the grandson argues. "'What about the Christmas Truce?'" According to his grandfather, however, the younger man had "drawn the wrong conclusions and didn't want to be put straight." To correct these misconceptions, the grandfather convinces an old friend to tell the story of the truce, with all its standard details, including a football match in which the Germans "'beat us 3–2,'" and follows it up with the tale of the second (albeit very muted) armistice in 1915.[21]

Graves added some surprising touches to his story, including a complimentary word for Field Marshal French, who "'commanded the B.E.F. at the time—decent old stick. Said afterwards that if he'd been consulted about the truce, he'd have agreed for chivalrous reasons.'" Graves, more predictably, also had the fictitious colonel who allows his troops to participate in the 1915 cease-fire punished for his actions, as Colquhoun was, except that Graves imposed a more severe penalty on the unfortunate officer. Haig, Graves wrote, ordered a court-martial on Colonel Pomeroy, who "'wasn't shot'" for permitting fraternization, "'but got a severe reprimand and lost five years' seniority.'" The lesson to be learned from the two separate cease-fires, the veteran argues, was that if another Christmas truce could not have happened "'in the days when "mankind," as you call 'em, was still a little bit civilized, tell me, what can you hope for now?'" The soldier concludes that the threat of nuclear attack was the only thing that prevented a third world war and therefore refuses to march against "the bomb."[22]

Though Clark saw the truce as a rebellion by the brave frontline soldiers against the uncaring and inept military leadership, the character in Graves's story viewed it as proof that pessimism about the future of mankind was justified. To complicate this conclusion, however, the grandson of the veteran responds to the story of the holiday armistice by observing that "'there wasn't any feeling of hate between the individuals composing the opposite armies. The hate was all whipped up by the newspapers.'" After the grandfather presents his opinion on the significance of the truce, the second soldier advises the grandson that he shouldn't "'be talked out of your beliefs'" and should make up his own mind on the subject. This double narration, which provides conflicting views of the cease-fire, enabled Graves to avoid providing an unambiguous moral to the story of the Christmas truce, which was consistent with his refusal in his autobiography to credit the event to rebellion against the war he despised.[23]

In the year after this story appeared, Peter Jackson, another veteran of the fighting, recorded a version of the truce that, like Graves's fiction, avoided the simplifications of Clark and Taylor but also included certain inaccuracies. Jackson described seeing heads emerge from the German trenches on 24 December, which "was a very dangerous thing to do," but as the British were aware there were Bavarians opposite, they held their fire. An officer came forward, and Jackson ventured out to meet him. Jackson had instructed his men not to fire, but if the Germans started, then they should respond "with everything you've got." The two officers arranged to bury the "one hundred and fifty bodies of our men who had died in an abortive attack about ten days previously," and Jackson was able to collect their identity disks. One of the British soldiers got in an argument with a German, and Jackson had to order him back to the trench to prevent him starting "another private war." The two sides began socializing enthusiastically, but "things were getting a bit out of hand," and Jackson was beginning to feel "a bit sorry that I had ever started this fraternization business," when he suggested a football match as a distraction. The two sides played what Jackson described as "a melee" rather than a proper match, which ended only when the football was impaled on barbed wire.[24]

The truce continued the next day, with more fraternization, and Jackson conversed with a German officer, who told him that they expected to be in London in two months. Jackson's reply to this was the mild statement that "if you get past this bit of trench that's as far as you are going to get." After two days of truce conditions, the Bavarian battalion was replaced during the night by a Prussian one, and the war started again with "very heavy fire" from the German trenches. That, according to Jackson, "concluded the unofficial armistice which was frowned upon by all the brass-hats afterwards, they said of course it should never have happened but it did happen." Jackson's truce, although recalled forty-nine years after the event, displayed many of the elements of contemporaneous accounts: an obvious ambivalence toward the enemy, the idea that the "brass-hats" did not approve of the armistice, although there was no record of any punishments, a football kick-about that actually seems to have happened, and the inaccurate but often expressed theory that troops were shuffled in the front line in order to restart the war. Jackson, however, did not credit any of the soldiers involved with a desire to end the war, noting, in fact, that tensions existed between the two sides even in the midst of fraternization, and that, in this case, a football match between the Germans and British was seen not as a shared pastime, but as a way to distract attention from an argument between two enemy soldiers.[25]

The diaries of Brigadier General James Jack, edited by John Terraine, which were published in the same year that the BBC series *The Great War* was aired, also demonstrate how opinions that contradicted the increasingly predominant narrative of the war and truce were sidelined. Jack, whose battalion, the 1st Cameronians, did not participate in the armistice, only heard of it afterward. Remarking on the "extraordinary" stories being told about the "unofficial Christmas truce," including a football match between the 2nd Argyll and Sutherland Highlanders and the Saxons, Jack noted on 13 January 1915 that these incidents seemed to suggest that, "except in the temper of battle or some great grievance, educated men have no desire to kill one another; and that were it not for aggressive National Policies, or the fear of them by others, war between civilized peoples would seldom take place." Jack's level-headed view of the war, which men were fighting because of a "great grievance" rather than because they had demonized the other side, stood in direct contrast to Williamson's disingenuousness, but in the end it was Williamson's interpretation of the truce that was granted a national audience, whereas Jack's diary was no doubt perceived as just another war memoir.[26]

George Coppard, whose memoir, *With a Machine Gun to Cambrai*, was edited and printed by the Imperial War Museum in 1969, also swam against the tide of the emerging First World War and Christmas truce discourse.[27] Coppard, who joined the 6th Queen's Royal West Surreys at the start of the war, did not leave for France until May 1915, when Kitchener's Army arrived at the Western Front. Coppard's battalion was in the trenches at Festubert on 23 December 1915, and the wet conditions and continuous rifle fire took their toll on the soldiers, who were immediately "reduced to a state of exasperating misery and discomfort."[28] Although the troops they relieved told the new battalion that "they could hear the Germans talking," Coppard did not feel any sense of fellowship with the enemy soldiers whose trenches were so close and who were suffering under the same terrible conditions.[29]

On being reminded of orders that "there was not to be any fraternizing with the enemy on Christmas Day," Coppard scotched all notions that the British were in the mood for another truce. "Speaking for my companions and myself," he observed, "I can categorically state that we were in no mood for any joviality with Jerry. In fact, after what we had been through since Loos, we hated his bloody guts. We were bent on his destruction at each and every opportunity for all the miseries and privations which were our lot." In spite of the collective memories of the Christmas 1914 truce, which he acknowledged was widely known, and the speculation among frontline troops in 1915 "whether a repeat performance would develop," Coppard's anger at the enemy would not have permitted any recurrence of fraternization or even friendly conversation across No Man's Land. In fact, on noticing that the Germans were being careless about exposing themselves on Christmas night, Coppard and his mates reckoned that "if we were careful we could bag a good many of them," and they opened fire on an enemy wiring party.[30]

The bitterness of the continued war, which Coppard believed made the "age-old sentiment of 'goodwill to all men' " untenable, had destroyed the desire for further truces on the part of at least one soldier. In the same year as Coppard's work appeared, J. Davey, a former sapper with the Royal Engineers who was in the front line in late December 1914, reported a relatively happy memory of the truce. Writing that the Imperial War Museum might "care for" information on the "1914 Christmas 'truce,' " Davey recalled the "fancy lights" on the enemy's trenches, the Germans "constantly calling out to this effect—'Don't fire, it's Christmas; if you don't, we won't; come over and talk,' " and the subsequent fraternization in No Man's Land. Davey received a field postcard with a Christmas greeting from a German soldier, which he had kept ever since; he recollected that the truce "went on for 2½ days" and mentioned a hare chased by the two sides. "In all, this was a most interesting experience," Davey concluded mildly, "and quite true in spite of many times such happenings have been discredited."[31]

The transformation during the 1960s of the narrative of both the war and the truce culminated in the film production of *Oh! What a Lovely War,* directed by Richard Attenborough. Though the film was neither an unqualified critical or commercial success—it won some BAFTAs and a Golden Globe for Best English-Language Foreign Film in 1970, but few other accolades—*Oh! What a Lovely War* did present a cinematic vision that echoed the antiwar narrative of the earlier stage production and similarly resonated with the public. In it the Christmas truce received a more thorough treatment than it had in the 1963 play. In fact, the film's dramatization of the event, which lasted for over six minutes of screen time, drew heavily on Hulse's letter about the cease-fire, but, quite predictably, it did not include any instructions from headquarters not to fire on German soldiers.[32]

Considering that Richard Attenborough's directorial style had always leaned toward the heavy-handedly explicit, the Christmas truce scene in *Oh! What a Lovely War* is surprisingly understated. Although one German soldier asks, rather discreetly, whether the British are "sick of the war," the majority of the dialogue between the enemy troops remains superficial. The two sides joke mildly with each other; for example, a British soldier, saying good-bye to his German counterpart after a shared drink of schnapps, offhandedly tells him, "Thanks very much, mate, and give my love to the kaiser." The movie is famous for its final scenes, which feature a soldier who was killed just before 11:00 A.M. on 11 November 1918, as he walks through a room where the leaders of the belligerent nations are drawing up the peace treaty; they all look up as the soldier walks by, but he remains invisible to them. The soldier then goes out into a field, where he lies down with other victims of the war while his mother, wife, and daughter picnic nearby. At the end, his daughter asks her mother what her father did in the war, while the camera pulls back to show 16,000 white crosses planted evenly in a field and in the background a male chorus sings:

And when they ask us, and they're certainly going to ask us
The reason why we didn't win the Croix de Guerre
Oh, we'll never tell them, oh, we'll never tell them
There was a front, but damned if we knew where.

After a period in the 1940s and early 1950s when both the First World War and the Christmas truce were mostly ignored in favor of the all-encompassing Second World War, the earlier conflict returned to the public's attention with the approach of the fiftieth anniversary of August 1914. The renewed notice that the First World War received could not avoid taking into account the knowledge of the Second World War, which made it clear that the Great War had not, in fact, achieved its stated purpose as "the war to end all wars." Not only had the 1914–1918 conflict conspicuously failed to bring an end to all disputes between nations, but it now, in the light of the destruction and misery caused by the Second World War, became blamed for the new war that had engulfed the world, caused an estimated 55 million or more deaths, and spawned the seemingly endless Cold War, with its threat of nuclear annihilation. The last major campaign on the Western Front, the BBC documentary *The Great War* maintained, "resulted finally in the collapse of German resistance and deep humiliation for

them in the signing of the Treaty of Versailles: a humiliation which festered in the German psyche until a man called Adolf Hitler promised
an end," a statement that closely ties the two conflicts and blames the
first for the second.[33]

Burdened with this now deadly reputation, it was difficult for the
First World War to maintain the pre–Second World War image that
many held of it as a conflict that had occurred, quite rationally, in
response to German aggression and that had been fought by leaders trying their best under miserable conditions. Additionally, the pre-
1939 beliefs that the soldiers who had served in the 1914–1918 war
had understood the reasons for their service and the terrible sacrifices
they had been asked to make were also now held to be myths. With
the ascent in the early 1960s of the waste-and-futility narrative of the
war, which drew on elements that had previously been a part, but not
a whole, of the interwar discourse, other views of the war were driven
to the sidelines and largely negated.

With this shift, the Christmas truce, which previously had been
noted by historians as an interesting but insignificant event, started
to move to the forefront of the narrative and was increasingly used as
proof of the antiwar feelings of the soldiers who had participated in it.
This use of the armistice was most blatant in the works of Clark and
Taylor and was further emphasized in the stage and screen versions
of *Oh! What a Lovely War.* In a sense, the truce, which had formerly
been a small part of the general narrative of the First World War, now
became a crucial element in the chronicle of resistance to that same
war. At the same time, while histories of the war that subscribed to
the senseless-and-futile view of the conflict began to feature the truce
more prominently, those historians, such as Woodward and Terraine,
who took a more "old-fashioned" attitude toward the war, a view in
which the truce had never been more than a minor curiosity, ignored
the event altogether.

The focus on such flawed versions of the armistice as Williamson's
account, and the insistence by Clark and Cameron that truce participants were punished for joining in the event, ensured that the myths
of the truce, propagated by those who promoted an altered view of
the war, became enshrined as fact during this decade. Although the
evidence from the 1960s demonstrates that many of the legends about
the 1914 armistice, such as the falsehood that the public was largely
unaware of it before *The Great War* and *Oh! What a Lovely War* brought
it into national prominence, were untrue, the sources from that period,

such as Taylor's work on the First World War, also illustrate how those myths became the new reality of the truce. As the decade that saw the great transformation of the British public's view of the conflict ended, the Christmas truce was steadily moving from its old place in the war narrative to its new position as a crucial part of the antiwar narrative.

9

"The Legendary Christmas Truce"

The First World War, the Christmas Truce, and Social History, 1970–1989

> Against that background, the Christmas Truce of 1914 stands out with particular poignancy. While there had been truces for religious and secular holidays since classical times, the events that occurred 90 years ago this week were a spontaneous, unled cry for sanity before the advent of industrialized war.
>
> —David Brown, "Remembering a Victory for Human Kindness: WWI's Puzzling, Poignant Christmas Truce," *Washington Post*, 25 December 2004

> I don't think we discussed the war itself all that much, and I am quite sure that we didn't say that this is silly, let's chuck it altogether, neither side talked like that at all, we all remained absolutely loyal to our side, and it was perfectly clear to both sides that at the end of the day we would go back and we would start killing each other again.
>
> —M. Leslie Walkinton, Queen's Westminster Rifles, interview (1985)

The Christmas truce, as described by Malcolm Brown in the documentary *Peace in No Man's Land*, "is an event still vivid in the minds of those who took part in it." The program, which aired on Christmas Eve 1981, was the first work that focused on the holiday armistice as a separate event rather than as just one episode within the larger story of the war. The thirty-five-minute broadcast consisted almost entirely of excerpts from interviews with three veterans who had participated in the 1914 cease-fire. By featuring these soldiers so prominently in his presentation of the truce, Brown's documentary followed the trend begun in the 1960s and pursued more thoroughly in the two following decades, in which accounts of the war, particularly histories and documentaries, were refashioned as part of a rejection of "top-down history." That approach to studying the past, where politicians and generals were perceived as the guiding forces behind events and therefore the only figures worth examining in depth, was largely swept aside by the innovative focus of social history. This new historiography emphasized a broader understanding of the past through the study of social groups and the expansion of historical enquiry to "cultures and mentalities," or, as E. P. Thompson labeled it, "history from below."[1]

This method of examining the past, however, was not entirely novel, particularly within the context of a contemporaneous understanding of the First World War. As early as 1914 the British press, by featuring letters written home from those on active service (and the closer to the front line, the better) as a vital component of the conflict's narrative, had conditioned the public to believe that the words of ordinary soldiers provided the "truth" about the war. The spate of memoirs in the late 1920s and early 1930s written by literate and articulate junior officers who made the horrors of life in the trenches of the Western Front vivid and accessible to interested readers not only contributed to the diversity of the interwar discourse, but also favored frontline experience over political or military analysis as a way of understanding the 1914–1918 conflict. In other words, historians could argue over the causes of the war, or condemn the generals' tactics, but only a soldier who had served in the front lines could say what it was like actually to fight in that war. The emphasis on eyewitness accounts undoubtedly influenced the interpretation of the First World War in the 1960s and beyond, when the narrative of the conflict was increasingly constructed on the basis of what the common soldier felt and remembered.

Peace in No Man's Land used the words of three "average" Tommies, H. G. R. Williams, an N.C.O. with the 1/5th London Rifles at Christmas 1914, Albert Moren, a private serving with the 2nd Queen's Royal West Surreys, and Leslie Walkinton of the 1st Queen's Westminster Rifles, to offer a version of the truce that underlined the futility of the First World War. Brown chose carefully from the recollections of these three soldiers to present a Christmas truce that tallied with the version that had become standard by the end of the 1960s, which featured a belief that if the cease-fire had continued the conflict would have come to a halt, enraged generals threatening courts-martial, battalions being pulled out of the front line as punishment for fraternizing, and the troops' humanity eventually becoming "lost in bigger battles." In their interviews, which are available in their entirety in the Imperial War Museum archives, the veterans who appeared in the documentary recalled the carol singing on Christmas Eve and fraternization the next day, when the two sides exchanged chocolate and cigars. *Peace in No Man's Land,* however, disregarded certain other aspects of the armistice that the men remembered, demonstrating how an account purportedly based on the direct recollections of participating soldiers—those in a position to speak the truth about the Christmas truce—could, with careful editing, instead support a narrative that contradicted many of their recollections.

Williams, who served in the 1/5th London Rifles, Henry Williamson's battalion, noted in his interview that the truce may have been frowned on in other areas, but "in our sector, anyway as far as brigade was concerned, it was encouraged because it enabled us to work on the trenches and also on various fortifications which were being built in Plugstreet Wood without the nuisance of continual machine gun fire." That subversive statement, however, did not make it to the final broadcast. Moren's contention that the armistice "could have finished the war" was, predictably, highlighted in the first few minutes of the documentary, whereas Williams's claim that the cease-fire had not changed his attitude toward the enemy—that "while the truce was on it was quite all right to be friendly with them, but directly it ended, we just went back to normal, I say, being shot at or shooting at the other people was one of the jobs we were out there to do and we sort of took it as a matter of course"—was left out. In fact, as Williams noted casually, "Even on the next day after the truce if there had been an attack or anything we should quite cheerfully have shot them and they would have quite cheerfully shot us I am sure of that"—yet another statement that failed to make the final cut. Walkinton was even willing to consider the truce from the point of view of the leadership, observing that the troops' fraternizing was "very unpopular with the staff of course, but it would have been a bit awkward for the generals if the Germans had decided to attack." This sort of evenhandedness was, however, also not deemed suitable for inclusion in Brown's "twentieth-century story of temporary peace."[2]

As he demonstrated in his interview of Moren, in addition to choosing the statements that were most apt to prove his overall point about the truce and the war, Brown was also at times determined to guide the veterans in the direction he wanted the armistice's interpretation to flow—even to the extent of placing words in an interviewee's mouth. The following exchange between the two illustrates the attempts Brown made to shape Moren's version of the truce:

> MOREN: Only one German could speak English. He had a wife and two children, he was thinking of them, he was definitely against it.
>
> BROWN: And he said it was a silly war, didn't he.
>
> MOREN: Yes, he was definitely against it.
>
> BROWN: I'd like you to go on if you would, and you said to me, I'd like you to say this, that if it had gone on much longer—if you could tell us—
>
> MOREN: Well, there was a mention of that, they said it was a silly war, and I felt in the way he spoke that it could have gone on, it could have stopped all fighting. You know, the feeling of the troops that day, felt on both sides. Could have gone into, sort of, you know, we don't want to fight any more. Who knows?
>
> BROWN: If it had been left to the troops—
>
> MOREN: I think so, yes, because the conditions were appalling, water, mud, poor rations and no laundry, no cleaning up or anything.
>
> BROWN: And none of you really wanted to fight?
>
> MOREN: I don't think so, no.

Such pointed questioning and later selectivity in editing the veterans' memories for the broadcast resulted in a documentary that appeared to be based on recollections of the soldiers involved, but in fact led to a deliberately molded narrative of the truce that ignored many of their memories. When the armistice was presented by a participant as an opportunity that could have ended the war, Brown featured the statement in the broadcast, while the words of a soldier who enjoyed the fraternization but saw no special significance in it were not included.[3] Brown's views on the truce, as expressed in *Peace in No Man's Land*, built on his 1978 history, *Tommy Goes to War*, in which he argues that "the Tommy had no wish to be in trenches killing Germans and he realized that the German almost certainly had no wish to be in trenches killing Tommies." What Brown describes as the "camarade-rie of the victim" led to "the legendary Christmas truce of 1914," the only time "when British and German soldiers saw each other face to face and did *not* fire." Brown takes this approach toward the armistice even further in *Christmas Truce,* his 1984 collaboration with Shirley Seaton. In that history, Brown and Seaton, drawing heavily on letters and diary entries written at the time of the truce, as well as a number of interviews conducted between 1960 and 1980, readily acknowledge that the vast majority of the misconceptions that have arisen in con-nection with the holiday armistice—many of which were promoted by Brown to begin with—are untrue. They note, for example, that offi-cers as well as privates and common soldiers took part, that uncensored letters about it were published in the newspapers, and that "contem-porary histories of the war included it as a matter of course." Brown and Seaton further concede that the "special circumstances" of the new type of warfare contributed to the atmosphere that allowed the truce to happen, that burial of the dead was an important part of many cease-fires, that there was no armistice in many parts of the line, and that many high-ranking officers, while not "conniving at fraterniza-tion," used the "lull to improve what all commanders knew were very inadequate lines of defence." They disclose the fact that no battalions were taken out of line and that no punishments were handed down as a result of the truce, although they make as much hay out of Ian Colquhoun's court-martial as possible. Brown and Seaton even admit that the truce could not possibly have ended the fighting, acknowledg-ing that "there was no chance that this could have happened."[4]

Even while conceding that it was "a relatively obscure event," however, the authors continue to insist on the truce's real and last-ing importance. "But what gives it greater historical interest and sig-nificance," Brown and Seaton argue forcefully, "is that it happened so soon after a violent explosion of nationalist hatred, the result—and the intention—of which was to inspire the peoples at war with a loathing and contempt for their opponents." The Christmas truce—according to these two historians—negated the initial outbreak of blind antipa-thy that accompanied the start of the war, and therefore continues to serve as a source of inspiration. In fact, as Brown wrote in the preface to the 1999 edition of the book, the 1914 armistice "can genuinely be seen as a precursor, a portent indeed, of the spirit of reconciliation now powerfully abroad as one century ends and a new age begins." As Brown and Seaton declare, "While it would be easy to dismiss the events of that far-off Christmas as little more than a candle in the darkness," they in fact "offer a light where no light might have been, and are thus a source of encouragement and hope that should not be overlooked and forgotten, rather acknowledged and, indeed, celebrated."[5]

In spite of having access to, and citing as sources, the accounts of such truce participants as R. J. Armes, Edward Hulse, Wilbert Spencer, and Lieutenant Colonel Laurence Fisher-Rowe, all of whom strongly contradicted the inferences offered at the end of their history, Brown and Seaton resolutely refuse to view the holiday cease-fire as anything other than the "candle in the darkness" that illuminates the moral of their work. Like those used in Brown's documentary *Peace in No Man's Land*, the interviews conducted for the book were carefully screened to avoid memories that contradicted this monolithic narrative of the truce. Brown, for example, spoke with another veteran for *Christmas Truce*, Ernie Williams of the 6th Cheshires, but he got little from him in the way of the preferred story of the cease-fire. When asked to explain the truce, Williams, although stating that he thought the conflict was "crackers actually," believed that "we had a sense of duty and loyalty to our country and they would have the same idea, and they were fighting for their own country, or thought they were." As a result, he had no issue with the Germans themselves, but he still thought it important to win the war. For inclusion in their work on the truce, however, Brown and Seaton preferred to quote Williams on the subject of a football game, during which he noted that "there was no sort of ill-will between us," rather than his desire to support his country by fighting the war in which it had engaged.[6]

Brown's various attempts to force the discourse of the truce into the pattern of the now-standardized narrative of the First World War, in which the soldiers had become the war's victims and fraternization a manifestation of their fellow feeling for the enemy troops, were at least ostensibly based on the recollections of the veterans themselves, a historiographical methodology that was considered essential to the authenticity of any account of the conflict. The interest, therefore, in interviewing and collecting memoirs from soldiers who had served in the First World War arose not only from the realization that it would be wise to get their recollections down on tape or in print while they were still alive, but also as part of the growing interest in social and cultural history and the need to reexamine the war in the context of the views of the men who had taken part in it. As a result, the focus in works about the First World War written after the 1960s shifted to those who had experienced the conflict firsthand, moving the spotlight from the politicians and generals who had directed the war to frontline soldiers or junior officers. Paul Fussell's *The Great War and Modern Memory* exemplifies this new approach, in which the words of those who had served in and written about the war were adopted not only as the "truth" about the war, but also as the only valid way to understand what had actually happened between 1914 and 1918. For Fussell, soldiers' recollections of the conflict were the sole point of view through which the war could be correctly perceived. As Leonard Smith, in his critique of this work, points out, "'Memory' is a wonderfully unproblematic and self-evident concept in Fussell's book. Memory always seems a clear window on the nature of reality, one opened by the hand of the war writer." Through an examination of the works, generally fictional, written by soldiers about their experiences in the First World War, and an underlying assumption that they were the most accurate possible representation of that war, Fussell argues that memory *is* history, because only these soldiers could accurately convey what the First World War was like, and knowing what the war was like is the only possible way to understand it.[7]

That the truth of war lies in the experience of war is a point of view that has informed the narrative of the 1914–1918 conflict ever since Fussell first articulated it. Although previously the memoirs and poetry of soldiers such as Graves, Owen, Sassoon, and Blunden were considered an important part of the war's discourse, they were never taken to be the literal truth about the war and were always offset by histories and other writings that provided more of an overview of the conflict. Fussell, however, strikes no such balance. He is a professor of English rather than a historian and as a result often relies on sources that were not completely accurate and points of view that were far from universal. Fussell, for example, discusses the "prewar summer," which "was the most idyllic for many years," during which Sassoon played cricket, Graves walked in the Welch mountains, and urbanites enjoyed "splendid evening parties, as well as a superb season for concerts, theatre, and the Russian ballet," without further noting that this was hardly the representative experience of ordinary soldiers, who far outnumbered these privileged few and whose experiences of both peace and war were often very different. Most important, Fussell, while acknowledging that the works he used to support his argument were fictionalized and generally written well after the war ended, does not appear to question their validity as genuine and reliable artifacts. In fact, the poems and novels from which Fussell so liberally quotes were intended mostly to convey general "truths" about the First World War, and more largely the experience of fighting in a war itself, but they were not necessarily meant to be directly representational.[8]

As a result of this selectivity in the use of primary sources, Fussell has no trouble making his case. Because the soldiers whose works he has examined saw only senseless massacre and horror in the 1914–1918 conflict, he concludes that "the German and British are not enemies; the enemy of both is the War." Consequently, the Christmas truce, which according to Fussell "outraged" the military leadership, is taken as proof that the soldiers' adversaries were not on the other side of No Man's Land, but were instead their own leadership sitting behind the lines directing the troops' movements with callous disregard for the lives they threw away. Fussell even stretches this moral to the following year, 1915, when repeating an anecdote related by Stephen Graham in the postwar polemic *The Challenge of the Dead* regarding a 6th Black Watch sergeant, who was shot "when he went forward in violation of orders" and fraternized with the Germans at Christmas, although this anecdote is fiction rather than fact, as the 6th Black Watch were not in the front line on 25 December 1915 and in addition sustained no casualties during that entire month.[9]

As Fussell notes in the preface to his work, by focusing on "places and situations where literary tradition and real life notably transect," he tries to understand "the simultaneous and reciprocal process by which life feeds materials to literature while literature returns the favor by conferring forms upon life." By taking the antiwar literature written by an articulate and disaffected group of junior officers and extrapolating those attitudes to all involved in the war, as well as using that literature to define soldiers' experiences in the First World War in general, Fussell permanently shaped the narrative of that conflict, underlining the belief that it was, as Graves put it, "wicked nonsense." The Christmas truce, with its rebellious, victimized soldiers and murderous leaders, provided Fussell with further proof that the war could be comprehended through the ideas and actions of the men involved rather than the views of their leadership.[10]

The problem with this approach to the analysis of the First World War is that memory, while it can convey some of the emotions felt at the time, is far from "wonderfully unproblematic and self-evident." In fact, at the same time that veterans were being lionized as the best source of truth about the war and probed for every last detail of the conflict, their recollections often refused to fall into line with the First World War's prevailing narrative, or were so influenced by the modern discourse that they, too, imposed new meanings on the truce and the war. Interviews with soldiers who had been in the front lines in Flanders in 1914 demonstrate how problematic memories could be in trying to determine what happened during Christmas of that year. For example, R. G. Garrod, a soldier with the 20th Hussars during the First World War, wrote sceptically about the truce in the early 1970s, observing that "although it was said that on Christmas Day there was an unofficial armistice, I myself have never met a man who took part in it."[11]

Garrod's assertion that he had never known anyone who participated in a truce, however, actually demonstrates how the previous decade had informed not only the narrative of the First World War, but also that of the armistice itself, as he then went on to describe his experiences in the front lines of Flanders on 25 December 1914, when "some Germans exposed themselves and a few of our chaps did the same, each side called out 'Happy Christmas' to each other and although no order was given, no firing took place." Nevertheless, since on that day "certainly no one went across to actually meet the enemy," Garrod did not understand that he had indeed taken part in the Christmas truce, the event that had become so famous. Though Gilbert Smith, who served with the 1st Queen's Royal West Surreys, did recall participating in the truce, during which British soldiers who had died during the 18 December attack were buried, he observed very little fraternization on that day, except when "some men did go over to the German wire but they kept on their side and received cigarettes from our fellows."[12]

A. Self, who served with the 2nd West Yorkshires, also discussed the truce in his privately printed memoir, *A Gunner at a Ring Side Seat*. Self's armistice consisted mainly of a cease-fire to bury the bodies in No Man's Land. "You have read all sorts of stories, ciggarettes, football etc; on what has been termed the 'Armistice,'" Self wrote, but "here are the facts in my sector, this was at Bois Grenier, South of Armentiers." He described the burial of a "L/Sgt. Friend," who had been killed during the German counterattack on 19 December, "in a grave about four yards behind our front line." The burial took place "in full view of the German front line—no mourners—no chaplain— just myself, a shallow grave, and a small wooden cross." Once Self had finished burying his friend, he "jumped down into our trench thankful that Fritz had kept faith to the truce." For the rest of Christmas, the two sides faced "each other in the muddy trenches" in the "uncanny" quiet of the cease-fire. Philip Neame, who served in the Royal Engineers, described a similarly low-key event when he was interviewed in 1974 about his memories of the conflict. Prompted by the interviewer, who referred to the armistice as "one of the most publicized events of the winter," Neame recalled that, on the front to which he was posted, "there was a complete cease-fire, and I would remember walking along our own front line, but there was no fraternizing, both our own infantry stood up and strolled about and the Germans did too, but they never got together and talked to each other at all."[13]

These four veterans, all of whom were recalling their war experiences more than fifty years after the conflict had ended, referred to their respective armistices very offhandedly, clearly believing that the cease-fires and mutually agreed-on burials in which they participated on Christmas Day 1914 did not in fact constitute a "real" truce, as the event had been described in so many histories and documentaries, and therefore weren't worth dwelling on. Only a decade after the narrative of futility had generally overtaken the discourse of the First World War and the armistice had become a prime example of the soldiers' rebellion against that hated war, the belief that participation in the holiday truce meant fraternization with the enemy, a game of football, and threats from authorities to resume the war, as well as a cynical attitude toward the conflict, had become so ingrained that even veterans who had been in the front lines at Christmas 1914 could not recognize their individual armistices as part of the legendary "Christmas Truce" about which they had heard so much.

Veterans of the conflict were also often confronted with the prejudices of their interviewers, which in turn complicated their struggles to provide unbiased memories of the war and the truce. In 1975 Colin Wilson, a former Grenadier Guard, was interviewed about the armistice by someone who made no bones about being an impartial questioner. The interviewer began the session with the statement that "what interests me very much is that episode of the First World War where you had that wonderful thing on Christmas Day, it's the most wonderful thing of the war, and I've never had the privilege of meeting anybody who was actually there." Thus encouraged to claim a part in "the most wonderful thing of the war," Wilson related a truce in which he had participated that took place on 31 rather than 25 December, when the Germans sang in their trenches and the two sides called back and forth to each other, and then met and fraternized in No Man's Land. Wilson recalled how other battalions in the 7th Division, particularly the Scots Guards and Gordon Highlanders, also socialized with the enemy, and that the "truce was then spreading, by then the general headquarters behind the line had found out that there was a truce on, and that didn't go down very well, so they issued an order that fraternization was to cease forthwith and any German soldiers that were seen to leave their trenches for the purpose of fraternizing was to be fired on"—in spite of the fact that the Grenadier Guards were part of the 7th Division of IV Corps, whose leadership was so tolerant of the truce. Wilson was also ready to fall in with the by-then expected moral of the armistice: when the interviewer concluded that the "episode of that unofficial truce was to me the most wonderful thing that occurred in the whole war and I wish it could have stopped the whole war," Wilson most cooperatively responded that "if it had been left to the soldiers it probably would."[14]

In the same year that Wilson's memories of the truce were recorded, J. H. Acton, who was with the 1st Devonshires on the Western Front from 1914 through 1918, described a much more conventional truce in his interview. Acton noted that the armistice lasted seven days, during which time there was no shooting, and that it had begun on Christmas Eve, when "during the night Jerry came out and shouted, it's Christmas, if you no shoot we no shoot." One of the Devons' soldiers went over to the German trenches, exchanged cigarettes with the Germans, and agreed to a cease-fire for the rest of the night. "Well, the next day at daylight on our right and on our left everyone was out in no-man's-land," Acton continued, describing the burial of two British soldiers who had been killed the night before when the Devons rotated into the trenches, and how "a German officer read the burial service." When questioned about the repercussions of the truce, however, Acton obviously did not react as the interviewer expected. "I believe the higher authorities frowned upon it afterwards, didn't they?" the interviewer asked. Acton shrugged off the question. "Ours didn't," he said. "I believe it went right along the line after, right along the line."[15]

As the recollections of these six veterans, whose written and oral memoirs were produced before 1976, reveal, the influence of the 1960s on the discourse of both the truce and the war itself is plain: four former soldiers more or less disavowed their cease-fires, as they did not fit into the pattern of the familiar narrative of Germans and

British meeting in No Man's Land, and one soldier claimed to observe fraternization that he had only heard about, whereas only one veteran discussed a truce that echoed the contemporaneous versions of the event, including a leadership that did not seem too much bothered by the impromptu armistice. This pattern of inconsistencies in soldiers' recollections of the event was to continue throughout the 1970s and 1980s as the memories of First World War veterans were probed for the details of their service in the conflict.

Major Leslie Walkinton, who served with the Queen's Westminster Rifles, was another soldier who, like Acton, did not buy into the general shift in the truce's narrative, as his 1979 interview about his experiences in the war (featured in the Brown documentary) illustrates; this was followed by the 1980 publication of his autobiography, *Twice in a Lifetime*. In that memoir, Walkinton noted that although officers had previously warned the soldiers "against fraternization with the enemy," Christmas was viewed by the troops as "a time of friendship and goodwill towards men." In any case, the veteran observed, the British soldiers had "nothing against" the enemy: "He shot at us and we shot at him—but that's what we were there for after all." He discussed previous cases of friendly behavior, such as the two sides singing to each other from their respective trenches, and remarks shouted across No Man's Land "generally with less venom in them than a couple of London cabbies after a mild collision." Walkinton even speculated that, during the war's first winter, the two sides might have been able to settle things between them: "How furious the politicians and generals would have been if the John Citizens of both sides had got together and said 'This is too damn silly, and it's very cold and uncomfortable. Let's chuck it and go home.' But no! I must admit that it is an impossible dream. If the plain man had tried to start a pow-wow some well-meaning lance-corporal, anxious for a second stripe, would have opened fire and spoilt everything."[16]

Walkinton then described how the British and Germans gradually eased into a truce in the evening of 24 December, with a cease-fire arranged for a twenty-four-hour period, singing on Christmas Eve, and fraternization on Christmas Day, including the exchange of food and drink. Walkinton recalled speaking with a German who "seemed a very pleasant sort of lad." The two soldiers "tried talking war, but I found he was full of newspaper propaganda, as I suppose I was, and we couldn't make any sense of it." The Queen's Westminster Rifles' truce ended, as Walkinton noted, when they were relieved by the 1st

Royal Fusiliers, but he retained the same attitude toward the Germans throughout the war and even afterward, noting that it was important "to realize that much of the devotion and bravery of the common soldiers was definitely the result of love of friends rather than hatred of the enemy's soldiers." Walkinton's acknowledgment that his views of the enemy had changed since the early part of the war was more than most veterans would admit to, although he did not necessarily acknowledge that many of those changes owed much to the postwar narrative.[17]

John Wedderburn-Maxwell, whose account of the truce had been published in the *Daily Telegraph* in January 1915, was also interviewed in 1985 about his memories of the war. Although at the time he had written that the truce was "the most extraordinary show" and "if we don't take care there will be a permanent peace without generals or COs having any say in the matter," his attitude seventy years later proved quite resistant to the modern narrative. "How did you feel about firing at these people to whom you had been talking to?" the interviewer asked him, to which the veteran responded fairly casually, "Oh, that was our job." Wedderburn-Maxwell also maintained that the truce had no "psychological effect on us, no, I think it was just an event," and that he did not believe that anyone was punished for fraternizing with the enemy. In fact, the only negative thing Wedderburn-Maxwell could recall about the Christmas armistice was that he got "an awful dressing down" for the publication of his letter in the newspaper, as his superior officer was able to figure out who wrote it from the details involved, and he was most annoyed with Wedderburn-Maxwell "for daring to write to the press."[18]

Major Walkinton, not yet squeezed dry on the subject of the truce, was interviewed again in 1985 but this time was even more adamant about not falling in with the prevalent view of the event. While acknowledging that the two sides, during fraternization, "couldn't have been friendlier," he scotched all notions that the cease-fire could have led to the conflict's end. In response to a question regarding any disciplinary action taken after the truce, Walkinton again punctured this myth, noting that there was "none whatever in my battalion, nothing at all, we were just told, look, you—don't do this again, we said we wouldn't." He summed up the entire experience as a "damn good joke," that is, a "way of laughing at one's superiors," as they could do nothing to prevent the truce, but in any case they did not even try: "they had the sense to keep away."[19]

George Ashurst, who was interviewed in 1987, the same year that his memoir, *My Bit: A Lancashire Fusilier at War, 1914–1918,* was published, discussed the truce in both accounts. Ashurst complained, both in the interview and in his book, about the "comfortably housed and well fed 'Heads' in the rear" who ordered the British artillery to fire, thus ending the armistice, and how "a few days afterwards when we got our letters and papers from home we read of the British public's horror at their troops actually fraternizing with the horrible German troops." He was particularly bitter about the "parsons" who "condemned us for such un-British conduct." Of course, there is no way to tell what was in any letters Ashurst may have received after the event, and possibly a friend or relative may have written this, but as noted earlier, no major newspapers condemned the truce and, in addition, no other soldier reported receiving communications from home denouncing the fraternization.[20]

Similarly, Cyril Drummond, who served as an artillery officer on the Western Front in 1914, wrote in a 1976 memoir that the ceasefire in his area had gone on for a week, "but of course the war was becoming a farce and the high-ups decided that this truce must stop." A bombardier with the Royal Field Artillery, Colonel Harold Lewis, when interviewed in 1986, had a completely different take on the truce: he doubted "whether anything of the nature or magnitude that had been claimed for it took place at all." In fact, he thought that, because of the discipline prevailing in the British and German armies, "the whole thing borders on the fairy tale and may be classed with the Russians with snow on their boots and the angel of Mons."[21]

As Todman aptly notes, "Just because a veteran has said it does not mean that it is true." The interviews and memoirs that were recorded or written during the 1970s and 1980s by elderly survivors of the First World War demonstrate that some of the soldiers involved were just as susceptible to the shifting elements of the narrative of the conflict and the Christmas truce as historians and the general public, and they were often equally vulnerable to the pressure from less than impartial interviewers in pursuit of a predetermined narrative. There were veterans who believed that those involved in the armistice had been punished and soldiers who maintained that British civilians had condemned the truce, while others insisted that the event had never happened. The focus on the recollections of soldiers during this time illustrates the pitfalls of histories that emphasize personal narratives and rely on the recollections of individuals about events long past. The memories of the war recorded by veterans in these decades reinforced many myths about the conflict, not least through the preconceptions of those who were interviewing the veterans or selecting the topics on which they spoke. At the same time, although many of the soldiers' recollections about their service in the Great War diverged sharply from what had become the conventional narrative, these deviations were glossed over and largely ignored in the rush to endorse a homogeneous discourse, as the many histories produced during these decades demonstrated.[22]

John Ellis's *Eye-Deep in Hell: Trench Warfare in World War I*, like Fussell's work, focuses on the war as experienced by the soldier in the trenches on the Western Front. Not content with noting that "in their letters home, soldiers were usually reticent about describing conditions as they really were," Ellis goes on to conclude that this voluntary behavior led to an antipathy on the part of the frontline troops to civilians. "As the war progressed," he observes, "this reticence began to express itself as a positive dislike of the home front *as a whole*." Ellis contrasts this with the "definite sense of comradeship that united the whole army," which was "doing a task that people at home could not even understand." This feeling of "common identity" was, however, confined "to the select brotherhood of the damned who had to suffer all the miseries of trench warfare." In the "us versus them" camaraderie of the front lines, "both sides were quite prepared to adopt a policy of live and let live" when lack of pressure from "higher commands permitted."[23]

Ellis, in *Eye-Deep in Hell,* notes that the "most famous example of fraternization" came about at Christmas 1914, when "up and down the whole line, Frenchmen, Germans and Englishmen spontaneously emerged from their trenches and met in no man's land where they exchanged cigarettes, drink, food, photographs and addresses," and the Lancashire Fusiliers even played the Saxons at football. Ellis's account of the armistice quotes an officer of the London Rifles, who volunteered that he now had " 'a very different opinion of the Germans,' " and includes the paragraph from Hulse's letter in which he discussed the inherent unlikelihood of the event, although he omits the orders Hulse received from headquarters telling him not to fire on the Germans. "But when news of these meetings reached the High Command," Ellis continues, "they were utterly appalled at the seeming disintegration of the 'fighting spirit.' " He also quotes the information from Field Marshal French's memoir noting how upset he was when he first heard of the truce, his immediate issuance of orders to prevent its recurrence, and the "trouble" that resulted for those commanders whose troops had participated in the event. Ellis, however, does not mention the accompanying passage from *1914* that expressed French's regret that he had not endorsed the armistice at the time, thereby supporting the conventional view of the cease-fire through selective use of participants' words to create the impression that the " 'absolutely astonishing' " truce, which changed the mind of at least one officer toward the enemy, was suppressed by the army's leaders.[24]

Alan Lloyd's *The War in the Trenches* went even further, observing that any temporary cease-fires in the trenches were feared by the military leadership, who believed that "lack of aggression in the proximity of the enemy—a live and let live attitude among the troops—once condoned might become habitual."[25] As proof of this, Lloyd maintained that the "fraternization at Christmas had quickly been condemned by British generals, and a number of the participants court-martialed." As these examples demonstrate, the parts of the armistice's history that were inconsistent with the new narrative of the war were gradually being swept aside in favor of a new discourse that emphasized the punishments meted out to participants while ignoring the contemporaneous evidence that no such disciplinary measures were implemented. At the same time, therefore, that historians were so heavily focused on using soldiers' documents and memories to present their histories as authentic, they were busy editing out the parts that did not fit their theories, creating a monolithic discourse that apparently captured the public imagination and drove out all dissenting views.[26]

Tony Ashworth, in *Trench Warfare, 1914–1918: The Live and Let Live System,* also examined the war through the eyes of the frontline soldiers. In this work Ashworth advanced the theory that it was the lack of hatred for the other side that enabled men to survive in the terrible conditions of the trenches. The live-and-let-live system, "a process of reciprocal exchange among antagonists, where each diminished the other's risk of death, discomfort and injury by a deliberate restriction of aggressive activity, but only on condition that the other requited the restraint," was, according to Ashworth, "the antithesis of the official kill or be killed." He compares the Christmas truce, which he maintains was neither the first nor the last unofficial armistice on the Western Front, "to the sudden surfacing of an iceberg, visible to all including non-combatants, which for most of the war remained largely submerged, invisible to all save the participants." For the validity of Ashworth's argument, which is that the soldiers in the front lines had worked out their own method of survival in defiance of the leadership, however, any visible manifestations of insubordination had to be ruthlessly punished. The truce, with its lack of subsequent penalties, did not support Ashworth's theories as well as he would like, so although he does maintain that the "reaction of high command to these truces was immediate and negative," he is at the same time forced to admit that "on the whole [it] appears to have taken the form of admonishment and warning." The abbreviated 1915 truce is much better suited to Ashworth's hypothesis, as orders had been issued in advance preventing it, and "two officers of the Scots Guards were court martialed; one was acquitted, and the other convicted and reprimanded." Ashworth, however, does not mention the quashing of Colquhoun's reprimand, or the fact that at least three battalions participated in the 1915 truce, from which only two junior officers were brought up on charges. The 1914 and 1915 Christmas truces, which were ostensibly well suited to Ashworth's theory that the soldiers in the trenches on both sides were keen to defy their commanders by "thwarting" their instructions to fight, did not in fact lead to the kinds of punishment that he believed such "unofficial and illegal" actions were supposed to result in, and more than a bit of manipulation was required to make these two events fit his premise.[27]

Another important work on the First World War that used the truce to prove its point, Modris Eksteins's *Rites of Spring: The Great War and the Birth of the Modern Age*, approached the conflict from an entirely different angle. Although his view that the war heralded the birth of modernism is not unprecedented, having already been advanced by Fussell and others, Eksteins further theorizes that Germany was, "on the eve of the war, the foremost representative of innovation and renewal," while "Britain was in fact the major conservative power of the *fin-de-siècle* world." Britain, as a result, was fighting to maintain not only its "pre-eminence in the world" but also its "entire way of life." Under this scenario, Britain's involvement in the war turned it "from a continental power struggle into a veritable war of cultures." For Eksteins, therefore, the First World War was not a fight for more colonies or a greater place in the sun, but rather a battle for the soul of the world, a struggle that Germany dominated until the end of 1945.[28]

In *Rites of Spring*, the Christmas truce represents neither the communal feelings that the British had for their opponents across No Man's Land nor a manifestation of their hatred of war, but is instead a stand-in for conservative British principles: "stability and responsibility." In fact, the British were fighting for civilization itself, which "was possible only if one played the game according to rules laid down by time, history, precedent, all of which amounted to the law." Since for the British the war represented "a struggle to preserve social values, precisely those values and ideals which the prewar avant-garde had so bitterly attacked: notions of justice, dignity, civility, restraint, and 'progress' governed by a respect for the law," participation in the truce embodied those ideals of "fair play," those "time-honoured courtesies" whereby "one saluted one's opponent and paid one's respects." Eksteins also credits the armistice to the Britons' "sporting spirit," which had guided their decision to enter the war and in which "most of the British participants joined in the Christmas truce. The war was a game, deadly earnest, to be sure, but a game nevertheless."[29]

But what of the Germans, who joined equally in the truce and in most cases appeared to have initiated it? Eksteins attributes their participation to the fact that "some of the Germans who had spent time in England—and there were a surprising number of them—clearly had acquired the British passion" for sport, without noting that, however many Teutonic waiters London hotels had employed, there could never have been sufficient numbers to sway the attitudes of the entire army. Eksteins also tosses in the influence of their Bavarian and Saxon heritage on the German peoples as a whole, for whom "history was not subservient to a vision of the future, as it was for so many Prussians. . . . The German quest for modernity was led by Prussia. The Christmas truce of 1914 was, by contrast, a celebration of history and tradition." For Eksteins, the holiday armistice represents the traditional values of the British, Bavarians, and Saxons, which took some time to be broken down by the modern conflict: "That such massive fraternization was never to recur during the war suggests," Eksteins maintains, "that it was not the 'guns of August' but subsequent events that shattered an old world."[30]

Eksteins discusses the sequel to the impromptu truces, when the event was extensively reported in the British press and less so in the German newspapers, while the French "muzzled all mention of fraternization." Afterward, "strict orders went out to troops in all armies that a recurrence of such incidents would have drastic repercussions; and since headquarters in each army pursued the matter for a time, seeking names and all available information, soldiers did become wary of further contacts with the enemy." Even though the live-and-let-live

system continued to allow mutual accommodation between the opposing forces, truces later became rare, as the "enemy became increasingly
an abstraction," with whom no relationship, sporting or otherwise,
was possible.[31]

For Eksteins, as for Montague sixty-odd years earlier, the war
had transformed European society, destroying its previously shared
social and ethical standards. For both, the Christmas truce, "with its
tales of camaraderie and warmth between supposedly bitter enemies
in the crater-scarred territory of no man's land," represented the last
gasp of the old values before they were shattered in the dehumaniz-
ing trenches that ushered in the new world of anti-traditionalism and
total war. Modernism, Eksteins argues, was imposed on the world by
the First World War; Fussell similarly maintains that the "essentially
ironic" mode of "modern understanding" had originated "largely in
the application of mind and memory to the events of the Great War."
These two influential writers saw in the First World War the origin of
a worldview that perceived events through a lens of irony, one that
contrasted expectations with disillusioning reality. The application of
this modernist outlook to the "memory" of the First World War has
since informed the narrative of the conflict in a way that renders such
interwar works as Hutchinson's *Warrior* and Thompson's *Lions Led by
Donkeys* not only obsolete but almost unreadable. The praise in those
works for the army's "courageous and sympathetic leadership" and
complaints that the Germans "did not play the game" support modern
criticisms of the conflict by demonstrating the naïveté of early twentieth-century views. In fact, after the narrative shift during the 1960s
and the hardening into established fact of the futile discourse of the
war in the decades thereafter, the conventional way to view the First
World War as the 1980s drew to a close was with despair at its waste
and stupidity, along with a large dose of sardonic wit to wash the bitterness down, attitudes exemplified in popular culture by the famous
BBC television series *Blackadder Goes Forth*.[32]

In that comedy series, the quintessential modernist and cynic Cap-
tain Edmund Blackadder, stuck in the endless stalemate of the Western
Front, fights a rearguard action, armed with only his wits and his ability
to see through the futility of the war, against the moronic leadership
(Colonel Melchett), the mindless upper-class officers (Lieutenant the
Honourable George Colthurst St. Barleigh), and the gullible common
soldiers (Private Baldrick). Noting that an order to advance means that
"Field Marshal Haig is about to make yet another gargantuan effort

to move his drinks cabinet six inches closer to Berlin," and remarking that the whole conflict "would be a damn sight simpler if we just stayed in England and shot fifty thousand of our men a week," Blackadder was perceived as speaking the "truth" of the war to an audience that, having been fed the popular narrative of the conflict for the previous thirty years, was well primed to receive it.[33] The series' representation of the Christmas truce begins with Lieutenant St. Barleigh reminiscing about the "wonderful" armistice and Blackadder quickly deflating him by observing that more ground was gained "during one Christmas piss-up than they managed in the next two-and-a-half years of war." The show, therefore, manages to present both a romantic and a cynical interpretation of the truce while reinforcing what had become the mainstream view of the futile fight on the Western Front.

By the end of the 1980s, the narrative of senseless waste that had overtaken the previously varied discourse of the First World War had almost completely driven out opposing opinions. Histories, memoirs, interviews with veterans, documentaries, and various manifestations of popular culture all reinforced a view of the war and the truce that was increasingly homogeneous, in which Malcolm Brown's perceived "camaraderie of the victim" led bitter enemies to cross No Man's Land and shake hands with those they had been trying to kill for the first five months of the war, and only threatened punishment from army leadership was able to force the men to fight each other again. While Eksteins argues that the 1914 holiday cease-fire was, in fact, the dying breath of the nineteenth-century values that were later destroyed by the war, the sophistication of his theories was no match for the breathtaking simplicity of the iconic last scene of *Blackadder Goes Forth,* when the doomed soldiers, invited by "General Insanity Melchett" to participate in "a mass slaughter," go over the top to face certain death. With such images the new orthodoxy of the war captured the public imagination and led to reliance on a narrative of the conflict that left little room for disagreement.

Although the new approach toward history during the 1970s and 1980s emphasized the importance of the views of the common soldier in understanding the war, the voices of the soldiers themselves either became increasingly lost in the drive to establish a more monolithic discourse of the conflict, or were reliant on the new discourse of the war as a touchstone for their own memories. The well-intentioned efforts to let the words of the veterans themselves drive the narrative of the war and produce genuine "history from below," which would allow their voices to be heard above the rhetoric of politicians and the analysis of the generals' tactics, failed to take into account the fallibility of soldiers' memories and the possibility that they could also rewrite the past either to suit a predetermined narrative or to please a ready audience for their war stories.

As a result of the new emphasis of historiography, the generally accepted elements of the First World War's conventions—stupid and callous generals sending the helpless frontline victims to be slaughtered in a war that had no purpose and made no sense—were apparently reinforced by the survivors of the conflict. The influence of the 1960s on the narrative of the war, together with the new emphasis on the role of the truce as a soldiers' rebellion against the conflict, came to inform not only popular culture but also the memories of those who fought in the war itself. Many veterans of the war, when recalling the cease-fires in which their battalions had participated, succumbed to the discourse that had developed around the armistice and, because they had not fraternized with the enemy in ways that echoed the myth, did not perceive that they had nonetheless been a part of the famous Christmas truce.

By 1990 the image of British and Germans meeting each other in No Man's Land had become so ingrained in the public consciousness that it defined the official holiday truce, and there were few variations on this theme available to counter the conventional wisdom. Although some surviving soldiers still insisted on the armistice they remembered—in which there were no punishments handed out and there was no desire to end the war—it was Albert Moren's belief that the truce "could have finished the war, if it was left to the men" that was broadcast on Christmas Eve 1981. The selectivity in the use of earlier sources employed by those writing about the war, and equally selective reliance on the memories of those who had experienced it sixty or seventy years earlier, meant that during the 1970s and 1980s the Christmas truce had become increasingly mythologized in support of a greater narrative that consistently reinforced the idea of the First World War as a senseless conflict.

10

"Memories of Christmas 1914 Persist"

Orthodoxy, Revisionism, and the Christmas Truce, 1990–2014

Some of the British officers took a dim view of such sport, and when the game came to its exhausted end, the men were encouraged back to their trenches for a carol service and supper. . . . Boxing Day passed without a game. The officers were alarmed at what had happened on Christmas Day. If such friendly relations continued, how could they get the men to fight again? How could the war continue?

—Michael Foreman, *War Game: Village Green to No-Man's-Land* (1993)

The Christmas Truce of 1914, however, was unique. While some senior officers went out of their way to "look the other way," most officers worked hard to put an end to it. The fact that the men under them defied these orders is extremely unusual. In addition, this truce lasted much longer and involved many more soldiers than any other previous truce.

—Jim Murphy, *Truce: The Day the Soldiers Stopped Fighting* (2009)

On the quiet Western Front in early 1915, Lyn Macdonald writes in *1915: The Death of Innocence,* the state of affairs between the opposing sides was so peaceful that "such belligerence as there was at present was largely directed by officers towards their own troops." The hostility that Macdonald believes was shown by army leadership toward its soldiers was the result of the 1914 truce, during which "authority on both sides of the line had strongly disapproved of the Christmas spirit of goodwill that had brought the front-line soldiers of both sides out of their trenches to swap greetings and gifts." This unauthorized fraternizing led to "rebukes that had passed down the chain of command through discomfited Brigadiers, Colonels and Majors to the rank and file."

Although the holiday armistice took place just before the chronological beginning of her history of the second year of the war, Macdonald's 1993 work opens on the Western Front in early 1915 with the aftermath of the truce. In fact, as Macdonald claims, the junior officers in the front lines "who had cast a benevolent eye on the friendly gatherings in No Man's Land and been glad of the chance to bury the dead in places where there had been an attack, spent the days after Christmas miserably composing the written explanations for these lapses of discipline which had enraged higher authority and for which higher authority was holding them personally responsible." The officers in the 5th Division, in fact, produced their very brief descriptions of the armistice within a day after receiving Smith-Dorrien's order to do so, and those in the other divisions faced no such requirement, but Macdonald, who writes about those soldiers who "might otherwise have gone unheard, the voices of a traumatized generation," is intent on proving that truce participants were punished. Disregarding the lack of consequences for those who joined in the widespread fraternization, the fact that Smith-Dorrien's order applied to only a very small percentage of truce participants, and the extensive reporting of the truce in regimental diaries, Macdonald uses the 1914 armistice to prove her point: that the "enraged" and callous authorities, condemning what they perceived as antiwar sentiment, had punished the officers who had allowed the truce to happen.[1]

Macdonald's work, driven by the senseless-and-futile narrative of the war, emphasizes the enthusiasm for the conflict among the willfully ignorant civilian populations of Britain and Germany and characterizes the British military establishment as hidebound, inflexible, and shortsighted. She closes *1915: The Death of Innocence* with the horror with which the army leadership, who had issued orders "which forbade any contact with the enemy," greeted the 1915 truces by three Guards battalions. As a result of the generals' anger over these mini-truces, Macdonald claims, "the junior officer who condoned the meeting in No Man's Land was sent home in disgrace," while "First Army Headquarters thundered its determination to get to the bottom of the sorry episode and threatened dire retribution." Macdonald then refers to the

urgent memo from headquarters asking for a report on the fraternization by the 2nd Coldstream Guards and 1st and 2nd Scots Guards,
and she follows this with the statement that the Guards' fraternization
was "hushed up," as the British public would have not appreciated the
story. "The comical Germans of the year before," Macdonald wrote,
"were now the hated Boche, progenitors of all the horrors and misery
that had dashed the hopes and expectations of a long and harrowing
year."[2]

The omissions in Macdonald's account of the 1915 truce are
easily refuted. Colquhoun was certainly not sent home in disgrace;
rather, he received permission to return to Britain while his wife gave
birth to their child. The threatened "dire retribution" for the 1915
truces was never implemented. No mention is made of the fact that
the sentence handed down in the Colquhoun court-martial was only
a reprimand (or of Haig's quashing of that mild punishment), or that
a second officer was also court-martialed and immediately found not
guilty. Macdonald also does not acknowledge that, though two other
Guards battalions participated in truces, no officers from those units
were punished. Moreover, the 1914 truce had not been condoned
by the British public because they found the Germans "comical," but
was instead readily accepted by the home front as an unusual Christmas celebration by its troops. Macdonald's view of the war, however,
presumes overreaction on the part of the British military establishment to any peaceable behavior from the soldiers they commanded,
and as a result, Colquhoun had to be banished to England by a furious leadership and severely punished for his actions while the news of
the 1915 truce—but not the one a year earlier—was covered up by
the government.[3]

A completely different view of both the war and the truce, however, was presented by Gary Sheffield less than a decade after Macdonald's work was published. Sheffield, who argues in *Forgotten Victory*
that "the Great War was seen by the vast majority of British people
as a just and worthwhile war—while it was still going on," believes
that it was the failure of the conflict to bring prosperity and security
to Europe that contributed to its reputation as futile. So prevalent
is this myth, he remarks, that "the First World War is often used as
shorthand for stupidity, blind obedience, failures of leadership, appalling physical conditions and deadlock." According to Sheffield, the soldiers in the front lines tried to make their lives more bearable "by
informal truces and tacit agreements that developed between opposing

sides," the Christmas truce being the "most famous" of these temporary cease-fires.[4]

After 1990, in spite of the presence of dissenting voices such as Sheffield's, there was little room in popular culture for variation in the narrative of the truce, or indeed of the First World War as a whole. The soldiers who fought the war were by this time generally perceived to be the traumatized victims of the callous and stupid British generals, and, as a result, the 1914 Christmas truce evolved into an unorganized but powerful rebellion against the war, which in turn had been suppressed by the callous military leadership. This interpretation of the conflict, based in part on the attitudes of the famous antiwar poets and in part on the selective use of the views of the soldiers who had participated in it, was also scrutinized by some revisionist historians, who looked at contemporary sources and drew different conclusions about the First World War. In response to this opposition, the supporters of the conventional view dug in their heels and insisted even more firmly that their interpretation of the conflict was accurate. The 1990s and 2000s became, in a sense, a new battleground of the war, as the orthodox narrative of the conflict, while under attack from revisionist forces, had become so firmly entrenched in the public consciousness that no new offensive could easily uproot it.

The conventional view of the war, in fact, continued to be promoted by a number of historians. Martin Gilbert, in *The First World War: A Complete History*, believes that the war started because "the European sovereigns lacked the will to try to halt" it. He describes the "moment of peaceable behavior" in the front lines at Christmas 1914, when "a spontaneous outburst of pacific feeling took place in the war zones." Gilbert also quotes various truce participants before turning to Field Marshal French's statement, taken from his memoir, *1914*, that he had issued orders to prevent further fraternization and " 'called the local commanders to strict account,' " without noting French's subsequent admission that he regretted doing so, or the lack of punishments handed out following the holiday armistice.[5]

In *The Great War and the Shaping of the Twentieth Century*, Jay Winter and Blaine Baggett also emphasize the conflict's inexorable progress, as the countries involved felt bound to honor their obligations under various treaties: "As soon as armies mobilized, war was unavoidable." They include the story of the "unofficial truce," which some saw "for what it was: a reassertion of decency by men who, as 1915 dawned, persisted in the belief that, while their enemies were misguided and dangerous, they were still men like themselves." The British generals, however, "were appalled at the news of the Christmas truce. Explicit orders threatened serious punishment should any similar incident ever happen again." Gerard De Groot, who argues that the "German invasion of Belgium was a godsend to the British government," as it enabled its leaders to "sell" the war to the British people and transform a "war of hegemony" into a "war of morality," also sees the conflict as inescapable, as mobilization led quickly to declarations of war. "No one wanted to miss the train," De Groot declares, enlarging on A. J. P. Taylor's theories. "Once war became inevitable, the European nations obeyed the dictates of the stationmaster's whistle." In spite of the dehumanization of the conflict through the use of technology, "shared sufferings encouraged a common humanity" across No Man's Land, and "civility occasionally sprouted like a flower in the desert." As an example of the common soldiers' resistance to the mechanized "business of killing," De Groot offers the "famous Christmas truce of 1914," which "inspired a football match between Germans and British, much to the dismay of the commanding officers who deemed it bad for morale."[6]

While all these accounts provide details that could be found in certain of the 1914 holiday truces, they tend to treat the armistices as more consistent and homogenized than they actually were. The Christmas truce was certainly a moment of "peaceable behavior," as Gilbert notes, but participation was motivated more by the holiday season than by a desire to lay down arms. Certainly the cease-fire was inspired partly by the idea that the enemies opposite were men like themselves, but few soldiers participating in the truce would have believed that, by fighting a war that they perceived as necessary, they were not behaving decently the remainder of the time they spent in the trenches. The football match that De Groot claimed was inspired by the atmosphere of the truce did occur, but it was the exception rather the rule. Additionally, French's memoir is cited by a number of works, all of which note that he was against the truce at the time, but they fail to report either the lack of punishment handed out after the 1914 truce or French's retrospective change of heart toward the cease-fire.

The *Horrible Histories* books, known for their popularity among British schoolchildren who doubtless remember their "facts" after what was taught in classrooms is long forgotten, describe the First World War as "a story of what happens when machines go to war and human beings get in the way." Terry Deary and Martin Brown, the authors of *The Frightful First World War,* compare the European combatants to "two big gangs" who "started collecting weapons, making threats and swapping insults, the way gangs do. All it needed was for one gang member to throw the first stone and a huge punch-up would follow." While observing that the assassination of the Austrian archduke in Sarajevo was the "first stone" thrown, Deary and Brown, astonishingly, focus on *France*'s responsibility for the war, contending that "Germany smashed France in the Franco-Prussian War of 1870–71 and it was just a matter of time before France tried to take its revenge." They refer to the famous truce that occurred on 25 December 1914, when "enemies stop fighting for a day or two and even play friendly football matches," a state of affairs that "can't last, and it won't be repeated," before concluding that the "*real* tragedy" of the war was that it "*didn't* solve any problems and it *didn't* bring peace. It led to the Second World War and far, far more misery, death and destruction."[7]

Peter Simkins, in *Chronicles of the Great War,* agrees that technology promoted a depersonalized conflict, which made any further armistice between enemy troops impossible after the first year of the war. "At Christmas 1914," he writes, "there was a spontaneous unofficial truce in Flanders, when British and German troops fraternized openly between the front lines, exchanging souvenirs and taking photographs." But "as the war became ever more impersonal and insatiable in its demands for men and material, there would be no more such incidents on this scale, although a 'live and let live' attitude existed on both sides in many 'quiet' sectors throughout the conflict." John Simpson, as befits a journalist, sees the armistice in terms of the government's infamous censorship, which, surprisingly, "did not prevent British newspapers printing full accounts of the Christmas truce of 1914, even though GHQ disapproved of soldiers fraternizing with the enemy." After Christmas, "all the main newspapers published letters from front-line soldiers to their families at home, describing the truce. The censors failed to stop them." Simpson, however, does not question whether the censors in fact did try to intervene and prevent these reports from reaching the British public, apparently believing that if the army leadership had disapproved of the truce, then the government as a matter of course would have wanted to supress the news of it.[8]

All these histories written between 1990 and 2010 refer to a narrative of the war that appears to have been literally unquestionable, as if a single interpretation of the conflict had been in place since the moment the guns stopped firing at 11:00 A.M. on 11 November 1918, and no doubts about its validity had ever existed. The Christmas truce, in this monolithic discourse, was understood variously as a reassertion of dignity, a rebellion against mechanized warfare, an outburst of pacifism, or a revolt against the army leadership. During this time, however, some historians began to push back against the homogenized narrative of the First World War, providing not only a revisionist view of the causes of the war, a reappraisal of the tactics of the generals, and a defense of the postwar settlement, but also explanations for the development of the assorted myths about the conflict. These authors, however, while challenging the standard discourse of the war, correspondingly discount the story of the truce, which appears to have no place in their less conventional interpretations of the conflict.

Niall Ferguson's controversial history, *The Pity of War*, argues that the image of a "bad, futile war," gained "academic respectability" through A. J. P. Taylor's *History of the First World War*, and was thereafter constantly reinforced by media representations such as *Blackadder Goes Forth*, which added "to the folk memory of donkey-like leadership." As a result of this general preoccupation with "the notion of the wickedness of the Great War," Ferguson contends, "disproportionate attention has been paid to the famous Christmas truce of 1914, when British and German soldiers 'fraternized' with one another in no man's land, and even more to the so-called 'live and let live' system which developed in certain sectors of the Western Front in 1914 and 1915." Michael Neiberg, on the other hand, maintains that the "aggression of the Kaiser's foreign policy in causing the war and the crimes of the German army in conquered territory conveniently became submerged" in the 1920s and with it an understanding of the conflict's origins. In Neiberg's view, the "continued fascination with the relatively minor and inconsequential Christmas truce of 1914 reflects the idea that the war was an aberration in an essentially fraternal Europe," a theory that reinforces the view of "the soldiers as victims who would have preferred to commiserate and celebrate with the 'enemy' but were instead forced to fight by vainglorious generals."[9]

John Morrow considers the First World War the result of centuries of imperialism, which, by allowing Europeans to massacre natives without remorse, had prepared the Continent for the slaughter of the 1914–1918 conflict. "European youth set off to war in 1914 with romantic images of glory and honor in their heads," Morrow states, as "their intellectuals and authors had spent a generation romanticizing their slaughter of other peoples; they presumed to continue this tradition in August 1914." Describing a typical truce, including shared "rations, liquor, and addresses, playing rugby and soccer," Morrow also notes that, to bring the armistice to an end, "commanders reminded their men that the other side was a perfidious enemy with whom fraternization should not recur." It was this dehumanization of the opposing side, Morrow contends, that imperialism had encouraged among Europeans, and which now not only brought an abrupt end to the truce, but enabled them to engage, without compunction, in more than four years of carnage.[10]

In *An Intimate History of Killing: Face-to-Face Killing in Twentieth-Century Warfare,* Joanna Bourke finds a place for the truce in her central hypothesis on modern combat. While arguing that the "characteristic act of men at war is not dying, it is killing," Bourke maintains that though " 'love' might be too strong a word, many combatants were surprised to find themselves feeling intensely affectionate towards their foe." As a result, soldiers "at the frontlines frequently expressed respect for their opponents—even to the extent of fraternizing with them. Fraternization between German, British, and French soldiers during that first Christmas 1914 became such an important war myth that practically every soldier claimed to have defied High Command to participate." The soldiers who participated in the truce might have been surprised to hear their feelings for the enemy described as "intensely affectionate," but Bourke is certainly correct that, as the regimental histories of battalions that fought in the First World War demonstrate, many more claimed a part in the truce than had originally joined in the holiday cease-fires.[11]

Janet Watson further argues that the focus "away from the cooperative and diverse effort presented from 1914 to 1918 and primarily toward the view of useless sacrifice on the part of soldiers in the trenches" has greatly influenced the way the public has come to view the war. Trench warfare, the most common experience of war for British soldiers serving in the First World War, was "what most civilians heard about, whether from members of their own families, friends and neighbors, or the press." In *Fighting Different Wars: Experience, Memory, and the First World War in Britain,* Watson maintains that this emphasis on the experiences of soldiers in the trenches has obscured many truths about the conflict, among them the different attitudes and beliefs that those fighting the war brought to their service. Watson also delineates the "different wars" fought by many soldiers, including those who were already serving in the army at the time the war broke out. The professional attitudes of these men in particular, Watson contends, "may go far to explain the famous Christmas Truce." Since the "volunteers who were fighting the war for a cause rather than because it was their job were still in the training camps at home" in December 1914, "the professional soldiers, both British and German, exchanged common courtesies and mutual respect." Watson further characterizes the General Staff's orders against future fraternization as "unnecessary. The conditions had altered, the soldiers had changed, the war had advanced, and there was little interest in befriending the enemy among the more service-oriented junior officers controlling the front lines."[12]

For historians with a less orthodox view of the conflict, as these examples demonstrate, the Christmas truce is a minor and easily explained event. Ferguson and Neiberg believe the emphasis First World War historians place on the armistice is a manifestation of the conventional narrative of the war and the complementary idea that soldiers rebelled against it by fraternizing with the enemy at Christmas 1914. Sheffield argues that the truce was nothing more than an attempt by the troops to make frontline service more bearable, and Morrow contends that the armistice ended because of contempt for the enemy, whereas Bourke and Watson both press the cease-fire into the service of their theories about killing and professionalism. In all these works, the truce is removed from the center stage it occupies in more orthodox histories of the war, while the meanings ascribed to it in these revisionist histories are more reminiscent of the diversity of discourse found in writings about the armistice during the 1920s and 1930s. On the other hand, those earlier memoirs, polemics, and histories all noted the importance of the truce to the men who had participated in it. These later attempts to challenge conventional notions about the war push the Christmas armistice off to the side, rendering it devoid of significance and barely worth a mention.

With the exception of Ferguson, whose work has been widely read (although few of his theories have been generally adopted), these revisionist historians, while often disputing the image of the war as wasteful and senseless, have had little influence on the conflict's orthodox discourse, which continues to be reinforced by popular culture, in the form of books, films, documentaries, songs, and websites. As Hanna observes, novels such as Sebastian Faulks's *Birdsong* and Pat Barker's *Regeneration* trilogy, which promote the idea that the war was misguided and tragic, "have enjoyed great commercial success because they resonate with what the readership expects to read: mud, blood, poetry and utter futility." In addition, by this time there were few veterans left to challenge the conventional narrative: the last available Imperial War Museum interview with a soldier who had participated in the Christmas truce took place in March 1990. Stanley Archibald, who served with the 1st East Kents (the Buffs) on the Western Front, recalled that on 25 December, after building up their parapets, "all of us just walked together and we met in No-Man's-Land." He spoke with a German who told him, in a very familiar accent, "Oh, blimey, mate, I was in a London 'otel when the war broke out," and the two sides exchanged tins of "bully beef for cigars." According to Archibald, his battalion's truce ended the next day, when a recently commissioned officer shot a German soldier who was still out in the open.[13]

Although Archibald's truce ended in a fashion designed to endear it to the hearts of those who support the orthodox discourse of the war, with a callous officer shooting an unarmed German, his overall view of the conflict is not so easily categorized. He felt, for example, that long before 1914 the army was aware that it would eventually have to fight Germany: "That is why we were so well trained," Archibald maintained. He believed that the British "had no choice" but to declare war, and that the "majority had to accept" that fact. After the 1990s, however, the statements of veterans such as Archibald, who saw the First World War as a necessary evil, were no longer part of the living narrative. This lack of personal testimony allowed others to continue to impose an interpretation on the conflict that would be unrecognizable to many who had fought in it.[14]

After *Blackadder* aired in 1989, dramatizations of both the war and the truce followed a set narrative. The play *A Christmas Truce*, written by William Douglas Home and first performed in the same year that Stanley Archibald was interviewed, offers one such interpretation. In Home's play a British junior officer advances the theory that if everyone refused to fight, as the soldiers were doing on Christmas Day, "the war would have to end because there is nothing anyone could do about it." Another British officer agrees, "That's what ought to happen," but unfortunately, "We all get taken in by bloody politicians telling us that this war is the one to end all bloody wars and that we've got to win it, whereas it's quite obvious that, if we win the bloody thing— or if you win it—never mind which, all it will achieve, apart from all us poor sods getting killed—will be to sow the seeds of the next bloody war." Home's dramatization contains all the now-standard elements of a Christmas truce: the German offer of an armistice, the burial of the dead, and soldiers discussing the foolishness of the war, and it additionally features both a football match and a German soldier who used to be a waiter in London. In the play, the truce concludes on Christmas afternoon when a colonel comes down from headquarters to "make sure the whole escapade ends double-quick and without any trouble." The soldiers who fraternized, the colonel states, should count themselves "damned lucky" because the brigadier in charge, "unlike lots of other Brigadiers . . . [is] not planning to have anyone court-martialed. Just so long as this truce ends at midnight." A junior officer asks if those who are court-martialed will be shot. "Hung, drawn and quartered, I'd say," the colonel responds grimly. This representation of the truce, so at odds with the contemporaneous accounts of it, completely encompasses the popular view of the event.[15]

The other major dramatic representation of the truce from this era, *Joyeux Noel,* as chapter 1 discusses, also situates the Christmas truce firmly within the orthodox narrative of the war: a rebellion by the soldiers against the futility of the conflict, punished by commanders who had to ruthlessly stamp out any defiance. As this film asserts, the Christmas truce was so shocking, so offensive, and so threatening to the status quo that even the British king and the German crown prince felt obliged to interfere to help punish the men involved. *Joyeux Noel,* like Home's *A Christmas Truce,* promotes two myths about the cease-fire that have increasingly become accepted as fact: that those soldiers who were involved in the event were penalized for their participation, and that the news of the cease-fire was suppressed, kept from a public that would have been horrified to hear that their soldiers had willingly fraternized with the enemy.[16]

The companion book to that film, *Meetings in No Man's Land: Christmas 1914 and Fraternization in the Great War,* jointly written by Marc Ferro, Malcolm Brown, Remy Cazals, and Olaf Mueller, promises to reveal "a story of the Great War that has long been forgotten or lost in censored official reports or officer journals." Admittedly, the French press, as Eksteins noted, prevented mention of the truce in their newspapers at the time, but German and British papers printed many details of it, and the story of the truce remained public knowledge after the war ended. "At last the story could be told," according to Brown's introduction, of the event that "has slipped across the divide between myth and reality, seizing the imagination of many people in the process." Not only could the tale finally be disclosed, "it could be revealed to a new generation in a new Europe as evidence of a step forward in terms of international understanding and reconciliation." Brown praises *Joyeux Noel* as "a worthy, honourable and brave" film, "despite its bold inaccuracies and certain other liberties that had been taken with the story"—as if there were something particularly courageous about making a twenty-first-century antiwar film that was based on a well-known interpretation of a very familiar story. He also reassures readers that "the curious story of the festive season at the front in 1914 might sound bizarre, or crazy, or incredible, but it's not another *Christmas Carol* or a historical leg-pull, it really did take place. There will always be incredulity: there can no longer be doubt."[17]

Although the appearance of the French as fellow fraternizers is certainly a welcome inclusion, their participation was well known long before the premiere of *Joyeux Noel* or the publication of *Meetings in No Man's Land*. Moreover, Brown's continued crusade to have the Christmas truce accepted as fact rather than fiction seems increasingly odd: the reality of armistice, which remained in public sight from 1915 onward and has been perpetually described as "famous" or "legendary" since its occurrence, may have been doubted by a few skeptics but has never been seriously questioned at any point since 1914. Brown also advances some of his favorite First World War tropes: that, under the grim circumstances of the trenches, "it is almost natural that enemies cease to be enemies; rather they become fellow human beings soaked by the same rain, frozen by the same frost, whitened by the same snow," who evolve into "companions in adversity, allies fighting the same grim conditions, and therefore, at a basic human level, almost friends." While admitting that the war diaries of the battalions involved did, in fact, refer to the truce, he also reports Smith-Dorrien's call for the names of officers involved, and he deems it "curious" that "no one was court-martialed" after the fraternization. Brown even reproduces a story about a Saxon battalion that, following fraternization with British troops, refused to fire on the men "with whom over the past two days they had become instant close friends," an action that he describes as "a virtual mutiny." Brown's account of the truce in *Meetings in No Man's Land,* therefore, merely expands on his earlier theories about the event, while adding little in the way of new material, aside from the information about the purported German mutiny.[18]

The increasingly simplified narrative of both the truce and the war also made these subjects particularly suitable for children's literature. Michael Foreman's *War Game: Village Green to No-Man's-Land,* published in 1993, concerns a group of "Suffolk lads" who, pressured by the local vicar and squire, join the King's Royal Rifles at the beginning of the war. The new soldiers are immediately sent to France and the front and "ordered to attack across No Man's Land, even though many lives were always lost and little or nothing was achieved." The proximity of the two lines of trenches meant that "each army could hear the other's voices and could sometimes even smell their breakfasts. They all knew that they were sharing the same terrible conditions." On Christmas morning, the British soldiers wake up to a world white with frost and quiet, where the "clock of death had stopped ticking." The Germans offer a cease-fire, the British accept, and fraternization ensues. The four Suffolk volunteers, who were all eager footballers before the war, join in a match where the goalposts are marked by caps. "Apart from that, it was wonderfully disorganized," Foreman writes, "part football, part ice-skating, with unknown numbers on each team. No referee, no account of the score." Those in charge disapproved, of course, and soldiers were instructed not to leave their trenches again, although Foreman adds that "there were a few secret meetings here and there along the Front, and gifts and souvenirs were exchanged."[19]

Once the "friendly Germans from Saxony" opposite are replaced by "fresh troops from Prussia," the war starts again with a "full-scale attack" at dawn. When the British are ordered to counterattack, one of the Suffolk villagers kicks a football into No Man's Land, and the soldiers are mown down by machine-gun fire, an appropriate end to an account so thoroughly informed by the conventional narrative. Fictional works such as *A Christmas Truce, Joyeux Noel,* and *War Game* encapsulate the contradictions of the orthodox discourse of the Christmas truce. Fraternization was a sign that those in the trenches hated the war and didn't want to fight it—in spite of the fact that they then went back, apparently quite willingly, to fighting it for four more years. The truce was proof that soldiers were eager to defy the orders of their officers—even though, when ordered not to fraternize, troops mostly obeyed those orders, and those who did not were careful to keep their cease-fires very low-key rather than advertise them as acts of open defiance. The armistice still acts as a beacon of hope for the world—which has, since it occurred, engaged in many wars, large and small, with no Christmas truces to leaven the violence. This conventional narrative emphasizes the punishments handed out to those who participated, even though no penalties followed the 1914 cease-fires, and generally suggests that news of the truce was suppressed, in spite of its prominent appearance in British newspaper columns. Within the parameters of the accepted discourse of the conflict, the tale of the truce is taken as clear proof that the futile First World War had been despised by the soldiers fighting it, and is rarely now presented any other way.

Stanley Weintraub's history of the cease-fire, *Silent Night: The Story of the World War I Christmas Truce,* follows the predictable story of "that remarkable moment" without deviation and, in an attempt to present a seamless antiwar discourse, mixes fact and fiction while presenting both as equally valid. Henry Williamson's *A Fox under My Cloak* is extensively quoted, the truce scene in Bairnsfather's *Bullets and Billets* segues neatly into the one in *Oh! What a Lovely War,* and even Blackadder's irritation at a German referee's "decision that placed him off-side" gets featured among the letters and diaries written by truce participants. Somewhat defensively, Weintraub notes that "the Commonwealth War Graves Commission lists six dead surnamed Blackadder," as if this will magically transform the television show's story line into demonstrable reality, and to underline the point, he then refers to the football game in Home's play *A Christmas Truce,* a fictional match the Germans won 3–1 in equally fictional overtime.[20]

"The Christmas Truce of 1914 has lingered strikingly in the memory even when its details have disappeared into myth," Weintraub argues, while making no attempt to distinguish between the reality of the truce and the falsehoods that have grown up around it, even including Graves's short story about the truce and Foreman's *War Game* among the "accounts" of the event. Weintraub's work also features John McCutcheon's 1984 ballad "Christmas in the Trenches." Although the song details the experiences of a fictional soldier, John Tolliver, who participated in a truce on Christmas Day 1914, Weintraub claims that it in fact relates the story of Sir Iain Colquhoun, whom the song alleges joined in the 1914 truce and was court-martialed and sentenced to death for that participation. The only problem with this version of events, Weintraub concedes, is that it is "inaccurate on almost every count." In spite of this admission, Weintraub concludes that, however "erroneous the song's specifics were, the conclusions were not," demonstrating that he intends to support the myths of the truce in the face of any and all contrary evidence.[21]

Illustrating his bias in favor of the conventional narrative of the truce, Weintraub reproduces a story about the XIX Saxon Corps, in which he claims "there was almost a mutiny in one regiment when it received orders to begin shooting again." For this regiment, the difficulty began on the 26th, when the order to fire was given, for the men *struck*. Herr Lange says that in the accumulated years he had never heard such language as the officers indulged in, while they stormed up and down, and got, as the only result, the answer, "We can't—they are good fellows, and we can't." Finally, the officers turned on the men with, "Fire, or we do—and not at the *enemy!*" Not a shot had come from the other side, but at last they fired, and an answering fire came back, but not a man fell. "We spent that day and the next," said Herr Lange, "wasting ammunition in trying to shoot the stars down from the sky."

This anecdote, the only documentation produced by anyone that alleges that participation in the truce was followed by an outright refusal among soldiers to obey orders and fire on the enemy, comes from a thirdhand account of very dubious provenance, yet Weintraub reports it faithfully as gospel truth, including it as such alongside the fictional works of Williamson and McCutcheon. In Weintraub's view, "Christmas 1914 evokes the stubborn humanity within us, and suggests an unrealized potential to burst its seams and rewrite a century"; as a result, he is willing to rely on fiction and highly questionable "facts" to support the truce myths in which he believes.[22]

The uncorroborated story of the German soldiers' rebellion, which was also cited by Brown in *Meetings in No Man's Land*, where he used it as proof that the Germans in the front lines on 25 December 1914 were, in the words of one participant, " 'certainly sportsmen if they are nothing else,' " was taken to another level in the aforementioned *Days That Shook the World* series. That documentary shows a Saxon regiment that "takes the truce further than anyone dares—to the very edge of mutiny. Sergeant Lange recalls that his men went on strike. There is no record of what sparked the revolt, except perhaps for these conscripts, the great patriotic cause had become nothing to the bond they felt with fellow soldiers just thirty yards away." The documentary further embellishes Weintraub's version of this event by showing the German officer cocking his revolver and pointing it at the head of a soldier while barking out an order in German. "The men realize that their protest can be nothing more," the narrator relates while the soldiers begin reluctantly shooting. "The strike is over." Of course, the reason that there is "no record of what sparked the revolt," is that there is no record of any such revolt at all, beyond a thirdhand belated version told to an Australian living in Germany during the war. The willingness of the *Christmas Truce* documentary to ignore readily available facts and accept unfounded accounts of the armistice in order to prove a point about the war—that the truce was a demonstration of the soldiers' hatred of a futile and destructive conflict—was echoed eight years later in an ITV series, one episode of which also focused on the Christmas armistice. *Find My Past*, which promised to "reveal how three people are related to someone from a significant historical event by searching the records on findmypast.co.uk" and "follow their journey as they discover who their ancestor is and the part they played in history," featured three survivors of truce participants in an episode that simultaneously promoted both the genealogy service that sponsored the series and a very conventional view of the First World War.[23]

A number of military historians were enlisted to provide the relatives with graphic accounts of what their ancestors had endured between 1914 and 1918. George Ashurst's descendent, for example, is told by Max Arthur, a military historian, that "in the entire time your great-uncle was at war, he was in two feet of water in the trench," in spite of the fact that Ashurst's memoir, *My Bit,* details extensive periods of time spent back in England on assignment and leaves. Another historian states that the Saxons "were prepared to have a truce, where the Prussians, who were from the north of Germany, much more militant, were really prepared not to play." The documentary notes that the armistice, when "men put aside their weapons and they just go back to being men," was in contravention of the orders Smith-Dorrien had issued on 4 December 1914, and, through a confusing lapse in the episode's time line, implies that Smith-Dorrien learned about the truce from the reports printed in the British papers on Boxing Day.[24]

Carol Smith-Dorrien, granddaughter of the famous general (who the narrator inaccurately claims was in charge of half of the B.E.F. at Christmas 1914), tries to place his 26 December 1914 orders in the best possible light, observing that "he was in overall charge of the troops and had to make the very difficult decision when the Christmas truce broke out, to say no more fraternizing." She further contends that the fact that Smith-Dorrien did not punish anyone for participation in a truce "shows that he understood that there was a desire to fraternize obviously, and even to admire each other, but this was not going to win the war," and she believes that it must have been "horrendous" for him to have to order the truce to cease. The episode also describes the truce as a day of "spontaneous peace" and reports, on the sole basis of George Ashurst's later account, how furious the soldiers were to have the cease-fire broken up by the military leadership. It further maintains that in some places in the line the truce lasted until March. What the *Find My Past* episode does not do, however, is admit that most of the soldiers in Smith-Dorrien's II Corps did not fraternize with the enemy, or that the commanders of the III and IV Corps, whose battalions much more frequently entered into truces, did not find it necessary to issue orders threatening punishment, as the cease-fires ended on their own.[25]

By 2012, the orthodox narrative of the First World War was so firmly established in popular culture that a military historian could, without fear of contradiction, tell the descendant of a soldier that his great-uncle had spent his "entire" war in two feet of water, although Ashurst's memoir (referred to in the episode) talks freely about time spent in the reserve lines, intervals out of line in France, and periods spent in England, including the last three months of the war. Similarly, the conflict's conventional discourse enabled the granddaughter of a famous general to transform her ancestor into a victim of a war that required him to make distressing decisions.[26] These views, however erroneous, are reinforced by numerous Internet sites about the truce, including its Wikipedia page, which notes that the holiday cease-fire is "often seen as a symbolic moment of peace and humanity amidst one of the most violent events of human history" and further describes it as "the most dramatic example of non-cooperation with the war spirit that included refusal to fight, unofficial truces, mutinies, strikes, and peace protests." This version of the Christmas truce, which few of its participants would recognize, is now being widely disseminated via the Internet, which circulates many of the armistice's myths while rarely providing alternative views about either the truce or the war itself. The Christmas truce of 1914, the History Channel website claims, "was never repeated—future attempts at holiday ceasefires were quashed by officers' threats of disciplinary action—but it served as heartening proof, however brief, that beneath the brutal clash of weapons, the soldiers' essential humanity endured." "The Soldiers Truce: A Hidden History from the First World War" assures the reader that the story of the truce, while "once largely unknown, has become widely circulated on the internet."[27]

From 1990 through 2014, the truce gained further ground in a narrative of the 1914–1918 war that contended, however weak or contradictory the evidence, that it "proved" that the soldiers involved in the conflict would have preferred to make peace with each other than to fight. Even if the facts did not actually demonstrate this, as Colquhoun's failure to be shot for allowing fraternization illustrates, then a fictionalized truce always trumped reality, as the moral drawn from it was infinitely more interesting. As a result, the lack of punishments handed out after both the 1914 and 1915 truces is truly an inconvenient truth, and one that will never be read in a work promoting the conventional narrative of the war. As Todman argues in *The Great War: Myth and Memory*, mainstream ideas about the conflict "have achieved the status of modern mythology and as such are knitted into the social fabric," which makes it nearly impossible to challenge the modern discourse of the First World War. As the famous Sainsbury's December 2014 Christmas advertisement demonstrates, the story of the armistice has become firmly embedded in the narrative of the conflict and is therefore inexorably linked to the conventional view of the war. With the centenary of the Christmas truce behind us, the orthodox narrative of the 1914 armistice, however it may deviate from the experiences and attitudes of the soldiers involved, has become the version entrenched in the British public's memory of the war, generally accepted without contradiction or contention, and cited in support of the First World War's discourse of waste and futility.[28]

11

"It Was Peace That Won"

The Christmas Truce and the Narrative of the First World War

Most higher-ups had looked the other way when scattered fraternization occurred earlier. A Christmas truce, however, was another matter. Any slackening in the action during Christmas week might undermine whatever sacrificial spirit there was among troops who lacked ideological fervor.
—Stanley Weintraub, *Silent Night*

By the way I don't know whether I told you there has been a Peace with the people opposite our section since Xmas Eve and it is still going on though the Germans sent in this morning to say they would begin sniping at 11.30 AM, but they haven't done it yet. 2 PM, I don't think they want to start more than we do as it only means a few of each side being hit and does not affect the end of the War.
—Lieutenant Colonel Fisher-Rowe, commander, 1st Grenadier Guards, to his wife, 28 December 1914

In 1983 Paul McCartney applied his famous optimism to the subject of the Christmas truce. "In love our problems disappear," the former Beatle sang in "Pipes of Peace," which was accompanied by a video depicting the 1914 armistice, complete with a spontaneous football match. The video casts McCartney as both a German and a British soldier—emphasizing the point that "the people here are like you and me"—who exchange family photographs, while the lyrics remind us that we should raise our children well by "help[ing] them to see" and teaching them "how to play the pipes of peace." In the video the truce ends when the soldiers fraternizing in No Man's Land are shelled, presumably by orders of the coldhearted but absent generals, and must run back to the "safety" of the trenches. Once behind cover, the doppelgängers look longingly at the photographs of each other's children, thus underlining the implicit moral that the soldiers of the two sides had the same feelings and sensibilities, and therefore had no reason to wage war on each other. The McCartney song pulls exactly the emotional levers it intends to: a comment on the video posted to YouTube.com notes that the song "shows you that they didn't want to fight each other, but politics dictated that they had to."[1]

This 1980s variation on "All You Need Is Love" demonstrates how an appealing and straightforward story can promote a clichéd view of the truce while simultaneously reinforcing certain myths about the First World War. As Alan Clark similarly maintained in his introduction to *The Donkeys,* the story of the 1914–1918 conflict really "was as simple as that." He was wrong. The war was never that uncomplicated, and the problems of trench warfare were never that amenable to an effortless solution, but Clark's superficial portrayal of the conflict was easy to grasp, which is how many of the myths about the First World War took root in the 1960s: by presenting a narrative that was straightforward, had obvious heroes and villains, and offered a clear moral. Having captured British cultural memory, that view of the conflict has become so ingrained that any attempts to dispute it arouse scorn and revulsion, as Michael Gove, the Conservative secretary for education, found out in early 2014 during the course of a very public spat over the narrative of the First World War.

Gove's clumsy and misguided attempts to reframe the First World War in heroic terms, as a victory for Britain and therefore a cause for public celebration, inspired headlines and censure in roughly equal quantities. His assertion that "our understanding of the war has been overlaid by misunderstandings, and misrepresentations which reflect an, at best, ambiguous attitude to this country and, at worst, an unhappy compulsion on the part of some to denigrate virtues such as patriotism, honour and courage" characterized the orthodox narrative of the war as a creation of "left-wing academics" whose purpose is "to belittle Britain and its leaders." In addition, he criticized the use of *Blackadder Goes Forth* as a teaching tool in school curricula relating to the war and condemned the popular television series as leftist propaganda. Although Gove's initial intention was to assert that "the conflict was a 'just war' to combat aggression by a German elite bent on domination," his comments were seen as a deliberately inflammatory attack on both the conventional discourse of the war and the historians who support that interpretation.[2]

Following this opening salvo in the debate about the First World War's narrative, Gove's detractors—and occasional supporters— quickly leapt into the fray. The *Observer* featured a rebuttal from Tristram Hunt, Labour's shadow education secretary, who called Gove's arguments "crass" and "politically motivated." In the *Mail Online*, Sir Tony Robinson, who played Private Baldrick in *Blackadder Goes Forth*, labeled Gove's comments "very silly," while strongly refuting the idea that the series supported any party line. Regius Professor of History Richard Evans, at the University of Cambridge, who had already crossed swords with Gove in 2013 over recommended changes to the British schools' history curricula, pointed out in the *Guardian* that Niall Ferguson, Alan Clark, and Max Hastings, the historians who were most famous for promoting a critical attitude toward the war and the failed military tactics of its generals, were all noted conservatives. Boris Johnson, Conservative mayor of London, then took up arms on Gove's behalf in an editorial in the *Telegraph*, provocatively titled "Germany Started the Great War, but the Left Can't Bear to Say So." In this piece Johnson argued that "it is a sad but undeniable fact that the First World War—in all its murderous horror—was overwhelmingly the result of German expansionism and aggression," but he contended that the modern Labour Party, out of misplaced political correctness, found it impolite to mention this inconvenient truth.[3]

Shortly after Johnson's contribution to the debate, Mark Steel, a commentator and stand-up comedian, weighed in on the controversy in the *Independent*, asserting sarcastically that Gove's statements about the conflict should prevail over the "poncey academic types who criticised the war, like Wilfred Owen and those poets. Just because they spent a few years being gassed and shot at, they thought that gave them a right to criticise it. Well, if they'd joined the real world, like Michael Gove, they might not be so full of airy-fairy pacifist nonsense." Brian Reade, a commentator on sports and current affairs for the *Mirror*, also added his two cents to the debate. "Michael Gove's Attempt at Rewriting Great War History Would Make My KKK-Supporting Uncle Bud Proud" was the title of Reade's piece, in which he declared that "anyone with half a brain knows no single country was totally to blame. It was more about Europe's ruling classes callously sacrificing 16 million lives in their dispute over who should have the biggest empires."[4]

The Christmas truce, the event that so many assume proves that the soldiers fighting the war found it futile and wished to bring it to a halt, plays a large part in the general mythmaking about the war. Margaret MacMillan, in an article entitled "The 1914 Christmas Armistice: A Triumph for Common Humanity," featured in the *Financial Times* on 20 December 2013, highlights that widely accepted view of the truce. Her account, which traces the development of the First World War's narrative of "the horrors of the trenches, the senseless waste of lives, and the meaninglessness of a war that apparently settled nothing," discusses how that interpretation of the conflict came to prevail over all others. While endorsing an orthodox view of the war, MacMillan nevertheless reminds the reader that "at the time people on all sides thought they had a just cause. It is condescending and wrong to think they were hoodwinked." Yet in spite of admitting that the war's widely accepted narrative was not endorsed by many of the soldiers who fought in it or the populations of the countries involved, MacMillan still represents the truce in conventional terms, noting that it is remembered now as "a moment when ordinary soldiers reacted against their leaders and the monstrous folly of the first world war." As a result, while she calls for "a new international approach to the war," MacMillan does not challenge the 1914 cease-fire's orthodox interpretation, leaving the impression that, just as she wishes that "the first world war cemeteries where the soldiers still remain separated into friend and foe will gradually crumble away," she also subscribes to the standard view of the Christmas truce, the event that provides such a useful lesson about a war that was not "glorious or noble," but was rather a conflict "where men were killed from a distance by an enemy they rarely saw," which makes the moment when they fraternized in No Man's Land all the more striking.[5]

Although MacMillan's article admits that the orthodox discourse of the war is not representative of beliefs held a century ago, she still maintains that the Christmas truce represents "a small reminder of a common humanity." Jeremy Rifkin, in his 2010 work *The Empathic Civilization: The Race to Global Consciousness in a World in Crisis,* argues that on 25 December 1914 the British and German soldiers who fraternized in No Man's Land made a conscious decision when leaving their trenches: they "chose to be human." As their letters and diaries demonstrate, however, the soldiers who took part in the truce were, and remained, human from the day they entered the trenches to the day they left them. What drew the men out of the trenches on that

Christmas was not, as Rifkin contends, "empathy for one another," but rather a combination of curiosity, sentimentality, boredom, and homesickness. Although there was a sense of shared suffering between the opposing armies on the front, this did not prompt the actions of the soldiers who participated in the armistice, as the joint miseries of the trenches would hardly become less apparent during the remaining four years of the war, while inciting no further large-scale episodes of fraternization. Nor was the truce inspired by resentment of the army leadership, who in most cases condoned it for the sake of both morale and necessary repairs to the trenches.[6]

The website www.firstworldwar.com goes even further in its support for the conventional narrative of the truce, acknowledging the facts about the cease-fire while asserting that, in fact, these troublesome particulars are irrelevant. The site maintains that the "most important legacy" of the Christmas truce is not the actual armistice—with its readily available details about the "many high-ranking officers who took a surprisingly relaxed view of the situation," the way the truce was "wildly [sic] reported in Britain and to a lesser extent in Germany," and the willingness of the soldiers involved to resume the war and fire on the troops with whom they had fraternized—but instead the ideas that have overtaken its reality. The website's authors freely admit that the truce has been romanticized but argue that the myths about it are so much more "comforting to believe" than the more prosaic truth asserted by pragmatists, which is that the event was "a temporary lull induced by the season of goodwill, but willingly exploited by both sides to better their defences and eye out one another's positions." The orthodox narrative of the senseless and futile conflict that was the First World War is firmly reinforced by the idea that participation in the Christmas armistice, "an effort by normal men to bring about an end to the slaughter," was a sign of mutiny by rebellious soldiers. The desire to believe in this myth overrides all evidence to the contrary, even for those, such as the authors of this website, who admit to the truce's troublesome realities.[7]

The Christmas truce, shorn of its mythology, is impossible to categorize simply, yet even those who, like MacMillan, challenge the conventional narrative of the war can't seem to resist the conventional narrative of the truce. The myth of the 1914 armistice is based on the belief that the soldiers who took part in it shared our modern sensibilities, hated war as we hate war, and rebelled against that futile conflict as we are certain we would have rebelled against it. The truce resonates with us today because we have long since decided where our sympathies lie, which is with the poets who represented the soldiers in the trenches and who captured their plight in such vivid language. As a result, the story of what really happened during the two weeks that started on Christmas Eve 1914 and finally ended about 10 January 1915 rarely cites the letters and diaries of the men involved, but relies instead on postwar memories that reinforce what we already believe. Christmas was celebrated in the trenches on 25 December 1914 as a sentimental rather than a religious holiday, and the widespread but not universal cease-fires and fraternizations were entered into in that spirit by a largely professional army composed of men who supported the war that they were fighting. To comprehend that viewpoint, it is necessary to reject much of what we now believe about the First World War, but to continue to impose a narrative on the truce that is contradicted by the accounts written home by those who took part in it does a disservice to the very soldiers whom we now view as victimized. They did not see themselves in that way, and imputing to them a consciousness that thoroughly misrepresents their perception of the conflict does not help us understand either the war or the truce.

One hundred years after the 1914 cease-fires on the Western Front ended, the varied elements of the Christmas truce have coalesced in public memory into one idealized armistice. This event rarely includes the burial of the dead, suspicion of the enemy, or a refusal to participate out of hatred for the opposing side, although all were features of the 1914 cease-fires. In the new composite truce, soldiers meet in No Man's Land, share cigarettes, food, and drink, and find time for a football match before being ordered back to their trenches by their callous generals. By consorting with their opponents, they make a mockery of the unwanted and purposeless conflict and create an example that will eventually inspire many with admiration for their defiance of a war they hated and the humanity they displayed toward their enemies.

The insistence on a standardized view of the war and the 1914 truce, as well as the proliferation of misinformation about both, ensures that many of these myths about the Christmas armistice not only remain unchallenged, but are constantly being reinforced. As the contemporary accounts of the truce demonstrate, the armistice was hardly the monolithic event now portrayed in the various media that feature it. The letters written home by soldiers, even before the truce, illustrate the surprising frankness with which they wrote about their lives in the trenches, providing their correspondents with vivid details about mud, death, destruction, and the plight of the Belgians, while also including stories about mutual jokes with the enemy in the lines opposite. These particulars, freely shared with the home front, presaged both the candor they would display when writing about the truce and the way the civilians back in Britain were prepared to accept the truth about the events of Christmas 1914.

An examination of the accounts of the truce written by the British soldiers who had participated in the event shows that, while many found the unexpected holiday from gunfire and danger welcome and enjoyed meeting their German counterparts in No Man's Land, very few expected, or even desired, that any lasting peace would occur as a result of the unofficial armistice. At the same time, they saw no need to hide from those at home their willingness to join in the occasion, clearly expecting their friends and families to enjoy the story of their impromptu Christmas truce as much as they did. Sparing few details, they wrote home about the cease-fires, their meetings with the enemy, the burial of the dead, the sharing of gifts, and the German misinformation about the course of the war, as well as the occasional football match. Their letters were not subject to censorship nor did they record any actions taken against those who had joined in the meetings with the enemy.

The evidence of the official war diaries for those battalions that had participated in the truce further demonstrates the general lack of inhibitions frontline officers felt about admitting to involvement in the event. While battalions that were part of the B.E.F.'s 5th Division (II Corps) did tend to be cagier about the details of the truce—most recorded only "very quiet" times in the line over Christmas—the diaries of the battalions forming the 4th, 6th, 7th, and 8th Divisions (III and IV Corps) demonstrate a willingness on the part of frontline officers to feature the incident, often at great length, in the documents that constituted the official record of their activities during the war. It is true that some officers in the 14th and 15th Brigades (II Corps) were required by their leadership, a few days after Christmas, to write up a brief account of their truces, but no further action was taken either against any of these officers or against the soldiers whom they had allowed to participate in any truce activities, including actual fraternization with Germans in No Man's Land. In fact, an examination of the diaries from battalions in the front line in Flanders during December 1914 and January 1915 reveals that ongoing cease-fires were reported by some for two or more weeks after Christmas without disciplinary action being taken against the troops involved.

An examination of British newspapers reveals that accounts of the Christmas truce were reported openly in late December 1914 and early January 1915. Although the British press drew the line at writing articles discussing the event—no doubt finding it too difficult to reconcile with their overall war reporting—the many descriptions of the unofficial armistice that appeared in newspapers such as the *Times, Daily Telegraph,* and *Manchester Guardian* make it clear that the truce became well known in Britain shortly after it occurred. Further, an examination of the headlines and leaders that accompanied the soldiers' letters about the Christmas armistice shows that it was accepted by the British without censure: "Christmas Truce / Mingling with the Enemy," "A Christmas Truce at the Front / Enemies at Football," and "British and Germans Fraternize," to give a few examples, illustrate the nonjudgmental nature of the press coverage of the event. The numerous accounts published in the British newspapers until mid-January 1915 demonstrate the level of public interest in the truce, and the refusal to criticize those who participated in the episode illuminates the fact that the newspaper editors who published these accounts, as well as the civilians who read about the event, probably understood the reasons for the truce and did not disapprove of the idea of their soldiers enjoying a temporary holiday armistice.[8]

As the war ground on for four more long and painful years, not only did the Christmas truce remain an important memory for those who had participated in it, but it additionally was often used as proof of the professionalism of the members of the British Army, who were assumed to be fighting not out of hatred of the Germans, but rather out of a belief in the righteousness of their cause. Although it is true that many of those who served on the Western Front and other theaters of the war eventually found themselves disillusioned with the purpose and prosecution of the conflict, the majority of the soldiers involved believed in the reasons Britain had gone to war and the importance of winning that war. This is reflected not only in the histories of the war written between 1914 and 1918, but also in the letters and memoirs of the soldiers still serving on, or invalided home from, the Western Front.

A mild repetition of the 1914 cease-fires by three battalions in 1915 confirmed that, in spite of official warnings, the army's appetite for punishing overt fraternization with the enemy was to prove very feeble indeed. References to the truce continued throughout the inter-war years, as the histories of many of the battalions and divisions that had participated in the armistice appeared and they included accounts of the event that varied widely. Some regimental histories celebrated it at great length, whereas a few ignored the armistice altogether or passed over it briefly. In many of these chronicles, however, the Christmas truce was featured prominently, clearly retaining its meaning for participants as an event fondly remembered and a memory shared with fellow soldiers.

With the end of the Great War, a flood of memoirs, histories, and polemics that supported or condemned the war appeared, and no consensus was reached on either the significance or result of the conflict. The Christmas truce, instead of being consigned to oblivion by all but those who had participated in it, remained a vital part of the inter-war narrative and was increasingly employed by those who took a firm stance on the war's meaning. Many still credited the truce to the professionalism of the soldiers involved, or took it as proof that Britain had entered the war not out of hatred of the enemy, but rather for the justice of the cause. Some who condemned the recent war, such as Philip Gibbs or C. E. Montague, believed that the armistice demonstrated a fellow feeling for the enemy soldiers, or a manifestation of prewar values. Surprisingly, the antiwar novels and memoirs that began to appear during the latter part of the 1920s—*All Quiet on the Western Front, Good-bye to All That,* and *Memoirs of a Fox-Hunting Man,* which now constitute the trinity of the antiwar canon—either ignored the truce entirely or, in Graves's case, touted it as a tribute to his regiment's traditions. As a survey of books written about the Great War before 1940, including the official British history of the conflict, demonstrates, the narrative of the Christmas truce in the first two decades after the end of the war continued to lack coherence, much like the varied views on the conflict itself.

With the advent of the Second World War and its aftermath, the discourse of both the Great War—now rechristened as the First World War, to denote its place as the precursor to the deadlier conflict—and the truce began to undergo major revisions. The view of the earlier conflict as wasteful and futile, which during the interwar years had been merely one strand of its narrative, began to overshadow all other views of that war. The late 1950s and early 1960s works of historians such as Cameron, Clark, Taylor, and Tuchman, who all strongly endorsed this interpretation, both shaped and encapsulated the public understanding of the conflict, in which the incompetent "donkeys" of the British army leadership sacrificed the lives of the brave "lion" soldiers in a senseless and foolish war. The further connection drawn between the First and Second World Wars—Taylor in particular blaming the second conflict on both the inept prosecution of the first war and the mismanagement of the peace that followed it—hammered home the point that the First World War not only had killed and maimed millions of men for nothing, but also had brought upon the world the second, and even deadlier, war. With its reputation now firmly fixed, the First World War could never be viewed again as necessary or worthwhile, let alone successful in its achievements. As the antiwar narrative of the 1960s dominated all other views of the conflict, the Christmas truce became ripe for rediscovery as proof that, as early as 1914, the soldiers in the trenches had rebelled against their callous leadership and sought to make common cause with the equally abused soldiers opposite.

This view was reinforced in Britain during the 1960s through multiple media, including the works of the historians mentioned above, the 1964 BBC documentary *The Great War,* and the theater and film versions of *Oh! What a Lovely War.* In the 1970s these sources of information were augmented by many interviews with surviving veterans whose memories were prodded by those already persuaded by the conventional narrative. "Did you tell them the truth?" George Ashurst was asked in 1985 about letters he wrote home during the war. "Oh, yes, yes," he replied, obviously bemused by the question, but far too polite to ask what the interviewer thought he would have written instead. With the insistence, from the 1960s onward, on one interpretation of the First World War, reinforced by the emphasis on the experiences of the men involved as well as the works of the soldier-writers who wrote of their disillusionment with the conflict, the British view of the truce coalesced around a narrative that supported the antiwar message of the second half of the twentieth century.

Over the past forty years, revisionist historians have tried without success to counter this view of the First World War, but it appears to be too firmly fixed in the British consciousness to be easily dislodged, as is the orthodox narrative of the Christmas truce. An evaluation of sources written between 1914 and 2014 that refer to the armistice reveals that the conventional narrative of the truce, like that of the war itself, took many decades to develop. Once the myth of the Christmas truce, the widespread rebellion by traumatized soldiers against the war they hated, took root, however, the reality of the holiday armistice became obscured. By misrepresenting the words and feelings of the soldiers who had participated in the event, and ignoring the freely published accounts of it in regimental diaries and the British press or the lack of disciplinary action taken against those involved, many have created a truce that bears little resemblance to the one that numerous soldiers took part in on Christmas Day 1914 in Flanders. "In the end, however," Murphy declares in his children's book about the armistice, "it was peace that won the day as hundreds of thousands of soldiers simply decided, despite direct orders to the contrary, that they weren't going to fight." This is, of course, not at all what the men involved in the Christmas truce decided. Those soldiers, in fact, wanted a day off, a holiday celebration, a temporary respite from fear, and a break from the monotony of the trenches. They achieved all this, but only at the cost of having their actions and motivations misunderstood for the next century—in spite of the very clear record they left behind.[9]

Since even some men who shared in the Christmas truce eventually came to believe in the myths about it, it is hardly surprising that those who wish to press the temporary cease-fire into the service of the orthodox narrative of the war would also be inclined to distort both the reality and significance of the episode. As the accounts of the soldiers involved, many of which appeared in the British press, demonstrate, however, the truce was widely publicized and was received by the public in the same spirit in which it was undertaken by those who participated in it: "We went out and met them," Ernest Morley wrote matter-of-factly to a friend, and experienced "the curious pleasure of chatting with men who had been doing their best to kill us, and we them." The "most weird Christmas of my life," as another soldier described it, was just that: odd and unusual, a memory to cherish, a tale to relate in the letters written home, and a story to tell to grandchildren or reminisce about when meeting another veteran of the trenches, but not a reason to end the war.[10]

In his 1967 work on the conflict, *Great Britain and the War of 1914–1918,* Llewellyn Woodward wrote: "In the last years of the war, the futility, inevitable, outrageous in its necessity, overshadowed everything. I use the words 'inevitable' and 'necessary' because I still thought that a German victory would fasten on Europe chains from which there would be no hope of release except after even greater misery. If I did not expect a much better world to come out of it, at least, though at far too heavy a cost, our victory would have removed the threat of a mindless European tyranny." Wars are, by their very nature, senseless and idiotic: no one has ever started a sensible or justifiable one. If one nation, or an alliance of nations, is determined to begin a war, however, the countries attacked have few choices: either fight or give in. The First World War was indeed, as Llewellyn maintains, "outrageous in its necessity." The true outrage of the war arose from the facts that fighting it was essential for Britain and that so many men had to die to win it.[11]

The 1914 cease-fire, the day of peace that has been romanticized by so many who subscribe to the orthodox narrative of the war, was initiated by men who believed in the cause for which they fought, and, in most cases, went on believing in that cause long after the temporary armistice and even the war itself ended. The truce may encapsulate our modern view of a hated war, but the First World War, and the 1914 armistice in particular, was perceived very differently by those who participated in it. Bruce Bairnsfather, whose account of the truce is renowned, characterized the episode as being "just like the interval between the rounds in a friendly boxing match." The boxing match that was the First World War was in fact a deadly and tragic conflict, yet the spirit in which the Christmas truce was undertaken did generally reflect the attitudes of the soldiers who took part in it: determined to win the war, but at the same time very glad to take a break from the battle.

Acknowledgments

I would like to express my sincere appreciation to my academic advisers at the University of Kentucky, Drs. Phil Harling and Karen Petrone, who contributed so much to this work. They both offered vital support and feedback on the project, from its beginnings as a master's thesis through the final manuscript submission, and I am very grateful for the time they gave to this work. Additionally, I want to thank them both for their forbearance with the world's most willfully stubborn graduate student, as their patience has been stretched far too often to remain unacknowledged. I would also like to thank Dr. Pearl James for her interest and encouragement.

My colleagues in the Office of Legal Counsel at UK deserve much appreciation for their understanding when class times or research trips kept me out of the office, as well as their willingness to listen to me talk about the First World War. I am particularly grateful to UK's general counsel, Bill Thro, for his support for my academic endeavors and enthusiasm for this book. All my coworkers have been helpful, but I would especially like to thank Cliff Iler, Marcy Deaton, Shannan Carroll, and Thalethia Routt.

Others at UK have been very generous in their support for my work, and Bill Swinford deserves special gratitude for encouragement as well as for practical assistance. Cathy Masoud, Eduardo Santillan-Jimenez, and Skip van Hook all took an interest in this project at times when support was sorely needed and much appreciated, and I hope they know how much that meant to me.

I am most grateful to Steve Wrinn and Allison Webster at the University Press of Kentucky for their many kind comments and helpful suggestions throughout the process.

Peter Grant reached out to me about my work at a very opportune time, and since then has provided much assistance in the way of suggestions, corrections, and advice, for all of which I am most grateful. Anne Samson provided me with some research help and lots of encouragement, and I am very appreciative of both.

The staff at the Imperial War Museum (IWM), particularly the late Roderick Suddaby, were of great help with my research, and ditto for the indefatigable Inter-Library Loan folks at UK, who always found the books, however obscure, I needed to complete this work. Thanks also to Dick Gilbreath for the wonderful maps.

I am very grateful to all the IWM collections' copyright holders who took the time to correspond with me regarding their relations' letters, diaries, and memoirs and to provide me with many details of interest regarding the war service and memories of their relatives. I hope they all feel that I have represented the views of those soldiers and veterans accurately.

Thanks to Ruth Booher for her friendship and support and to Jamie Wilson for the same, as well as her kind comments on some of this work in earlier drafts. In spite of the fact that we have never met, Shelley Nass obligingly offered to read the entire book and suggested useful corrections. Pat O'Connor and I have met, many times, but that didn't stop him from not only reading some chapters but also providing comments on them that made me want to write a whole other book on the Christmas truce. I'm grateful to you all for your help and advice.

Lori Cresci, in her various roles as cheerleader, unofficial editor, sounding board, grammarian, intelligent ideal reader, and BFF, has been a rock throughout the three years it took to complete this work, and I can't imagine how I could have got through it without her. I also can't imagine how I would have got through the past forty years without her, but that's another story.

Thanks to Saskia for being the best daughter ever.

Finally, I would like to thank my husband, Mark, for everything he has done to help with this work. From sharing my passion for the subject to providing much-needed advice on the various drafts of the project, his support, insight, and understanding have proved invaluable. In addition, he is the only person who has read this work in its three forms—master's thesis, dissertation, and manuscript—although I doubt that is what he had in mind when he volunteered for better or worse thirty-three years ago. In gratitude for his patience and assistance, I therefore dedicate this book to him, with lots of love.

Notes

1. "A Candle Lit in the Darkness"

1. Christian Carion, director, *Joyeux Noel* (Sony Picture Classics, 2005), DVD liner notes.

2. "Merry Christmas (*Joyeux Noel*)," *Times*, 17 December 2005; Stephen Holden, "A Christmas Truce Forged by Germans, French, and Scots," *New York Times*, 3 March 2006; Matthew Leyland, "Merry Christmas (*Joyeux Noel*)," *BBC*, 13 December 2005; Roger Ebert, "*Joyeux Noel*," *Chicago Sun-Times*, 9 March 2006; Sheila Johnston, "The Astonishing War Story That a Nation Chose to Forget: Lessons in Humanity: *Joyeux Noel*," *Telegraph*, 2 December 2005.

3. For the conventional narrative of the 1914 truce, see, among others, Stanley Weintraub, *Silent Night: The Story of the World War I Christmas Truce* (New York: Penguin, 2002); Malcolm Brown and Shirley Seaton, *Christmas Truce* (London: Pan Books, 1984); John Keegan, *An Illustrated History of the First World War* (New York: Random House, 2001); Paul Fussell, *The Great War and Modern Memory* (New York: Oxford University Press, 1975); Alan Clark, *The Donkeys* (London: Pimlico, 1961); Lyn Macdonald, *1915: The Death of Innocence* (1993; repr., Baltimore: Johns Hopkins University Press, 2000); and Marc Ferro, Malcolm Brown, Remy Cazals, and Olaf Mueller, *Meetings in No Man's Land: Christmas 1914 and Fraternization in the Great War*, trans. Helen McPhail (London: Constable, 2007).

4. Weintraub, *Silent Night*, xvi. Although the various cease-fires and fraternizations were unconnected and should more accurately be described as "the Christmas truces" rather than "the Christmas truce," the singular term will be used throughout this work.

5. "Plugstreet," www.ww1battlefields.co.uk/flanders/plugstreet.html; "Kickabout That Captured Futility of First World War to Be Replayed for Centenary," *Guardian*, 8 February 2013; Malcolm Brown, "When Peace Broke Out," *Guardian*, 23 December 2001.

6. Laurence Fisher-Rowe, 1st Grenadier Guards, to Mrs. Fisher-Rowe, 27 December 1914, Private Papers of L. Fisher-Rowe, Imperial War Museum Collection No. 16978. All letters and diary entries are reproduced with original spelling and grammar intact. The letters and diaries cited in this work, aside from those published in the British press or in compilations of letters, come from the extensive Imperial War Museum collection of soldiers' private papers.

7. Adrian Gregory, *The Last Great War: British Society and the First World War* (Cambridge: Cambridge University Press, 2008), 3; Gerard De Groot,

The First World War (New York: Palgrave, 2001), 1; Martin Gilbert, *The First World War: A Complete History* (London: Orion Books, 1994), xv.

8. John Keegan, *The First World War* (London: Hutchinson, 1998), 3; Adam Gopnik, "The Big One: Historians Rethink the War to End All Wars," *New Yorker*, 23 August 2004, 81. Of course, because the agreements France had entered into with Britain did not guarantee British involvement if Germany attacked the French or if the French attacked Germany, the French could not know before entering the war that British help would be available. Gopnik was, however, fairly accurate about the German, British, and Russian motives.

9. Niall Ferguson, *The Pity of War* (London: Penguin Press, 1999), xxxviii; John Simpson, *Unreliable Sources: How the Twentieth Century Was Reported* (London: Macmillan, 2010), 115.

10. Fussell, *The Great War and Modern Memory*, 41. This tendentious figure is thoroughly incorrect: as Cruttwell notes, the number of British men who enlisted was, in total, 6,211,427, of which 744,702 died and 1,693,262 were wounded throughout the course of the war. C. R. M. F. Cruttwell, *A History of the Great War, 1914–1918* (Oxford: Clarendon Press, 1934), 630. Fussell's figures of 7,000 (at a minimum) dead and wounded daily would amount to, for the entire war, at least 10,500,000, or 150 percent of Britain's total army during the war. Even if some men were wounded on multiple occasions, or wounded and thereafter killed, this figure remains unrealistic. In addition, it should be noted that the term *wastage* did not reflect any callous attitude toward casualties on the part of army leadership, but was instead a standard military term for any event that lowered the strength of a unit. An outbreak of measles among the soldiers in a battalion would also be considered wastage if it took men out of line while they recovered.

11. John Ellis, *Eye-Deep in Hell: Trench Warfare in World War I* (Baltimore: Johns Hopkins University Press, 1976); Tim Travers, *The Killing Grounds: The British Army, the Western Front & the Emergence of Modern Warfare* (London: Routledge, 1993); Keegan, *The First World War*, 3.

12. Cate Haste, *Keep the Home Fires Burning: Propaganda in the First World War* (London: Penguin Books, 1977), 31; A. J. P. Taylor, *A History of the First World War* (New York: Berkeley Medallion, 1963), 103; De Groot, *First World War*, 147.

13. Arthur Marwick, *The Deluge: British Society and the First World War* (New York: Norton, 1965), 218; Simpson, *Unreliable Sources*, 133; Brian Bond, *The Unquiet Western Front: Britain's Role in Literature and History* (Cambridge: Cambridge University Press, 2002), 11.

14. Keith Robbins, *The First World War* (Oxford: Oxford University Press, 1984), 150; Simon Schama, "No Downers in 'Downton,'" *Daily Beast*, 16 January 2012. John Simpson similarly remarks that Lloyd George's son Gwilym, who was commissioned into the Royal Welch Fusiliers in 1914, "managed,

against the odds, to survive the war," without noting that the possibility of being killed in the war was approximately one in ten: hardly optimal, but not a certain death sentence either. Simpson, *Unreliable Sources*, 134. As Cruttwell noted, 5,466,725 of the 6,211,427 British soldiers who served in the war survived it. For casualty figures, see Cruttwell, *History of the Great War*, 630.

15. Barbara W. Tuchman, *The Guns of August* (1962; repr., New York: Presidio Press, 2004), 523; Gilbert, *The First World War*, xv; Jay Winter and Blaine Baggett, *The Great War and the Shaping of the Twentieth Century* (New York: Penguin Books, 1996), 392; Gilbert, *The First World War*, 511.

16. Peter Bradshaw, "Merry Christmas," *Guardian*, 15 December 2005. In fact, not a single truce began with a cry of "No more war!"

17. Fussell, *The Great War and Modern Memory*, 10; Taylor, *History of the First World War*, 39; Winter and Baggett, *The Great War*, 99.

18. Brown and Seaton, *Christmas Truce*, 194; Weintraub, *Silent Night*, 174.

19. Gregory, *The Last Great War*, 5; Gary Sheffield, *Forgotten Victory, the First World War: Myths and Realities* (London: Headline, 2001), xvii.

20. John Horne, ed., *A Companion to World War I* (Malden, Mass.: Blackwell, 2010), xx, xxii; John Terraine, *The Western Front, 1914–1918* (London: Hutchinson, 1964), 20.

21. Richard Curtis and Ben Elton, *Blackadder Goes Forth* (BBC, 1989); Gopnik, "The Big One," 79; Marwick, *The Deluge*, 10; Daniel Todman, *The Great War: Myth and Memory* (London: Hambledon Continuum, 2005), 122.

22. Gregory, *The Last Great War*, 44; Todman, *The Great War*, 124.

23. Terraine, *The Western Front*, 180; Gopnik, "The Big One," 83; Horne, *Companion to World War I*, xxii. Gopnik's theory would be more convincing had he chosen four military figures less well known for their willingness to ignore the "butcher's bill" in pursuit of victory.

24. Charles Edmonds, *A Subaltern's War, Being a Memoir of the Great War from the Point of View of a Romantic Young Man . . .* (1929; repr., New York: Minton, Balch, 1930), 120–121. It is worth noting that in the first year of the war, before Kitchener's Army came to swell the ranks of the British Expeditionary Forces (B.E.F.), battalions often spent longer periods in line waiting for relief or reinforcements. An examination of war diaries of frontline battalions from 1914 and 1915, however, shows that troops generally did rotate out of the lines regularly, and that four- to five-day stretches in the trenches became the norm after November 1914.

25. Samuel Hynes, *A War Imagined: The First World War and English Culture* (New York: Atheneum, 1991), xii; Emma Hanna, *The Great War on the Small Screen: Representing the First World War in Contemporary Britain* (Edinburgh: Edinburgh University Press, 2009), 12; Hew Strachan, *The First World War* (London: Penguin Books, 2003), xv.

26. Ferguson, *Pity of War*, xxxiii; Gregory, *The Last Great War*, 283; Sheffield, *Forgotten Victory*, x.

27. Horne, *Companion to World War I*, 280; Ferguson, *Pity of War*, pl. 13, between pp. 180 and 181; Gregory, *The Last Great War*, 133. Ferguson's observation contradicts his own stated view, expressed in *The Pity of War*, that the home front was presented only with a "sanitized" view of the war, which demonstrates that the conventional view of the war and a revisionist take on it can coexist even within one work. Ferguson, *Pity of War*, 354.

28. Ferguson, *Pity of War*, 412; Todman, *The Great War*, 127.

29. "Fighting the Myths of the First World War," https://networks.h-net.org/node/5293/blog/h-empire/6919/fighting-myths-first-world-war; Todman, *The Great War*, xii; Gregory, *Last Great War*, 3; Nicoletta F. Gullace, "Allied Propaganda and World War I: Interwar Legacies, Media Studies, and the Politics of War Guilt," *History Compass* 9, no. 9 (2011): 686; Michael S. Neiberg, "Revisiting the Myths: New Approaches to the Great War," *Contemporary European History* 13, no. 4 (November 2004): 506.

30. Hanna, *The Great War on the Small Screen*, 7; Gregory, *The Last Great War*, 4; Todman, *The Great War*, 18.

31. In fact, the influential 1964 BBC series on the 1914–1918 conflict, *The Great War*, begins with crowds cheering on the enthusiastic volunteers marching off to war in early August 1914—even though the soldiers embarking for France at that time were all professionals or territorials who had enlisted earlier—and ends with piles of corpses. Janet S. K. Watson, *Fighting Different Wars: Experience, Memory, and the First World War in Britain* (New York: Cambridge University Press, 2004), 5; Simpson, *Unreliable Sources*, 89.

32. Weintraub, *Silent Night*, xvi; Neiberg, "Revisiting the Myths," 506; R. J. Armes, 1st North Staffordshires, letter, 25 December 1914, Private Papers of R. J. Armes, Imperial War Museum Collection No. 16576. This work examines the attitudes of the soldiers involved in the holiday cease-fires rather than offering specific details of the 1914 and 1915 Christmas truces. For those interested in more information about the truce, including extensive reports from many firsthand accounts, *Christmas Truce* by Malcolm Brown and Shirley Seaton provides a wealth of detail about the event itself. Although the conclusions Brown and Seaton draw from the truce can be disputed, their research into the episode is impressively thorough, and they provide the most complete and factually reliable account to date of the armistice.

33. Hanna, *The Great War on the Small Screen*, 77–78.

2. "Absolute Hell"

1. Marwick, *The Deluge*, 135; Terraine, *The Western Front*, 17–18; Modris Eksteins, *Rites of Spring: The Great War and the Birth of the Modern Age* (Boston: Houghton Mifflin, 1989), 181; Todman, *The Great War*, 10.

2. Ellis, *Eye-Deep in Hell*, 138–139; Anthony Fletcher, "Between the

Lines: First World War Correspondence," *History Today* 59 (November 2009): 45; Robert Graves, *Good-bye to All That: An Autobiography* (1929; rev. ed., New York: Doubleday, 1957), 228.

3. Michael Roper, *The Secret Battle: Emotional Survival in the Great War* (Manchester, U.K.: Manchester University Press, 2009), 15, 21; Jessica Meyer, *Men of War: Masculinity and the First World War in Britain* (New York: Palgrave MacMillan, 2009), 16–17.

4. John H. Morrow Jr., *The Great War: An Imperial History* (New York: Routledge, 2004), 156.

5. George Ashurst, interview, 1987, Imperial War Museum Collection No. 9875. It should be noted that Ashurst, as a proponent of the conventional narrative of both the war and the Christmas truce, would be expected to support the notion that soldiers were prevented from sharing the truth of the war with those at home, but, when interviewed, he refused to fall in with this particular convention. Further, while some censorship of soldiers' correspondence did occur, it appears to have been confined mainly to excising the names of places where troops were stationed. As Cuthbert Lawson noted in a letter to his mother, "Judging by the extracts from Officers' letters which appear in the papers, you can say almost anything about the past, and if any of my efforts have been scrapped, it is more likely to be because they are so minute in writing, and so compressed in space, that any ordinary Censor would shy at reading them." Cuthbert G. Lawson, 3rd Royal Horse Artillery, to his mother, 6 October 1914, Private Papers of C. G. Lawson, Imperial War Museum Collection No. 7834. Certainly, the intermittent nature of army censorship was expected to act as an overall deterrent to soldiers sending too many forbidden details home, but as Lawson observes, it didn't appear to stop anyone from saying pretty much whatever he pleased as long as place names and battle plans were not provided.

6. The first recruiting appeal offered terms of service for a period of three years or "until the war is concluded," from which Marwick deduces that "Kitchener at least did not share the widely held belief that the war would be over within six months"; Marwick, *The Deluge*, 35.

It should be noted that, although trenches had been used as defensive measures during warfare in the American Civil War, the Boer War, and the Russo-Japanese War, they had never been as extensively employed as they were on the Western Front between 1914 and 1918. Compounding this issue was the fact that conventional military training in the early twentieth century emphasized grand tactics and mobile campaigns rather than defensive warfare, which left commanders on both sides ill prepared to fight the stationary battles of the First World War. Of course, lack of imagination on the part of the same military leaders certainly did not help ease the bottleneck. The passage quoted is from John A. Liddell, 2nd Argyll and Sutherland Highlanders, to his father, 26 November 1914, Private Papers of J. A. Liddell, Imperial War Museum

Collection No. 11126.

7. Cruttwell, *History of the Great War,* 107.

8. S. Thomas Lucey, 1st Loyal North Lancashires, to his mother, 25 December 1914, Private Papers of S. T. Lucey, Imperial War Museum Collection No. 15331; Arthur Pelham-Burn, 6th Gordon Highlanders, to "My dear Mathers," n.d. (ca. late December 1914), Scrapbook of Claude Buckingham, Imperial War Museum Collection No. 8632; E. R. P. Berryman, 2/39 Garhwal Rifles, to Jane Berryman, 1 January 1915, Private Papers of E. R. P. Berryman, Imperial War Museum Collection No. 17257.

9. Frank Black, 1st Royal Warwicks, to "Alf," 2 December 1914, Private Papers of F. H. Black, Imperial War Museum Collection No. 4333; H. M. Dillon, 2nd Oxfordshire and Buckinghamshire Light Infantry, to his sister Kathleen, 15 September 1914, Private Papers of H. M. Dillon, Imperial War Museum Collection No. 4430; E. H. E. Daniell, 2nd Royal Irish, to his mother, 26 September 1914, Imperial War Museum Collection No. 1329; Pelham-Burn to "My dear Mathers," n.d. (ca. late December 1914). It can be argued that the friends and relatives of professional and territorial soldiers—who constituted the vast majority of the British soldiers in the trenches in 1914—were probably more receptive to honest evaluations of the conditions under which their men fought than families of newly enlisted men would be, and that this influenced the way they wrote home in the first months of the war, but the willingness of the British press to publish these accounts belies the theory that this type of knowledge would be acceptable only to the relations of professional soldiers, a small minority of the population.

10. Percy H. Jones, 1st Queen's Westminster Rifles, to his brother, 20 December 1914, Private Papers of P. H. Jones, Imperial War Museum Collection No. 12253; Wilbert B. P. Spencer, 2nd Wiltshires, to his mother, December 1914, Private Papers of W. B. P. Spencer, Imperial War Museum Collection No. 1684; Liddell to his mother, 21 December 1914.

11. Maurice Mascall, Royal Garrison Artillery, to his fiancée, 1 December 1914, Private Papers of E. M. Mascall, Imperial War Museum Collection No. 11163; Dillon to his sister Kathleen, 29 October 1914; Lucey to his brother, n.d. (late December 1914). Mascall's fiancée was probably not at all comforted, either, to read a description of his regiment's first visit to the trenches, which featured "bullets singing over our heads, and a more or less continuous fire from snipers on both sides."

12. Kitchener's new army, which comprised units consisting solely of men who volunteered at the beginning of the war—although many of their officers were drawn from those who were already in the army when the war started—did not begin to arrive in France until May 1915; Gilbert, *The First World War,* 159.

13. B. H. Liddell Hart, *The Real War, 1914–1918* (Boston: Little, Brown, 1930), 81; Robert Graves, "Christmas Truce," in *The Shout and Other Stories*

(New York: Penguin Books, 1965); originally published as "Wave No Banners," *Saturday Evening Post*, 15 December 1962, 112; E. W. Cox, Intelligence Section, to his wife, 16 September 1914, Private Papers of E. W. Cox, Imperial War Museum Collection No. 8548.

14. Daniell to his mother, 26 September 1914; Lawson to his mother, 26 October 1914.

15. Alfred Dugan Chater, 2nd Gordon Highlanders, to his girlfriend, 13 December 1914, Private Papers of A. D. Chater, Imperial War Museum Collection No. 1697; Liddell to his mother, 21 December 1914.

16. Michael Holroyd, 1st Hampshires, letter, 23 December 1914, Private Papers of M. Holroyd, Imperial War Museum Collection No. 7364; F. E. Packe, 2nd Welch, to his mother, 9 October 1914, Private Papers of F. E. Packe, Imperial War Museum Collection No. 1653. "Atkins" is a reference to "Tommy Atkins," the common term for a British rank-and-filer; it is more customarily shortened to "Tommy."

17. Ashurst, 1987 interview.

18. Cox to his wife, 5 October 1914; Dillon to his sister, 24 October 1914; F. G. Chandler, 2nd Argyll and Sutherland Highlanders, to "My dear old man," 17 December 1914, Private Papers of F. G. Chandler, Imperial War Museum Collection No. 15460. In fact, Dillon died of pneumonia in London in January 1918, a condition no doubt brought on by his four periods of service on the Western Front. According to the Imperial War Museum website, he was a company commander in the 2nd Oxfordshire and Buckinghamshire Light Infantry from August to November 1914, and he participated in the Retreat from Mons and the Battle of the Aisne.

19. According to Philip Gibbs, some journalists made their way to the front in the early part of the war without authorization from the British War Office, but they were sent home early in the campaign. Philip Gibbs, *Realities of War* (London: Heinemann, 1920), 3, 7. "Guns and Airships / Allies' Fine Work / Increasing Ascendency," *Daily Telegraph*, 14 December 1914. As Percy Jones later ironically remarked about official British military information in the lead-up to the Battle of the Somme, "There is nothing like the truth!"; Jones, diary entry for 26 June 1916.

20. Whereas the *Times* was, most democratically, "glad to consider for publication letters received by relatives and friends from those serving with the Military and Naval Forces," and the *Manchester Guardian* was similarly grateful for letters "written by soldiers who are, or have been, taking part in any of the campaigns which are now being waged," both the *Morning Post* and the *Daily Mail* preferred to solicit their material from "relatives and friends of officers."

As Cate Haste notes about censorship in her work about British propaganda during the war, "Press articles were surveyed by the Censorship Department. Censorship was compulsory for cables, including press cables, but otherwise press censorship was voluntary, that is, editors were given the freedom to decide which articles to submit to the censor." It is clear, however, that Haste believes that the voluntary nature of the censorship did not prevent newspapers from stifling the truth wherever possible. She also writes, "Of the real nature of trench warfare and the horrific effect of modern weapons, the country remained largely in the dark"; Haste, *Keep the Home Fires Burning*, 30, 31.

21. "Letters from the Front," *Daily Mail*, 1 January 1915; "What Modern Shell Fire Is Like," *Daily Mail*, 11 December 1914.

22. Sergeant Woodcock, "Letters from the Front / 204 Left Out of 1,250," *Daily Mail*, 27 October 1914; "Letters from the Front / Tremendous German Losses," *Daily Mail*, 2 November 1914; "Soldiers' Letters Home / Ten Years Older / Mowing Down Germans in Belgium / Never a Grumble," *Daily Mail*, 9 November 1914; "Soldiers' Letters Home / Writing amid the Shells," *Daily Mail*, 11 November 1914. Although one of the conventions of First World War discourse is that all families of soldiers killed were told that they died peacefully and quickly after being shot in the head or chest, letters discussing men being "blown to pieces" show that the British public could not entirely avoid being aware of the way its soldiers died in battle.

23. "Campaigning in Many Lands / Soldiers' Varied Experiences Told in Letters and Interviews / Cheshire Territorials in the Trenches," *Manchester Guardian*, 31 December 1914; "Letters from the Front / Nervous Reaction / Physical Curiosities," *Daily Telegraph*, 22 December 1914.

24. "Letters from the Front," *Times*, 19 November 1914; Ferguson, *Pity of War*, 354.

25. "Letters from the Front," *Times*, 19 November 1914; "Soldiers' Stories," *Manchester Guardian*, 5 September 1914.

26. Private Rogan, "Letters from the Trenches / A German Request for Assistance," *Daily Mail*, 31 December 1914; "Letters from the Trenches / A German Who Was 'Fed Up,'" *Daily Mail*, 31 December 1914.

27. "Letters from the Front / The Heavy Losses at Ypres / Two Regiments Billeted in Two Houses / The Other Side of the Haystack," *Manchester Guardian*, 10 December 1914; "Editorial—the New Year," *Daily Mail*, 1 January 1915.

28. Editorial, *Manchester Guardian*, 24 December 1914.

29. Richard Attenborough, director, *Oh! What a Lovely War* (Accord Productions, 1969).

3. "A Great Day with Our Enemies"

1. Jim Murphy, *Truce: The Day the Soldiers Stopped Fighting* (New York: Scholastic Press, 2009), jacket copy, 10. Although Murphy asserts that "years of such government propaganda on each side conditioned European people

to distrust and hate their enemies, many of whom longed for war," the main thrust of his argument is that "the rush to war had been driven by the egos and ambitions of their national leaders, fueled by misguided popular support"; Murphy, *Truce*, 1, 6, 11.

2. Ibid., 46, 50–51, 69, 103.

3. Vicky Smith, review of *Truce: The Day the Soldiers Stopped Fighting*, by Jim Murphy, *Kirkus Reviews:* 1 October 2009, www.kirkusreviews.com/book-reviews/jim-murphy/truce/; Roger Sutton, "Five Questions for Jim Murphy," *Notes from the Horn Book: News about Good Books for Children and Teens* 2, no. 11 (November 2009), http://archive.hbook.com/newsletter/archive/2009/notes_nov09.html.

4. Brown and Seaton, *Christmas Truce*, xxii–xxiii.

5. Entry for 11 December 1914, battalion diary, 2nd Essex, WO 95/1505, National Archives (hereafter cited as NA); entry for 19 December 1914, battalion diary, 2nd Queen's Royal West Surreys, WO 95/1664, NA. The episode involving the 2nd Essex was also featured in its regimental history, which noted without censure that on 10 December 1914 "at 10 a.m. officers and men of 'A' and 'D' Companies met a party of the 181st Regiment, 19th Saxon Corps, midway between the trenches, and the latter stated, in the expressive language of the War Diary, that they were 'fed up.' Their trenches appeared to be held in about the same strength as those of the Essex and were in a similar state." John W. Burrows, *The Essex Regiment, 2nd Battalion (56th) (Pompadours)* (Southend-on-Sea: John H. Burrows & Sons, 1927), 119. Although two officers and two stretcher bearers from the battalion were taken prisoner during the 2nd Queens Royal West Surrey's cease-fire, the soldiers of that battalion did not seem to have taken offense: at least, it didn't prevent their participation in the Christmas truce a week later.

6. J. Selby Grigg, 1/5th London Rifles, letter, 27 December 1914, Private Papers of J. Selby Grigg, Imperial War Museum Collection No. 3881; Robbins, *First World War*, 150.

7. "The Pope's Efforts for Peace / Failure of the Christmas Truce," *Times*, 26 December 1914; Holroyd to his parents, 31 December 1914. The truce that Pope Benedict called for (in the hope that it would give the combatant countries time and perspective to sort out their differences) received little official publicity. With the exception of carol singing on Christmas Eve (generally by the Germans), the religious significance of Christmas seems to have been mostly ignored by the British soldiers in the front lines. The leadership made sure that the soldiers in the trenches all had as good a Christmas dinner—with a plentiful supply of plum puddings—as could be expected under the circumstances, and gifts from home, as well as the tobacco products supplied by Princess Mary, were much appreciated, but few soldiers noted any sort of religious services marking the occasion. In short, Christmas was treated by the soldiers in the trenches as a sentimental rather than a religious holiday, and there was

more mention of prayers accompanying the burial of the dead in No Man's Land than there was in connection with any observation of the birth of Christ.

8. Brown and Seaton, *Christmas Truce*, xx, 56. The evidence for this assertion includes the war diaries and regimental histories of the battalions involved, as well as letters written home and diaries kept by individual truce participants. The claims made in Brown and Seaton's work are borne out by the author's research. The descriptions regarding specific truces apply to the armistices in the British and German lines—the ones that took place between the French or Belgians and Germans were noted to be less frequent and considerably less interactive, and they consisted mostly of cease-fires and singing in the separate trenches.

9. The accounts of football matches that do exist frequently report them as happening in other units than the writers'.

10. H. J. Chappell, 1/5th London Rifles, to his parents, 27 December 1914, Private Papers of H. J. Chappell, Imperial War Museum Collection No. 1674; Chater to his mother, 27 December 1914; J. Hancock, 1st Royal Fusiliers, to Amy Griffiths, 3 January 1915, Private Papers of J. Hancock, Imperial War Museum Collection No. 8146.

11. Richard Lintott, 1/5th Battalion London Regiment (London Rifle Brigade), diary entry for 25 December 1914, Private Papers of R. Lintott, Imperial War Museum Collection No. 3394; Spencer, letter, 28 December 1914 (Spencer's German was less than fluent: the correct phrase is *Glückliche Weihnachten*); Grigg, letter, 26 December 1914; Chater to his mother, 25 December 1914.

12. E. W. Squire, 1/13th London Kensingtons, to his parents, 4 January 1915, Private Papers of E. W. Squire, Imperial War Museum Collection No. 369; Ted Lack, regiment unknown, to his niece Bab, n.d., Collection of Documents relating to Croydon Branch of the Old Contemptibles, Imperial War Museum Collection No. 9646; John Wedderburn-Maxwell, 45th Brigade R.F.A., to his father, 26 December 1914, Private Papers of J. Wedderburn-Maxwell, Imperial War Museum Collection No. 9362; Armes to his wife, 24 [and 25] December 1914.

13. Holroyd to his parents, 31 December 1914; Sam Lane, 2nd Wiltshires, diary entry for 25 December 1914, Private Papers of S. Lane, Imperial War Museum Collection No. 11686; Percy Jones, diary entry for 27 December 1914; Grigg, letter, 26 December 1914.

14. Squire to his parents, 4 January 1915 letter; unknown soldier (1), 1/16 Queen's Westminster Rifles, entry for 25 December 1914, Manuscript diary of unidentified soldier, Imperial War Museum Collection No. 1552; Black to Seamons, 31 December 1914.

15. According to the worldfootball.net website, there was a friendly match between England and Germany on 21 March 1913, resulting in an English win of 3–0. Wedderburn-Maxwell to his father, 26 December 1914; W. H.

Diggle, HQ 8th Division, to Liz, 27 December 1914, Private Papers of N. Noble, Imperial War Museum Collection No. 854; Liddell to his mother, 25 December 1914; H. D. Bryan, 1st Scots Guards, diary entry, n.d., Private Papers of H. D. Bryan, Imperial War Museum Collection No. 13833.

16. Lintott, diary entry for 25 December 1914; Grigg, letter, 26 December 1914; Armes to his wife, 24 [and 25] December 1914. The correct German spelling is *Für Vaterland und Freiheit*.

17. D. Lloyd-Burch, Ambulance Corps, diary entry, n.d., Private Papers of D. Lloyd-Burch, Imperial War Museum Collection No. 1423; Cecil Lothian Nicholson, 2nd East Lancashires, diary entry for 25 December 1914, Private Papers of Cecil Lothian Nicholson, Imperial War Museum Collection No. 9975; Pelham-Burn to Mathers, n.d.

18. Jones, diary entry for 27 December 1914; unknown soldier (2), 2nd Borders, diary entry for 25 December 1914, Transcription of diary of unidentified soldier, Imperial War Museum Collection No. 8631.

19. Spencer, letter, 25 December 1914; Pelham-Burn to Mathers, n.d. In spite of the negative emotions aroused by the sight of so many dead bodies, the soldiers quoted here all wrote home about the burials and memorial services without hesitation. Their unwillingness to communicate in a few cases appears to have resulted mostly from a wish to avoid providing descriptions of the decomposed corpses, rather than from a desire to shield their correspondents from information about the truce, the burial parties, or the fact that there were so many British dead.

20. Grigg, letter, 26 December 1914; C. G. V. Wellesley, 2nd Lincolnshires, letter, 25 December 1914, Private Papers of C. G. V. Wellesley, Imperial War Museum Collection No. 15579; W. J. Chennell, 2nd Queen's Royal West Surreys, to his wife, Sally, 29 December 1914, Private Papers of W. J. Chennell, Imperial War Museum Collection No. 16627.

21. Diggle to Liz, 27 December 1914; Black to Seamons, 31 December 1914.

22. Bernard J. Brookes, 1/16th Queen's Westminster Rifles, diary entry for 24 December 1914, Private Papers of B. J. Brookes, Imperial War Museum Collection No. 10825; Armes to his wife, 24 [and 25] December 1914. In spite of the precautions taken, considerable intelligence was collected during the armistice by the participating battalions.

23. Liddell to his parents, 25 December 1914; Ernest G. Morley, 1/16th Queen's Westminster Rifles, to "Eg," 29 December 1914, Private Papers of E. G. Morley, Imperial War Museum Collection No. 2450; unknown soldier (2), diary entry for 25 December 1914 (apparently this particular British soldier had faith that, whatever lies the German press might be reporting, the British newspapers could still be relied on); M. Leslie Walkinton, 1/16th Queen's Westminster Rifles, to his family, 26 December 1914, Private Papers of M. L. Walkinton, Imperial War Museum Collection No. 12061.

24. Ralph Blewitt, 39th Brigade R.F.A., to Miss Henderson, 1 January 1915, Private Papers of R. Blewitt, Imperial War Museum Collection No. 8469.

25. Blewitt to Miss Henderson, 1 January 1915; Black to Seamons, 31 December 1914; Chater to his mother, 25 December 1914; Grigg, letter, 26 December 1914. On the issue of homesickness generally, on 22 December 1914, for example, Sam Lane recorded in his diary that his battalion was "on our three days rest and our billet is a barn, it is rotten, and I shall be glad to get back home." A few months later, Frank Black wrote home that he did "wish the silly old war would hurry up and finish. I feel I have done quite enough soldiering now to last a lifetime." It is not unusual to find these types of comments in soldiers' correspondence; in fact, it was practically unheard of for a soldier to say he was having a grand time and hoped the war would last forever. Most soldiers recognized the necessity of fighting, but of course they would rather have been safe at home with their families than stuck in a muddy and cold trench while being shot at by snipers. Lane, diary entry for 22 December 1914; Black to Dorothy, 7 April 1915.

26. J. S. Fenton, 2nd Field Company Royal Engineers, diary entry for 27 December 1914, Private Papers of J. S. Fenton, Imperial War Museum Collection No. 12033; John Ray, 1st Duke of Cornwall's Light Infantry, diary entry for 25 December 1914, Private Papers of J. Ray, Imperial War Museum Collection No. 4652; Harold Atkins, 1/5th London Rifle Brigade, to his father, 27 December 1914, Private Papers of Harold Atkins, Imperial War Museum Collection No. 16505.

27. Brown and Seaton, *Christmas Truce*, 93–94; Lloyd-Burch, diary entry, n.d.; Holroyd, to his parents, 23 [and 24] and 31 December 1914; Cox, letter, 27 December 1914. Although the instances were rare, there were some reports of Prussian soldiers participating in the holiday armistice, as evidenced by an undated diary entry of H. D. Bryan, who wrote that during his truce, a boxing contest was arranged between the German and British soldiers, but he noted that, although it promised to be great fun to watch, "I took no part not wishing to be knocked about by a big Prussian Guard. The best match was between one of our men measured 6'5½ ins and a huge Prussian Guard of about the same height. These two hammered each other and would not give in until stopped by us owing to their faces being smashed up so badly." This episode had a curious epilogue; as Bryan further observed: "Then Our men suggested that each should be given a rifle and only 1 Bullet, stand or lay at 1 hundred yards from each other and on the word being given fire. But this we would not allow seeing that we had called a truce for this day."

28. Brookes, diary entry for 25 December 1914; Morley to "Eg," 29 December 1914; Pelham-Burn to Mathers, n.d.; Wedderburn-Maxwell to his father, 26 December 1914; Jones, diary entry for 27 December 1914; Kenneth M. Gaunt, 1/16th Queen's Westminster Rifles, to Auckland, 25

December 1914, Private Papers of K. M. Gaunt, Imperial War Museum Collection No. 7490; Grigg, letter, 27 December 1914.

29. Spencer, letter, 25 December 1914; Mascall to his fiancée, 29 December 1914. The argument made by Brown and Seaton that ongoing diminished activity in certain areas of the line amounted to a de facto continuation of the truce is not borne out by the letters and diaries of the men involved, who cheerfully discussed at what point the shooting would resume. Brown and Seaton contend that "in certain sectors the mood inspired by the events of Christmas lingered on with incredible stubbornness," citing Ploegsteert Wood and an area south of Armentières as two places that remained quiet long after Christmas, possibly into February and March; Brown and Seaton, *Christmas Truce*, 157. It is much more likely, however, that, with the shortage of ammunition that plagued the Allied armies through mid-1915, and other parts of the line experiencing more volatility during this time, these were just not particularly busy areas. No soldier's letters or diaries examined reported any truce extending past the end of the year (even though in some cases, as war diaries demonstrate, cease-fires without fraternization did last until the first weeks in January), and most were over by 27 or 28 December 1914.

30. Lloyd-Burch, diary entry, n.d.; Blewitt to Miss Henderson, 1 January 1915; Pelham-Burn to Mathers, n.d.; Brookes, diary entry for 26 December 1914; Liddell to his mother, 25 December 1914; Wellesley to his wife, 25 December 1914; Chennell to his wife, Sally, 20 March 1915; Blewitt to Miss Henderson, 1 January 1915. Blewitt's remark, incidentally, represents one of the few observations that the fighting began again by orders of an officer. Most truces ended in a rather more desultory fashion; shooting by both sides picked up slowly as battalions rotated in and out of the trenches in the week after Christmas.

31. Frederick A. Brown, 2nd Monmouthshires, memoir, Private Papers of F. A. Brown, Imperial War Museum Collection No. 4401.

32. Brown and Seaton, *Christmas Truce*, 11.

4. "No War Today"

1. *Days That Shook the World: The Christmas Truce* (BBC documentary, 2004). Each day's 14,500 casualties total 23,490,000 for the entire war. The casualty figures more generally accepted for the war are 9–10 million military deaths and 6–7 million civilian deaths—still horrific, but not the more than 20 million asserted in this documentary. Of course, the civilian deaths would include women and children as well as men, whereas the documentary implies that the casualty numbers cited are military deaths only.

2. In this documentary, the assertion that soldiers in the line defied orders from junior officers to cease fraternization is based on the memoirs of Francis Philip Woodruff (alias Frank Richards), written many years after the event. See

chap. 7 for a discussion of Woodruff's work. Of course, no mention is made in the documentary of the leaders of III and IV Corps, whose battalions were much more heavily involved in the truces on 25 December 1914.

3. It is true that, after the British forces in France were reorganized at the end of December 1914, Smith-Dorrien was put in charge of the new Second Army, which comprised the former II and III Corps, but at the time of the truce he commanded only one of five British corps in France, and therefore the order he issued on 26 December 1914 was addressed to the II Corps only—not the entire army, as the documentary implies.

4. Arthur Bates, 1/5th London Regiment (London Rifle Brigade), to his sister Dorothy, 24 December 1914, Imperial War Museum Collection No. 10083. While Black, as already noted, did confess to being slightly apprehensive about being surrounded by the Germans by a ratio of four to one over British troops, he still had no compunctions about shaking hands and exchanging souvenirs with the enemy; Black to Seamons, 31 December 1915.

5. Fisher-Rowe to his wife, 25 December 1914; Chater to his mother, 25 December 1914; Liddell to his mother, 25 December 1914.

6. Tony Ashworth, *Trench Warfare, 1914–1918: The Live and Let Live System* (London: Pan Books, 1980), 10; General Staff, War Office, *Field Service Pocket Book* (London: His Majesty's Stationery Office, 1914), 210–211.

7. Of the fifty-four battalions involved, the war diaries for eighteen do not mention the truce at all—although most of these note that the front line was very quiet around Christmas—and one diary is missing from the National Archives, that of the 1st East Surreys.

8. Diary entries for 25 and 26 December 1914, 1/13th London Kensingtons, WO 95/1730/3, NA; diary entries for 25 and 26 December 1914, 2nd Royal Berkshires, WO 95/1729, NA; diary entries for 26 and 27 December 1914, 2nd Rifle Brigade, WO 95/1731, NA.

9. Diary entries for 25 through 31 December 1914, 20th Brigade, WO 95/1650, NA.

10. Diary entries for 24 through 30 December 1914, 10th Brigade, WO 95/1477, NA. This must have been an oral report, as the 2nd Royal Dublin Fusiliers' diary noted only that Christmas Day was "very quiet" and there was "no shelling or sniping heard"; diary entry for 25 December 1914, 2nd Royal Dublin Fusiliers, WO 95/1481/4, NA.

11. General Sir Aylmer Haldane, *A Soldier's Saga: The Autobiography of General Sir Aylmer Haldane* (Edinburgh: William Blackwood & Sons, 1948), 304–305, 287.

12. Richebourg, where the 1/39th and 2/39th Garhwal Rifles and the 2/3rd Gurkhas became so friendly with the Germans that, as one participant described it in a letter home, you "would never believe that we had been fighting for weeks," was only two miles north of Festubert, where the 4th Royal Welch Fusiliers, 1st Gloucestershires, and 4th Seaforth Highlanders had no

such contact with the enemy. Berryman, letter, 26 December 1914. Similarly, the 1st Bedfordshires, in trenches along the Wulverghem-Messines Road, fraternized with the Germans, whereas the 3rd Worcestershires, less than two miles north in Kemmel, did not. The brigadier general of the 12th Brigade (III Corps), to whom the 2nd Essex, which had reported an earlier meeting with the Germans, belonged, had also issued an Operation Order dated 13 December that forbade "further parlaying with the enemy in any form," adding that the "Germans will be informed of this as soon as possible but no further communication of any sort will be made to them." This was no doubt in response to a report of the 11 December meeting earlier in the 2nd Essex's diaries (see chap. 3). No other brigade-level orders prohibiting fraternization were found in the war diaries. 12th Brigade, WO 95/1501, NA. The 2nd Essex did, in fact, participate in the Christmas truce, but no indication that they did so can be found in their battalion diary or regimental history. No copy of Haldane's order was located among the 3rd Division diaries.

13. Smith-Dorrien, 14th Brigade, order, 4 December 1914, WO 95/1560, NA. Smith-Dorrien's primary aim at this point in the war was to seize the initiative in the conflict, which "has hitherto generally been with the enemy"; this order was clearly part of that effort.

14. In fact, the 14th Brigade papers did include a report from a sergeant in the 1st Devonshires who, on Christmas, "was able to go forward" and as a result "had some talk with an English speaking officer," a conversation that clearly could not have occurred had the battalion not been fraternizing with the enemy; 14th Brigade, report, n.d., and confidential memorandum, 26 December 1914, WO 95/1560, NA.

15. 14th Brigade, confidential memorandum, 26 December 1914; 5th Division, directive, 28 December 1914, WO 95/1510, NA.

16. 5th Division, reports, 26 and 28 December 1914, WO 95/1510, NA. The first Gleichen report was just a generally informative summary about the broad parameters of the truce, whereas the one written on 28 December appears to have been in direct response to Smith-Dorrien's order. Gleichen also included a note in his 26 December report from the commander of the 6th Cheshires about the numbers of Germans in the trenches opposite them, as well as a description of their appearance, their units, and their insignia.

17. 5th Division, 1st Norfolks and 1st and 6th Cheshires, reports, 28 December 1914, WO 95/1510, NA.

18. 5th Division, directive, 30 December 1914, WO 95/1510, NA.

19. In the same 26 December 1914 order, for example, under the heading "Comfort in the trenches," Smith-Dorrien spent as much time bemoaning the lack of boards for soldiers to stand on to keep them clear of the mud as he did blaming officers for the troops' involvement in the truce—hardly the attitude of someone who was determined to punish the men under his command for

participation in "a friendly gathering" in No Man's Land; 14th Brigade, confidential memorandum, 26 December 1914, WO 95/1560, NA.

20. Diary entry for 25 December 1914, 4th Division, WO 95/1440, NA; diary entries for 25 December 1914 through 1 January 1915, 6th Division, WO 95/1581, NA. After the reorganization of 26 December 1914, III Corps was part of the Second Army, under Smith-Dorrien.

21. Various reports from 6th Division diaries, WO 95/1581, NA.

22. Diary entries for 25 and 26 December 1914, 7th Division, WO 95/1627, 1634, NA.

23. Diary entries for 26 December 1914 through 4 January 1915, 7th Division, WO 95/1627, 1634, NA.

24. Diary entries for 25 and 26 December 1914, 8th Division, WO 95/1671, NA. The 8th Division diary also stated that the report of an interview with a German soldier who approached their lines was "forwarded to 4th Corps."

25. Diary entry for 25 December 1914, 2/39th Garhwal Rifles, WO 95/3945/3, NA; diary entry for 25 December 1914, Garhwal Brigade, WO 95/3930, NA; diary entry for 25 December 1914, Meerut Division, WO 95/3943, NA. An officer in the 1/39th Garhwal Rifles, Kenneth Henderson, wrote in the 1920s that the leaves of some officers in his regiment were stopped as punishment for allowing their men to fraternize. An examination of other records, including the war diaries and letters written by other members of the Meerut Brigade, shows that Henderson was mistaken, and that leaves proceeded after Christmas 1914 as previously arranged. Edward Berryman, for example, wrote to his sister Jane on 1 January 1915 that "the whole corps is now resting, & we all—as many as can—getting LEAVE." Although Brown and Seaton cite Henderson's assertions that leaves were stopped for Garhwali officers as proof that soldiers who participated in the 1914 truce were punished for their actions, this contention is not borne out by the evidence. Kenneth Henderson, 1/39th Garhwal Rifles, memoir, Private Papers of K. Henderson, Imperial War Museum Collection No. 10942; Brown and Seaton, *Christmas Truce*, 126–127; Nesham, *Socks, Cigarettes, and Shipwrecks*, 53.

26. The diary for the 2nd Gordon Highlanders did record that, on 4 through 7 January, a "sort of informal truce with the enemy during Xmas and the New Year having taken place strictest orders were issued that it must cease. All Germans above ground to be shot at," but this appears to have been the exception rather than the rule. Diary entries, 4 through 7 January 1915, 2nd Gordon Highlanders, WO 95/1656/2, NA. One explanation for this somewhat tardy order would be that the Highlanders were part of the 7th Division, which was rather more relaxed about the Christmas cease-fire.

27. According to multiple military histories, including that of the East Lancs, once Smith-Dorrien became head of the Second Army, in January 1915,

he "issued an order forbidding all informal understandings with the enemy, under penalty of trial by court-martial on any officer or non-commissioned officer who allowed such understandings." By this time, of course, just about every truce was over, and no one was ever prosecuted under this order for participation in any 1914 truces. C. Lothian Nicholson and H. T. MacMullen, *History of the East Lancashire Regiment in the Great War, 1914–1918* (Liverpool: Littlebury Bros., 1936), 34n.

28. Diary entry for 26 December 1914, 1st Royal Fusiliers, WO 95 1613/2, NA.

29. Brigadier General Sir James E. Edmonds and Captain G. C. Wynne, *History of the Great War, Based on Official Documents, by Direction of the Historical Section of the Committee of Imperial Defence, Military Operations: France and Belgium, 1915: Winter 1914–15: Battle of Neuve Chapelle: Battle of Ypres* (London: Macmillan, 1927), 1, 2–3, 28. The criticism of Sir John French is tactfully expressed: Edmonds noted that French "might have been wiser to wait until the New Armies were trained, and guns and munitions provided"; Edmonds and Wynne, *History of the Great War,* 2–3.

30. Ibid., 28.

31. No doubt the reason for the more frequent mention of joint burials was that the need to remove bodies from No Man's Land also provided useful official cover for officers who had allowed their battalions to participate in the truce.

32. Not every regiment produced an official history after the war: some regiments were disbanded or consolidated after the conflict ended and as a result were less likely to commission a history of the unit, particularly those whose losses had been so high that few veterans remained to take an interest in any publication offered.

33. Sir Frederick Maurice, *The History of the London Rifle Brigade, 1859–1919* (London: Constable, 1921), 74, 75, 76.

34. Colonel H. C. Wylly, *Crown and Company: The Historical Records of the 2nd Batt. Royal Dublin Fusiliers, Formerly the 1st Bombay Regiment,* vol. 2, *1911–1922* (Aldershot, U.K.: Gale & Polden, 1923), 36; Wylly, *The Border Regiment in the Great War* (Aldershot, U.K.: Gale & Polden, 1924), 14–15, 30.

35. F. Loraine Petre, *The History of the Norfolk Regiment, 1685–1918* (Norwich, U.K.: Jarrold & Sons, 1924), 13. In fact, the truce did spread throughout the British trenches, which was already known by those most likely to read the history, but at least Petre acknowledged that participation in the truce went unpunished, in spite of the 1st Norfolks' position in Smith-Dorrien's II Corps.

36. Reginald Berkeley, *The History of the Rifle Brigade in the War of 1914–1918,* vol. 1, *August 1914–December 1916* (London: Rifle Brigade Club, 1927), 46–47. The diary of neither the 1st nor 2nd Rifles recorded any information

about a German juggler, and the 3rd Rifles' diary contains no mention of the truce at all, so Berkeley must have gotten this information from a veteran who was present at the truce.

37. Rudyard Kipling, in fact, obviously regretted that the nonparticipation of the Irish Guards in the truce had cost him a good story: in *The Irish Guards in the Great War* he noted, "The Christmas truce of 1914 reached the battalion in severely modified form." Even Kipling's ability to spin a great tale faltered before the plight of the 1st Irish Guards, stuck in a "network of trenches, already many times fought over, with communications that led directly into the enemy's lines a couple of hundred yards away," who "spent Christmas Day, under occasional bombardment of heavy artillery, in exploring and establishing themselves as well as they might among these wet and dreary works." Although he reported that "Boxing Day was quiet, too, and only four men were wounded as they dug in the hard ground to improve their communications with the 2nd Coldstream on their left," even the great storyteller Kipling was unable to make any hay from these very flimsy bits of straw. Rudyard Kipling, *The Irish Guards in the Great War, Edited and Compiled from Their Diaries and Papers*, 2 vols. (London: Macmillan, 1923), 1:53.

5. "One Day of Peace at the Front"

1. Denis Winter, *Death's Men: Soldiers of the Great War* (London: Allan Lane, 1978), 15, 24, 25, 220. The weekly journal's full title was *The Sphere: An Illustrated Newspaper for the Home*.

2. Winter, *Death's Men*, 16, 212–213.

3. These five papers are representative of the British press as a whole, as they all had national exposure, were all widely read (the *Daily Mail* was the paper with the largest circulation at the time), and represented varying viewpoints, from the conservative and mainstream through the more liberal.

4. "Carols Sung by both Sides," *Times*, 26 December 1914. The truce was never officially acknowledged by the government in its briefings about the war, and with no correspondents at the front, it would have taken time for the letters about the truce written by the participants to reach England.

5. Ibid.; "Christmas Trees in German Trenches / Troops Feast While Belgians Fast," *Daily Mail*, 26 December 1914.

6. "Jangle of Bells and Guns," *Daily Mail*, 28 December 1914. It should be noted that the troops fighting at Nieuport (now Nieuwpoort, Belgium) were French, not British. "Guns and Airships / Allies' Fine Work / Increasing Ascendency," *Daily Telegraph*, 26 December 1914. In the second reference "we" must refer collectively to Allied troops, as there were no B.E.F. forces in the vicinity of Roye in December 1914.

7. "Christmastide in the Trenches / Greeting the Enemy / Unaccepted Challenges," *Daily Telegraph*, 31 December 1914.

8. "Christmastide in the Trenches / All Arms 'Downed,'" *Daily Telegraph*, 31 December 1914; "Christmastide in the Trenches / Friendly Arrangements / Germans from London," *Daily Telegraph*, 31 December 1914.

9. "A Christmas Truce at the Front / Enemies at Football / German Gets a Friendly Haircut," *Manchester Guardian*, 31 December 1914; "Christmas at the Front / An Interrupted Truce," *Morning Post*, 31 December 1914.

10. "Letters from the Front," *Times*, 1 January 1915.

11. Ibid.

12. Ibid.

13. "The New Year," *Daily Mail*, 1 January 1915.

14. "One Day of Peace at the Front," *Daily Mail*, 1 January 1915. Presumably, the *Daily Mail* was not going to allow that any more than a single day of peace could have been possible. On the basis of internal evidence, a member of the Scots Guard probably wrote this account, as it echoes the events presented in the famous Hulse letter discussed in chap. 6.

15. Ibid.

16. "Christmas Truce / Mingling with the Enemy," *Daily Telegraph*, 1 January 1915.

17. "Exchanging Cigars," *Daily Telegraph*, 1 January 1915.

18. "The Unofficial Christmas Truce / British and Germans Exchange Presents," *Manchester Guardian*, 1 January 1915.

19. "Christmas Truce in the Trenches / Colonel's Challenge / A New Year's Day Match" and "Sorry to Fight Us," *Daily Telegraph*, 2 January 1915.

20. "German Football Enthusiast," and "The Day of Intercession," *Morning Post*, 2 January 1915.

21. "Letters from the Front / More Tales of the Truce / Christmas Goodwill / Friendly Meetings with the Enemy," *Times*, 2 January 1915.

22. Ibid.

23. "More Tales of the Truce / Grave Suspicions," *Times*, 2 January 1915.

24. Ibid.

25. "More Tales of the Truce / A Belgian Point of View," *Times*, 2 January 1915.

26. "Christmas Day in the Trenches / Lancashires' Varied Experiences," *Manchester Guardian*, 6 January 1915.

27. "Christmas Day in the Trenches / A British Officer's Letter, Friend and Foe and the Dead," *Manchester Guardian*, 6 January 1915.

28. "A Busy Christmas," *Daily Mail*, 5 January 1915. Of the nearly seventy letters about the truce featured in the five main papers reviewed, over fifty were published between 31 December 1914 and 7 January 1915.

29. "A Sequel to the Truce / French and Germans Refuse to Fight Afterwards," *Manchester Guardian*, 6 January 1915; "Do the Germans Really 'Hate'? What Soldiers Say," *Manchester Guardian*, 14 January 1915. The first report may well be the origin of the persistent myth that soldiers who

participated in the truce were punished for their involvement by being moved to a different part of the line. As for the hint about the German distaste for further fighting, few British readers would be completely immune to the not-very-subliminal suggestion that the French were not overly enthusiastic warriors, either.

30. "The Christmas Truce/Stringent German Army Order," *Times,* 7 January 1915; "Truce in the Trenches/Fraternization of Germans with Allies Forbidden," *Daily Mail,* 9 January 1915.

31. "The Light of Peace in the Trenches on Christmas Eve," *Illustrated London News,* 9 January 1915.

32. "The Great War" and "Saxons and Anglo-Saxons Fraternizing on the Field of Battle," *Illustrated London News,* 9 January 1915.

33. Editorial, *Daily Telegraph,* 7 January 1915. As for what had appeared in the press generally through 7 January 1915, the only noncorrespondence accounts of British participation in the truce—namely, the brief synopses in the *Illustrated London News*—can hardly be characterized as "reporting."

34. Ibid.

35. Editorial, *Manchester Guardian,* 9 January 1915.

36. Ibid. It appears, however, that the author of this editorial never asked himself what participation in the truce said about the souls of the German soldiers, and whether they too had been granted a vision of an ideal during the event.

37. It is unclear whether in fact there was any British official reaction to the cease-fire, outside the internal military notice of the event.

6. "That Unique and Weird Christmas"

1. George Herbert Perris, *The Campaign of 1914 in France and Belgium* (London: Hodder and Stoughton, 1915), xx, xxiii, 391–392. Perris's attempts at evenhandedness were not always successful, as he could not resist crediting the war to standard German "frightfulness."

2. Ibid., 391–392.

3. Ferro et al., *Meetings in No Man's Land,* 76; "One Day of Peace at the Front," *Daily Mail,* 1 January 1915. The idea that the truce was forgotten almost immediately is a corollary to Brown's insistence that many believe that the 1914 holiday armistice itself was a myth, a viewpoint he has vigorously contradicted on many occasions, even though the number of those who appear to doubt the cease-fire's existence has always been few.

4. *Days That Shook the World.* The reason these two myths may coexist peacefully is that people tend to believe that Colquhoun was court-martialed for participation in the 1914 truce. M. Leslie Walkinton, in a 1985 interview, stated, "I think I have read since that, you see, some people went on with it a bit after Christmas Day, and I think that one Scottish officer was

court-martialed, but I don't think he was punished or anything, but I don't really know." M. Leslie Walkinton, 1/16th Queen's Westminster Rifles, interview, 1985, Imperial War Museum Collection No. 9132.

5. Diary entries for 2 through 5 January 1915, 2nd Lancashire Fusiliers, WO 95/1507, NA; diary entry for 3 January 1915, 2nd Yorkshires, WO 95/1659, NA; diary entries for January 1915, 1st Rifle Brigade, WO 95/1496, NA.

6. Diary entries for 1 through 11 January 1915, 1st Somerset Light Infantry, WO 95/1499, NA.

7. Atkins to his father, 27 December 1914; Dillon to his sister Kathleen, 17 January 1915. As no historian has ever been able to verify a case of troops being moved as a result of the cease-fire, it is most likely that the Saxon soldiers stationed opposite Dillon's battalion were just rotated out of the line, and fresh troops sent up in their place.

8. W. A. F. Foxx-Pitt, 2nd Cheshires, to his mother, 29 December 1914, Private Papers of W. A. F. Foxx-Pitt, Imperial War Museum Collection No. 18386; "Battlefield Stories," *Manchester Guardian*, 22 January 1915. Regarding Foxx-Pitt's continued cease-fire, it should be noted that as the 2nd Cheshires were in the 18th Brigade, 6th Division, they were part of the former III Corps, where attitudes toward the truce were more relaxed, and where longer cease-fires were tolerated as long as actual fraternization ceased after Christmas Day.

9. Lawson to his mother, 7 January 1915.

10. H. Ridsdale, 76th Field Company Royal Engineers, diary entry for 25 December 1915, Private Papers of H. Ridsdale, Imperial War Museum Collection No. 5186; W. Tate, 2nd Coldstream Guards, diary entry for 26 December 1915, Private Papers of W. Tate, Imperial War Museum Collection No. 4520.

11. Iain Colquhoun, 1st Scots Guards, diary entry for 25 December 1915, Private Papers of Iain Colquhoun, Imperial War Museum Collection No. 6373.

12. Iain Colquhoun, diary entries for 26 December 1915 through 5 January 1916.

13. Iain Colquhoun, diary entry for 17 January 1916. The granting of Colquhoun's request for leave to attend the birth of his child was certainly aided by the fact that his wife was the niece of Margot Asquith, the prime minister's wife. Brown and Seaton, *Christmas Truce,* 205. As Asquith wrote to his wife during the trial, "They took some more evidence yesterday, which turned out to be favourable to the other officer concerned, and I should not be surprised if they stop the Court Martial in his case, although I imagine they mean to proceed with it in the other"; Raymond Asquith, *Raymond Asquith: Life and Letters,* ed. John Jolliffe (1980; repr., London: Century Hutchinson, 1987), 233. Asquith described Colquhoun's court-martial in a letter to his

wife as "a pretty bloody and exhausting struggle," and he admitted that "the facts were sadly against us all the time." The facts were "against" Colquhoun, however, only to the extent that no one denied that fraternization took place, which led to the inevitable conclusion that Asquith may have been gilding the lily a bit in an attempt to portray his defense of Colquhoun as heroic; ibid., 235–236.

14. Iain Colquhoun, diary entry for 17 January 1915; Colquhoun, diary entry, n.d.; Brown and Seaton, *Christmas Truce*, 205–206; Asquith, *Raymond Asquith*, 236.

15. Brown and Seaton, *Christmas Truce*, 204; Weintraub, *Silent Night*, 171–172; www.clancolquhoun.com/. The story about Iain Colquhoun's court-martial and royal pardon was available on the Colquhoun clan website in early 2014 but had been removed by the end of that year.

16. Iain Colquhoun, diary entry, n.d. According to Brown and Seaton, Barne "was eventually promoted major but was killed in 1917"—sadly and ironically by a British airplane accidentally dropping its bombs on the British lines. Brown and Seaton, *Christmas Truce*, 206. The Scots Guards' regimental history also reported that the 2nd battalion participated in a lengthy truce at Christmas 1915. "During the night of the 24th–25th December, a lot of talking was heard in the enemy lines, and Germans shouted in English to our men. At dawn two German snipers began shooting, and one of them killed C. S. M. Oliver with a bullet in the head. The sergeant-major was an excellent N.C.O. and very popular with the men. Nevertheless, within ten minutes both German and British soldiers were clambering out of trenches and fraternizing in No Man's Land. News of this only reached the Battalion Headquarters by a message from Brigade, who had heard of it from Corps Headquarters. The C.O. himself at once went off to the trenches to put a stop to the fraternization, but by the time he got there it was all over, and the men were back in trenches settled down for the day's routine." F. Loraine Petre, Wilfred Ewart, and Major General Sir Cecil Lowther, *The Scots Guards in the Great War, 1914–1918* (London: John Murray, 1925), 130–131. The 2nd Scots Guards' truce was also described at length in a novel about the war by Wilfred Ewart, an officer in the regiment; Wilfred Ewart, *Way of Revelation: A Novel of Five Years* (New York: D. Appleton, 1922). The 1st Scots Guards' truce was not mentioned in the regimental history, but since it had ended in a court-martial for two of its officers, this is hardly surprising.

17. *The Times History of the War*, vol. 4 (London: The Times, 1915), pt. 45, 29 June, 225. Regarding references to the 1914 truce in later war diaries, the 1/16th Queen's Westminster Rifles, which had enthusiastically celebrated the 1914 cease-fire, recorded that 25 December 1915 "passed quietly, but there was no sort of repetition of last years truce." In fact, the Germans "shouted across to our men this morning but receiving no encouragement the conversation ceased," after which the enemy "shelled the school behind S.6.

about 12 noon and at 1 pm put some twenty whizz-bangs into the Potuize defences"; diary entry for 25 December 1915, 1/16th Queen's Westminster Rifles, WO 95/1616, NA. The 2nd Seaforth Highlanders, who relieved the Royal Irish Rifles in the trenches in the evening of 25 December, also noted in their diary that there were "no Xmas advances in this part of the line"; diary entry for 25 December 1915, 2nd Seaforth Highlanders, WO 95/1483, NA. By *advances*, they meant overtures from the enemy.

18. John Buchan, *Nelson's History of the War*, vol. 5, *The War of Attrition in the West, the Campaign in the Near East, and the Fighting at Sea Down to the Blockade of Britain* (London: Thomas Nelson and Sons, 1915), 28–29, 38–39.

19. *Times History of the War*, 4:221.

20. Ibid., 221–224. Some of the details given in the descriptions of the armistice were based on soldiers' letters that were published in the *Times* in January 1915 about the truce; see chap. 5 for more information about these letters. The war diaries discussed in chap. 4 confirm that it was most probably the 7th Division order not to shoot unless absolutely necessary that was the source for the *Times's* information.

21. Ibid., 225–227. Planting itself firmly on the moral high ground, the *Times* noted with disdain that, as the German government and newspapers "had taken particular care never to expose themselves to any personal danger, the value of their views as to the desirability of a little relaxation from the nerve-trying stress of a continued residence in the trenches, may be disregarded, perhaps with feelings not unmingled with a little contempt." The *Times* writers, themselves most likely strangers to the battlefields, probably ought to have avoided this particular bit of censure, but to be fair, the paper never chastised British soldiers for their participation in the truce, so perhaps its writers may be forgiven their preaching in this case.

22. Ibid., 227–228.

23. Cyril Falls, *War Books: A Critical Guide* (London: Peter Davies, 1930), 178–179; Bruce Bairnsfather, *Bullets and Billets* (London: Grant Richards, 1916), available at Project Gutenberg, www.gutenberg.org/files/11232/11232-h/11232-h.htm. All quotes attributed to Bairnsfather are from this Project Gutenberg document, which is unpaginated.

24. Arthur Conan Doyle, *The British Campaign in France and Flanders*, vol. 1, *1914* (1916; repr., Newcastle, U.K.: Cambridge Scholars Publishing, 2009), 8, 191–192.

25. Sir Edward Hamilton Westrow Hulse, *Letters Written from the English Front in France between September 1914 and March 1915* (1916; repr., Miami: HardPress Classics, n.d.), 49, 79. Hulse reported that in one raid "two German officers were found dead thirty or forty yards in front of their trenches, and all the men themselves dead *in* the trenches, showing that they will not follow their officers"; Hulse, *Letters*, 17.

26. Ibid., 58. Upon finding the Germans "a good, strong, and pretty healthy lot," Hulse speculated that "probably only the best of them had been allowed to leave their trenches"; ibid., 59.

27. Ibid., 60–62. It should be noted that Captain Paynter's career did not suffer for his part in encouraging the truce: he was made a major by August 1915 (*Supplement to the London Gazette*, 25 August 1915, 8505), and the Scots Guards' regimental history states that he finished the war with the rank of colonel.

28. Hulse, *Letters*, 62–64, 74. As will be seen in subsequent chapters, Hulse's main letter about the truce has been used repeatedly in later years (very selectively) to underline the conventional view of the armistice, whereas his second letter, describing the aftermath of the truce, has been largely ignored. In 1916, however, the letters merely provided another view of the well-known truce, one that emphasized the nonrebellious nature of the event.

29. *Days That Shook the World;* Hulse, *Letters*, introduction.

30. Major General Lord Edward Gleichen, *The Doings of the Fifteenth Infantry Brigade: August 1914 to March 1915* (Edinburgh: William Blackwood & Sons, 1917), available at http://archive.org/stream/thedoingsofthefi22074gut/pg22074.txt, unpaginated. See chap. 4 for Gleichen's two reports on the 1914 Christmas truce, the second in response to Smith-Dorrien's request for detailed accounts of the armistice from the officers involved.

31. Stephen Stapleton, "The Relations between the Trenches," *Contemporary Review* 111 (January–July 1917): 636, 638.

32. Diary entry for 25 December 1917, 2nd Seaforth Highlanders; Sir John French, *1914* (Boston: Houghton Mifflin, 1919), 345.

33. French, *1914*, 345.

34. Ibid., 347; Murphy, *Truce*, 82.

35. French, *1914*, 350; Brian Bond, ed., *The First World War and British Military History* (Oxford: Clarendon Press, 1991), 131.

7. "The Curious Christmas Truce"

1. Commons Sitting of Monday, 31 March 1930, 1929/30, House of Commons Hansard, George V year 20, 920–981, 5th ser., 237:923, 931, 936, 937–938. The Parliamentary debate was over whether the words "this House regrets that the policy of the Government with regard to conscientious objectors is contrary to the spirit of the policy adopted hitherto by successive Governments since the War with regard to ex-service men and constitutes a reversal of such policy" should be inserted into the rule overturning the restrictions on conscientious objectors. The question failed. Notably, conscientious objectors who undertook alternative service during the war were already exempted from rules restricting their promotions and pensions (http://hansard.millbanksystems.com/commons/1930/mar/31/

government-departments-conscientious). In regard to the general attitude toward the war outside Parliament, Benson reckoned that support for his past positions in his constituency was such "that being a conscientious objector gave me 5,000 extra votes." When another M.P. noted sarcastically that this was "a compliment to your constituency!" Benson replied succinctly, "It is."

2. Ibid., 943, 950.

3. Ibid., 950. Wood stated this his battalion's truce had lasted two weeks, which is consistent with the 2nd Gordon Highlander diaries, which do not report an order to resume firing until 4–7 January. The Gordon Highlanders were part of the 7th Division, which was quite relaxed about continuing cease-fires by its brigades and battalions.

4. Ibid., 929.

5. Edmonds, *A Subaltern's War*, 192–193, 205. Carrington published his memoir under the pseudonym Charles Edmonds.

6. Ludovic Kennedy, introduction to Alan Lloyd, *The War in the Trenches* (London: Hart-Davis, MacGibbon, 1976), 7.

7. Gibbs, *Realities of War*, 160.

8. Ibid., 64, 173, 455.

9. C. E. Montague, *Disenchantment* (1922; repr., London: MacGibbon & Kee, 1968), 16.

10. Ibid., 10, 16, 106–107.

11. Ibid., 106–107.

12. Strachan, *The First World War*, 339; Arthur Ponsonby, *Falsehood in War-Time: Containing an Assortment of Lies Circulated throughout the Nations during the Great War* (New York: E. P. Dutton, 1928), 59; Bond, *Unquiet Western Front*, 38. Although Brian Bond has effectively argued that as Sassoon was a noted warrior, Graves and Owen were neither conscientious objectors nor pacifists, and Sherriff had intended *Journey's End* to memorialize soldiers he knew, "the war literature of the 1920s was full of ambiguities and could not, taken as a whole, be held to support the 'anti-war' myth," his view is a minority one. Bond, *Unquiet Western Front*, 35.

13. Graves, *Good-bye to All That*, 137.

14. H. W. Wilson, *The War Guilt* (London: Sampson Low, Marston & Co., 1928), 345.

15. P. A. Thompson, *Lions Led by Donkeys: Showing How Victory in the Great War Was Achieved by Those Who Made the Fewest Mistakes* (London: T. Werner Laurie, 1927), 3, 23. The titles of the books by Thompson and Clark are taken from a quote attributed to the German general Erich Ludendorff on the bravery of British soldiers, who were "lions led by donkeys," the donkeys being the incompetent British generals. The quote is widely believed to be apocryphal.

16. Ibid., 127, 128, 139–140.

17. G. V. Carey and H. S. Scott, *An Outline History of the Great War*

(1928; repr., Cambridge: Cambridge University Press, 2011), 24, 33–34, 41. While conceding the tremendous losses that the British suffered at the First Battle of Ypres in November 1914, the authors still managed to find inspiration in the fact that sufficient British soldiers survived "to leaven the New Armies and to make them invincible, a result due in no small part to the memory of the brilliant achievements of these splendid soldiers"; Carey and Scott, *Outline History of the Great War,* 33–34.

18. Liddell Hart, *The Real War,* 11, 29, 81.

19. Graham Seton Hutchinson, *Warrior* (London: Hutchinson, 1932), 10, 12.

20. Ibid., 50, 52, 61, 62. As Hutchinson had been on leave over Christmas, he missed the main truce, but the Argyll and Sutherland Highlanders enjoyed noticeably quiet conditions in the line in early January 1915.

21. Ibid., 62–63. As the Argyll and Sutherland Highlanders were part of III Corps, which was incorporated into the Second Army under Smith-Dorrien after Christmas 1914, the order referred to is probably the one Smith-Dorrien issued early in January 1915—when just about all the truces and subsequent cease-fires had already come to an end of their own accord.

22. Frank Richards, *Old Soldiers Never Die* (1933; repr., East Sussex, U.K.: Naval and Military Press, n.d.), 65. On the other hand, Richards (real name Francis Woodruff) may not have been as indifferent to the attitudes of his superiors as he professed, as his memoir, although issued fifteen years after the end of the war, was published under a pseudonym.

23. Ibid., 65, 66–67. In fact, the 2nd Royal Welch Fusiliers had been in the front line, which according to their official diary was very quiet the entire month, since 3 December 1914. Their relief, therefore, by the Durham Light Infantry late in the day on 26 December can hardly have been as much of a surprise as Richards pretends. War diary, 2nd Royal Welch Fusiliers, WO/95/1365, NA.

24. Captain J. C. Dunn, *The War the Infantry Knew: 1914–1919, A Chronicle of Service in France and Belgium with the Second Battalion His Majesty's Twenty-Third Foot, the Royal Welch Fusiliers* (1938, repr., London: Jane's, 1987).

25. Ibid., v, vii.

26. Ibid., 101–103.

27. Cruttwell, *History of the Great War,* 3, 6, 11.

28. Ibid., 107, 108–109. Some French troops did participate in truces, but not as many as in the British and German part of the line.

29. Brown, memoir. All quotes attributed to Brown come from this manuscript. Obviously, not all First World War veterans regretted their service in that war. According to Todman, "When the appeal for volunteers to join the nascent Home Guard, the Local Defense Volunteers, was put out by Anthony Eden in early summer 1940, Great War veterans were the first to respond. By the end of June, there were nearly one and a half million volunteers. Numbers

in individual platoons varied, but it has been estimated that approximately 30 per cent were veterans." Todman, *The Great War,* 189.

30. The sergeant's death is recorded in the Monmouths' regimental history, but not its war diaries. Captain G. A. Brett, *A History of the 2nd Battalion the Monmouthshire Regiment* (Pontypool: Hughes and Son, 1933), 36–37.

31. Carey and Scott, *Outline History of the Great War,* 261.

32. Graves, *Good-bye to All That,* 249. It should also be noted that Sherriff, Blunden, Owen, and Sassoon all failed to use the truce as a symbol of disillusionment with the war—or even to mention it at all in their works, although, as demonstrated, it was an event that was familiar not only to every soldier who served on the Western Front, but almost equally to the civilian population.

33. Ephraim Lipson, *Europe, 1914–1939,* rev. ed. (London: Adam & Charles Black, 1944), 322; Irene Richards, J. B. Goodson, and J. A. Morris, *A Sketch-Map History of the Great War and After, 1914–1935* (London: George G. Harrap, 1938), 11.

34. Haldane, *A Soldier's Saga,* 278, 304–305. Haldane, probably unconscious of the way it would reflect on his reputation for heartlessness in the face of the war's immense losses, recalled that in early August 1914 he was very much concerned about how the British government would react to the German aggression, but he then heard, "to my intense relief, that war had been declared"; Haldane, *A Soldier's Saga,* 279.

35. Mary Renault, *The Charioteer* (1953; repr., New York: Bantam Books, 1959), 78.

36. Henry Williamson, *A Fox under My Cloak* (London: Macdonald, 1955), 57, 58, 61, 62; Henry Williamson society website, "Biography: First World War," http://www.henrywilliamson.co.uk/biography/firstworldwar.

37. From the Henry Williamson society website, "Biography: The Norfolk Farm," http://www.henrywilliamson.co.uk/biography/thenorfolkfarm. Williamson did, however, note that not all the moneylenders were "Jewish millionaires; many were Gentiles. Ah well!" Henry Williamson, 1/5th London Rifles, letter, n.d. (ca. 1969), Imperial War Museum Collection No. 1724.

38. Lieutenant General Molesworth, introduction to Arthur Henry Cook, *A Soldier's War (Being the Diary of the late Arthur Henry Cook, . . . during the Great War, 1914–18)* (Taunton, U.K.: Goodman & Son, 1957), 31. Molesworth in his introduction insisted that the "other ranks" remained cheerful through "good food and recreation," but he also more realistically noted that those same soldiers also had "doubts from time to time of the wisdom of the 'High Ups,'" both points of view that Cook depicted in his diary entries. According to the Somersets' diary, the battalion was in the line and fraternized on Christmas Day itself, so Cook's company must have been in reserves and took their place at the front on 28 December, when they "relieved C Company"; 1st Somerset Light Infantry, diary.

39. Arthur H. Booth, *The True Book about the First World War* (London: Frederick Muller, 1958), 18, 22–24; Cyril Falls, *The Great War* (New York: G. P. Putnam's Sons, 1959), 13, 14, 39.

8. "The Famous Christmas Truce"

1. Hanna, *The Great War on the Small Screen*, 21, 40; Tony Essex, Gordon Watkins, John Terraine, Ed Rollins, and Tom Manefield, producers, *The Great War* (BBC, 1964), episode 1, "On the idle hill of summer."

2. Essex et al., *The Great War*, episode 3, "We must hack our way through"; episode 5, "This business may last a long time." The title of each individual episode was a quote, rendered in lowercase letters. The title of the second episode was attributed to Queen Mary, but the full quote was in fact "God grant we may not have a European war thrust upon us, and for such a stupid reason, too—no, I don't mean stupid, but to have to go to war on account of tiresome Serbia beggars belief"; Queen Mary, July 1914. Of course, the war did not happen because of "tiresome Serbia," but taking the phrase "for such a stupid reason" out of context no doubt suited the producers' purposes. See chap. 7 for the full description of the truce in Williamson's *A Fox under My Cloak*.

3. Williamson's 26 December 1914 letter was reprinted in the biography written by his daughter-in-law, Anne Williamson, *A Patriot's Progress: Henry Williamson and the First World War* (Stroud, Gloucestershire, U.K.: Sutton, 1998), 38–39; Grigg, letter, 26 December 1914. Williamson's letter was sent by his father to the newspapers and printed in the *Daily Express* in 1915.

4. A. Williamson, *A Patriot's Progress*, 40, 123–124.

5. H. Williamson, letter, ca. 1969. This letter provides an interesting contrast to a current debate on the subject, which has the right attacking the left for demonstrating pro-German sympathies by refusing to blame the First World War on German aggression, which illustrates how easily a historical dispute can be manipulated for political points.

6. Essex et al., *The Great War*, episode 26, "And we were young"; Todman, *The Great War*, 36. For a more detailed exploration of *The Great War* and its effect on the narrative of the conflict, see Todman, *The Great War*, and Hanna, *The Great War on the Small Screen*.

7. Todman, *The Great War*, 121; Watson, *Fighting Different Wars*, 26.

8. James Cameron, *1914* (New York: Rinehart, 1959), 42, 74, 155, 203, 252–253.

9. Ibid., 262. The truce that was "refused" is no doubt a reference to the pope's suggestion for a Christmas cease-fire.

10. Clark, *The Donkeys*, 11. Clark asserts, for example, that at Neuve Chapelle, "many of the men, including the whole of the 25th Brigade, were going into action for the first time"; Clark, *Donkeys*, 51. An examination of the war

diaries of the battalions forming the 25th Brigade, however, demonstrates that many of them had been in the line since some time in 1914, that the 1st Royal Irish Rifles and the 2nd Rifles had been in the front line for varying rotations since November 1914, and that both had participated in the 18–19 December 1914 attacks on the German trenches.

11. Ibid., 41, 174.

12. Chris Wrigley, *A.J.P. Taylor: Radical Historian of Europe* (London: I. B. Taurus, 2007), 1. As Wrigley further notes, Taylor came in "first in a *Times* informal poll to ascertain the most influential British intellectual since the Second World War"; Wrigley, *A.J.P. Taylor*, 2.

13. A. J. P. Taylor, *Origins of the Second World War* (Middlesex, U.K.: Penguin Books, 1961), 41, 42; Tuchman, *Guns of August*, 523. Taylor further argues that "her opponents fought, though less consciously, to defend that settlement," which was hardly the case: the Allies, as in the First World War, were fighting against German aggression, which, if for no other consideration than their own safety, they could not allow to stand. Taylor, *Origins of the Second World War*, 41. As for Tuchman's estimate of Allied casualties on the Western Front, Cruttwell provides figures of 10,004,771 known deaths in the war, but this total includes 460,000 Italians, at least 1,700,000 Russians, and 1,200,000 Austro-Hungarians, none of whom fought on the Western Front. The horrendous casualties that British Empire troops suffered in non–Western Front battles such as Gallipoli should also be considered; they render Tuchman's casualty estimates quite fanciful—and certainly discredited. Cruttwell, *Great War*, 630–631.

14. Sheffield, *Forgotten Victory*, 17.

15. Ferguson, *Pity of War*, xxxii; Taylor, *History of the First World War*, 12, 13, 14; Taylor, *Origins of the Second World War*, 265–266. For a native of the country that produced British Rail, Taylor's faith in the immutability of railway timetables is rather touching.

16. Taylor, *History of the First World War*, 38.

17. Ibid., 39; Theatre Workshop, *Oh, What a Lovely War*, edited and introduced by Joan Littlewood, with commentary and notes by Steve Lewis (1965; repr., London: Methuen, 2006), xxvii–xxviii, xxxi, xli, xlii, 32. It should be noted that the soldiers of the First World War, so idealized by those writing between 1920 and 1939, were in this drama reduced to puppets manipulated by the monstrous generals and politicians, which demonstrates that Littlewood and the company saw the British troops as stand-ins for an exploited class rather than as individuals making conscious choices. Additionally, as the program for the original production demonstrates, *Oh, What a Lovely War* was as much about CND and the dangers of nuclear war as it was about the First World War.

18. "Group Panorama of the Kaiser's War," *Times*, 20 March 1963; Brown and Seaton, *Christmas Truce*, xxii.

19. Sir Llewellyn Woodward, *Great Britain and the War of 1914–1918* (1967; repr., Boston: Beacon Press, 1970), xiii.

20. Ibid., xxii–xxiii, xxiv, xxv–xxvi; Terraine, *The Western Front*. As Woodward acerbically observed about the Allied policy of attrition, "This plan, if one can call it a plan, did result in victory, but the victorious generals nearly destroyed European civilisation by the methods which they employed to save it. Fortunately for the Allies the enemy generals were equally obtuse"; Woodward, *Great Britain and the War of 1914–1918*, xxv.

21. Graves, "Christmas Truce," 101, 104.

22. Ibid., 105, 114, 115. Graves further noted that the punishment allotted to the colonel was irrelevant because he was killed in action the following year. Additionally, French, who was not consulted in advance, claimed to have condemned the truce at the time, and he regretted his attitude toward the cease-fire only after the war had ended.

23. Ibid., 109, 115.

24. Peter Jackson, interview, 1963, Imperial War Museum Collection No. 4138. Jackson's regiment is not given, but from his description of events from November 1914 onward, his battalion was clearly part of the 21st Brigade (7th Division, IV Corps), whose leadership took a very relaxed attitude toward the Christmas truce.

25. Ibid.

26. James L. Jack, *General Jack's Diary, 1914–1918* (1964; repr., Princeton: Collectors Reprints, 1997), 94. To be fair, Jack also found it "interesting to visualize the close of a campaign owing to the opposing armies—neither of them defeated—having become too friendly to continue the fight," but he did not seem to entertain this as a viable option. His take on the truce was in accord with that of those who believed the war was necessary—that it proved that the British were not motivated by hatred and prejudice.

27. George Coppard, *With a Machine Gun to Cambrai: The Tale of a Young Tommy in Kitchener's Army, 1914–1918* (London: Her Majesty's Stationery Office, 1969).

28. Ibid., 58–59.

29. Ibid.

30. Ibid., 59, 60.

31. Ibid., 61; J. Davey, 1st Royal Irish Rifles, to the Curator, Imperial War Museum, Private Papers of J. Davey, Imperial War Museum Collection No. 3643, 20 July 1969.

32. Attenborough, *Oh! What a Lovely War*; IMDb, "Awards," www.imdb.com/title/tt0064754/awards?ref_=tt_awd. (The exclamation point was added to the film's title.) On the perceived antiwar bias of the film, Pauline Kael argued that the "specific target" of *Oh! What a Lovely War* was in fact the "follies of the upper classes," and she maintained that the film's explanation of war was that "wars are made by the officers, who are homicidal

imbeciles interested only in personal position and indifferent to the death of their men"; Pauline Kael, *Deeper into Movies* (Boston: Little, Brown, 1973), 15. This would presumably have been consistent with Littlewood's interpretation of the event.

33. *The Great War*, liner notes from the DVD. The quote "the war to end all wars" has been generally attributed to H. G. Wells, who published a book in 1914 entitled *The War That Will End War* (London: Frank & Cecil Palmer, 1914), available at https://archive.org/details/warthatwillendwa00welluoft.

9. "The Legendary Christmas Truce"

1. Malcolm Brown, *Peace in No Man's Land* (BBC, 1981); Eric Evans, "Social History," www.history.ac.uk/makinghistory/resources/articles/social_history.html.

2. H. G. R. Williams, 1/5th London Rifles, interview, n.d., Imperial War Museum Collection No. 30545; Albert Moren, 2nd Queen's Royal West Surreys, interview, n.d., Imperial War Museum Collection No. 30546; M. Leslie Walkinton, 1/16th Queen's Westminster Rifles, interview, 1979, Imperial War Museum Collection No. 4519.

3. Brown repeated his questions and points throughout several takes of the interview with Moren; this selection is from the second round of questioning; Moren, interview.

4. Malcolm Brown, *Tommy Goes to War* (London: J. M. Dent & Sons, 1978), 100, 101; Brown and Seaton, *Christmas Truce*, xxiii, xxiv–xxv, 11, 45, 69, 103, 161, 163, 189, 204–206.

5. Brown and Seaton, *Christmas Truce: The Western Front December 1914*, rev. ed. (Oxford: Pan Macmillan, 1999), xxv, 1, 215–216.

6. Ernie Williams, 6th Cheshires, interview, n.d., Imperial War Museum Collection No. 25228. In their letters home, Armes noted that "of course" the war would start again, Hulse spoke contemptuously of the Germans, Spencer was filled with bitterness after the burial in No Man's Land of so many dead British soldiers, and Fisher-Rowe was quite happy for the battalion he commanded to go on participating in a truce for more than a week.

7. Leonard V. Smith, "Paul Fussell's *The Great War and Modern Memory*: Twenty-five Years Later," *History and Theory* 40, no. 2 (May 2001): 242.

8. Fussell, *The Great War and Modern Memory*, 23–24.

9. Ibid., 124, 245. Fussell grudgingly admits that Graham's story about the sergeant's grave, on which crimson roses are said to grow, is "English literature, we realize" but the anecdote could just as easily have been offered without the details of the soldier's rank and unit, which lend "an air of verisimilitude to an otherwise bald and unconvincing narrative." Stephen Graham, *The Challenge of the Dead: A Vision of the War and the Life of the Common Soldier in France* (London: Cassell, 1921), 81.

10. Fussell, *The Great War and Modern Memory*, ix.

11. R. G. Garrod, 20th Hussars, memoir, Private Papers of R. G. Garrod, Imperial War Museum Collection No. 6677. The memoir is undated, but internal evidence indicates that it was probably written during the 1970s. Although the reasons for most of the interviews featured in this chapter, which are held by the Imperial War Museum, are never given, they are assumed to be part of the general mission of the museum, which is to "seek to provide for, and to encourage, the study and understanding of the history of modern war and 'wartime experience'" (Imperial War Museum website, www.iwm. org.uk). Some of the interviews, however, were clearly recorded for inclusion in documentaries, such as the Henry Williamson 1964 interview featured in *The Great War*, and the Albert Moren and H. G. R. Williams interviews recorded for Malcolm Brown's *Peace in No Man's Land*.

12. Gilbert H. Smith, 1st Queen's Royal West Surrey, memoir, 1973, Private Papers of G. H. Smith, Imperial War Museum Collection No. 11396.

13. A. Self, 2nd West Yorkshires, memoir, n.d., Private Papers of A. Self, Imperial War Museum Collection No. 7753; Philip Neame, 15th Field Company Royal Engineers, interview, 1974, Imperial War Museum Collection No. 48.

14. Colin Wilson, 1st Grenadier Guards, interview, 1975, Imperial War Museum Collection No. 9083. Chronologically speaking, Wilson's memories of the armistice are fairly dubious: although it is true that the 1st Grenadier Guards rotated back into the trenches on 27 December, and that the cease-fire in their area lasted until the beginning of January, there are no records from any battalion or soldier of fraternization after Boxing Day. He could not possibly have seen the 2nd Scots Guards or 2nd Gordon Highlanders fraternizing with the enemy, as neither battalion did so beyond 26 December.

15. J. H. Acton, 1st Devonshires, interview, 1975, Imperial War Museum Collection No. 24881. Although the 1st Devons were part of the 5th Division, and therefore under the direction of Smith-Dorrien, it appears that Acton did not have any memories of displeasure on the part of the leadership to spoil his recollection of the truce.

16. Walkinton, 1979 interview, and M. L. Walkinton, *Twice in a Lifetime* (London: Samson Books, 1980), 43–44. The foreword to Walkinton's memoir, written by Field Marshal John Harding, Baron Harding of Petherton, who served, like Walkinton, in a London Territorial Infantry Brigade, unapologetically placed the First and Second World Wars on the same footing. "I often wonder if the younger generations of today realise how different, how difficult, how restricted and how tedious our lives would be," Lord Harding wrote, "if the author and his comrades and mine had not been prepared to face all the fearfulness of war rather than submit to the Kaiser and his Prussians or Hitler and the Nazis"; Walkinton, *Twice in a Lifetime*, 7. As Walkinton noted in relation to the soldiers' attitudes toward the Germans, "Every fighting soldier also discovered, if he stayed long enough to get the front line

mentality well into him, that the further from the line the greater the hatred of the enemy. At the real front he was called Fritz or Brother Boche"; Walkinton, *Twice in a Lifetime*, 43.

17. Walkinton, *Twice in a Lifetime*, 45, 179. Walkinton further added, "Of course we didn't delude ourselves that we had never hated each other's guts when our best friends were killed or maimed or our living conditions became unbearable, but we wanted to forgive and forget and do what little we could to avoid a repetition"; Walkinton, *Twice in a Lifetime*, 179.

18. John Wedderburn-Maxwell, 45th Brigade R.F.A., interview, 1985, Imperial War Museum Collection No. 9146.

19. Walkinton, 1985 interview. Walkinton did recall hearing that "one Scottish officer was court-martialed, but I don't think he was punished or anything, but I don't really know," although clearly he is mixing up the 1915 truce with the one in which he participated.

20. Ashurst, 1987 interview, and George Ashurst, *My Bit: A Lancashire Fusilier at War, 1914–1918* (Wiltshire, U.K.: Crowood Press, 1987), 42. Although Ashurst does not say exactly when his memoir was written—it seems unlikely that he had waited until the mid-1980s to record his memories of the war— he seemed very angry still at the time of writing it at "the men who did their fighting in big chateaux and their marching in motor cars" and the home front whom he believed had condemned the truce. He defended the armistice against those critics, arguing that the soldiers had done nothing wrong: "We had dared to stop the bloody game of war a few hours longer than the 'official' period. Men who were half starved, dirty, lousy, suffering unbelievable mental and physical tortures, for a purpose that not one in a hundred of them could definitely state—can one imagine the feelings of these men at this ingratitude from their own country? No wonder that the common and general wish of these men was that those well fed and comfortable critics were in the trenches opposite, in the place of a more friendly enemy"; Ashurst, *My Bit*, 42. At the same time, Ashurst was also, somewhat surprisingly, convinced that the truce had been authorized in advance by "somebody in authority"—he believed it was the Germans—who had decided that "we mustn't fight" for a few hours; Ashurst interview.

21. Cyril A. F. Drummond, 32nd Brigade R.F.A., essays, n.d., Private Papers of C. A. F. Drummond, Imperial War Museum Collection No. 1694; Harold Essex Lewis, 240th Royal Field Artillery, interview, 1986, Imperial War Museum Collection No. 9388.

22. Todman, *Great War*, 207.

23. Ellis, *Eye-Deep in Hell*, 169, 192 (italics in original), 196. In spite of the global emphasis of such documentaries as *The Great War*, the First World War was, during this period, increasingly understood to mean the war on the Western Front, but it also included the occasional attention-getting "sideshow," such as Gallipoli.

24. Ibid., 172–173.

25. Lloyd, *War in the Trenches,* 37–38.

26. Ibid. Lloyd also describes the second truce that occurred at Christmas 1915, observing that on that date "the trench soldier's inclination to make the most of seasonable lulls was demonstrated by a further outbreak of fraternization in No Man's Land, despite the orders against such behaviour. At least two officers who took part were court-martialled," without further noting that one officer was found not guilty and the other had his sentence quashed. Additionally, Lloyd generally ups the ante by stating that participants in the 1914 truce were court-martialed rather than the more vague "punishments" alluded to by Clark, Cameron, and company; Lloyd, *War in the Trenches,* 79.

27. Ashworth, *Trench Warfare,* 13, 19, 24, 32–33. Ashworth also alleges, on the basis of Wilfred Ewart's posthumously published diary, that "all leave in the battalion was stopped" for the 2nd Scots Guards following their 1915 fraternization. One page after the observation that "owing to the fraternization incident a week ago, all leave in the regiment is stopped indefinitely," however, Ewert noted that, three weeks later, he had just returned from leave in England. If leave was indeed stopped as punishment, therefore, it was for no more than a week or two, which Ashworth does not mention; Ashworth, *Trench Warfare,* 33; Wilfred Ewart, *Scots Guard* (London: Rich & Cowan, 1934), 80–81.

28. Modris Eksteins, *Rites of Spring: The Great War and the Birth of the Modern Age* (Boston: Houghton Mifflin, 1989), xv, 117, 118, 120.

29. Ibid., 117, 118, 123.

30. Ibid., 97, 123, 133. "But what the truce revealed, by its unofficial and spontaneous nature, was how resilient certain attitudes and values were," Eksteins theorized. "Despite the slaughter of the early months, it was the subsequent war that began profoundly to alter those values and to hasten and spread in the west the drift to narcissism and fantasy that had been so characteristic of the avant-garde and large segments of the German population before the war"; ibid., 98.

31. Ibid., 134–135.

32. Ibid., 97, 128; Fussell, *Great War and Modern Memory,* 35; Curtis and Elton, *Blackadder Goes Forth.*

33. Of course, Blackadder's casualty figures were as wildly inflated as everyone else's: 50,000 British dead a week would equal 11,440,000 for the entire war, almost twice as many as actually served in all the British forces. It is no surprise, however, that Blackadder's assertions passed without adverse comment, as the casualties of the war reported in various histories had been progressively increasing from 1960 onward.

10. "Memories of Christmas 1914 Persist"

1. Macdonald, *1915,* vii, 3–4, 5. The explanations written in response to Smith-Dorrien's 27 December request by the 5th Division officers involved in

the truce were all dated 28 December 1914. Macdonald, it should be noted, entirely failed to mention the Christmas 1914 truce in her work *1914: The Days of Hope* (London: Penguin Books, 1987).

2. Macdonald, *1915*, 599–600. (*Boche* is slang for Germans.) Information about Colquhoun's court-martial was not published in the British press, but this may have been for a number of reasons, only one of which was censorship by the leadership. Alternative suggestions are that the newspapers were unaware of the event or, as the minor 1915 armistices did not present the mass appeal of the previous year's extensive truce, uninterested.

3. See chap. 6 for a full account of the 1915 truces and their aftermath.

4. Sheffield, *Forgotten Victory*, 3, 5, 151–152.

5. Gilbert, *The First World War*, 25, 117, 119.

6. Winter and Baggett, *The Great War and the Shaping of the Twentieth Century*, 50, 99; De Groot, *The First World War*, 19, 20, 166. Winter and Baggett, however, fail to note that Italy, when reminded of its "treaty obligations" by Germany, declined to honor them but instead waited out the first year of the war and eventually entered on the Allied side.

7. Terry Deary and Martin Brown, *The Frightful First World War* [1998] and *The Woeful Second World War* (London: Scholastic, 2003), 8, 9, 15, 16, 129; the book is an entry in Scholastic's *Horrible Histories* series. Deary and Brown even theorize that the Germans lost the war because they had been too successful in their spring 1918 campaign. "But the Germans are rushing forward too quickly. Their supplies can't keep up with them and they soon run out," Deary and Brown assert. "When the Allies stop and turn, the Germans have nothing left to give. The Allies push on and on and on. All the way to Germany. The starved and feeble Germans are the losers . . . and all because they had been the winners"; Deary and Brown, *Frightful First World War*, 92.

8. Peter Simkins, *Chronicles of the Great War: The Western Front, 1914–1918* (Godalming, Surrey, U.K.: CLB International, 1991), 45; Simpson, *Unreliable Sources*, 135.

9. Ferguson, *Pity of War*, xxxii, 343; Neiberg, "Revisiting the Myths," 506. Ferguson further claims that, because of the animosity between the enemy armies, "orders not to fraternize . . . were quite willingly obeyed"; Ferguson, *Pity of War*, 344.

10. Morrow, *The Great War: An Imperial History*, 8, 69.

11. Joanna Bourke, *An Intimate History of Killing: Face-to-Face Killing in Twentieth-Century Warfare* (London: Granta Books, 1999), 5, 134, 136.

12. Watson, *Fighting Different Wars*, 9, 25–26. In addition, Watson argues that when we define "the war" as the conflict that took place on the Western Front, those who served on other fronts or in other nonfighting functions, such as women who built munitions in British factories, are denied their place in the history of the conflict.

13. Hanna, *The Great War on the Small Screen*, 13; Stanley Archibald, 1st

East Kents (the Buffs), interview, 1990, Imperial War Museum Collection No. 11340.

14. Archibald, 1990 interview.

15. William Douglas Home, *A Christmas Truce* (London: Samuel French, 1990), 45, 53. The colonel does acknowledge that they probably will "get away with it . . . because the top brass and the Government know damned well that the public at home wouldn't stand for it, if people were court-martialed over Christmas—sentimental buggers that they are! I'd say that half the British Army has already written home or to the newspapers about it." The only Christmas truce cliché that Home missed, therefore, was the censorship of news about the armistice. Home, *A Christmas Truce*, 54.

16. An opera by Kevin Puts, *Silent Night*, based on the narrative of *Joyeux Noel*, won a 2012 Pulitzer Prize for music, and has been frequently performed since; see "Schedule," http://silentnightopera.com/productions.html.

17. Ferro et al., *Meetings in No Man's Land*, 1, 2, 3, 5. The first quote comes from the jacket copy.

18. Ibid., 16, 17, 52, 54. The knowledge that the French participated in the truces is verified by stories in the British press in early 1915 and the mention in Cameron's history *1914*, which was published in 1959. The inclusion, however, on purportedly equal terms, of Russian fraternization—which was rare, did not tend to occur at Christmas (Easter fraternization on the Eastern Front being slightly more common), and by 1916 and 1917 was more indicative of revolutionary principles than holiday sentiment—is indeed pushing the envelope. Although the sections of the book dealing with the French, German, and Russian armistices will be more novel to English-speaking readers, they provide little that is new regarding the Christmas truce narrative.

19. Michael Foreman, *War Game: Village Green to No-Man's-Land* (1993; repr., London: Pavilion Children's Books, 2006). The book is unpaginated. Although Foreman dedicates his work to the memory of his uncles, "William James Foreman, killed aged 18; Frederick Benjamin Foreman, killed aged 20; William Henry Goddard, killed aged 20; Lacy Christmas Goddard, died of wounds Christmas Day 1918 aged 24," who all died in the war, and gives his characters the same names as his uncles, thus implying that they had all been in the truce, this scenario is unlikely. Even if the "Suffolk lads" had been sent to the front almost immediately after enlisting, which rarely happened, the King's Royal Rifles Corps, although at the front in December 1914, did not participate in the truce.

20. Weintraub, *Silent Night*, 109–111.

21. Ibid., 171–172, 173. Weintraub seems to have reached the conclusion that the ballad is about Colquhoun's court-martial and subsequent execution on the basis of stories McCutcheon tells when he sings the song live, rather than any connection drawn in the lyrics; see "Christmas in the Trenches," www.youtube.com/watch?v=sJi41RWaTCs.

22. Weintraub, *Silent Night*, 140–141, 174. Weintraub's lack of footnotes makes the source of the story about the mutiny particularly hard to trace: the reference to the book from which this account comes appears only in endnotes to a passage cited 125 pages earlier. The anecdote was repeated by a German soldier in late 1915 to an Australian woman, Ethel Cooper, who lived in Germany and remained there throughout the war. Internal evidence in the Cooper letters, which are collected in a volume entitled *Behind the Lines: One Woman's War, 1914–18: The Letters of Caroline Ethel Cooper*, however, demonstrates that the supposed mutiny was not participated in or witnessed by the soldier in question, and it is therefore undoubtedly based on nothing more than rumors and a desire to impress a foreigner with his distaste for the war. Cooper, *Behind the Lines: One Woman's War, 1914–1918: The Letters of Caroline Ethel Cooper*, ed. Decie Denholm (Sydney: Collins, 1982).

23. *Days That Shook the World; Find My Past* (ITV, 2012); see also www.findmypast.co.uk/. Weintraub's account of the Saxon mutiny does not identify the soldiers involved as being under Lange's command ("his men"). As Lange was a member of the commissariat, he could not possibly have been in charge of frontline soldiers.

24. *Find My Past*, November 2012.

25. Smith-Dorrien's command was extended on 26 December to II Corps of the reorganized B.E.F., but at the time of the truce he commanded only one of the B.E.F.'s five corps. The series' attempt to grant him an earlier promotion was presumably done to emphasize his power to order an end to the truce.

26. This was demonstrated by Smith-Dorrien's directive of 4 December 1914, which noted that the "rushing of a hostile trench at night and the scuppering of its occupants, though it will doubtless be attended with loss on our side, and though there may be no intention of holding the trench permanently, has incalculable results of a moral nature both on our own troops and on those of the enemy. Similarly, constant sniping on the enemy's trenches will have just as annoying effect on the enemy as their sniping has on us, and, and this is the important point, the enemy, owing to reduced numbers and the difficulty of providing reinforcements, will stand to lose far more on the balance than we shall."

27. "Christmas Truce," http://en.wikipedia.org/wiki/Christmas_truce; "Christmas Truce of 1914," www.history.com/topics/christmas-truce-of-1914; "The Soldiers Truce," www.newdemocracyworld.org/revolution/christmas_truce_thoughts.html. The author of the Christmas truce entry on the third website, Dave Stratman, also informs his readers that "the real goal of political leaders in provoking World War I was to destroy the international working class movement of the time, which threatened to overwhelm the governments of Western Europe and Russia"—which at least presents a different take on the subject. He reverts to a more conventional narrative when

discussing the truce, however, noting that "many of the officers on each side attempted to prevent the event from occurring but the soldiers ignored the risk of a court-martial or of being shot," though he offers no proof of these claims.

28. Todman, *The Great War,* xii; "Sainsbury's Official Christmas 2014 Ad," www.youtube.com/watch?v=NWF2JBb1bvM. As of May 2015, the famous Sainsbury's advertisement had garnered over 17,000,000 viewings on YouTube.

11. "It Was Peace That Won"

1. Paul McCartney, "Pipes of Peace," www.youtube.com/watch?v=J7ErrZ-ipoE.

2. Tim Shipman, "Michael Gove Blasts 'Blackadder Myths' about the First World War Spread by Television Sit-Coms and Left-Wing Academics," *Daily Mail,* 2 January 2014.

3. Toby Helm, Vanessa Thorpe, and Philip Oltermann, "Labour Condemns Michael Gove's 'Crass' Comments on First World War," *Guardian,* 4 January 2014; Tony Robinson, "Baldrick Hits Back at 'Silly' Gove in Great War Rumpus: Sir Tony Robinson Says Education Secretary Made a Mistake in Row over Showing Blackadder in Lessons," *Daily Mail,* 5 January 2014; Richard J. Evans, "Michael Gove Shows His Ignorance of History—Again," *Guardian,* 6 January 2014; Boris Johnson, "Germany Started the Great War, but the Left Can't Bear to Say So," *Telegraph,* 6 January 2014.

4. Mark Steel, "By Jingo, Gove's Right—Those Leftie Academics Have Hijacked the Great War: Remembrance Sunday Has Nothing on 'Blackadder,'" *Independent,* 9 January 2014; Brian Reade, "Michael Gove's Attempt at Rewriting Great War History Would Make My KKK-Supporting Uncle Bud Proud," *Mirror,* 11 January 2014.

5. Margaret MacMillan, "The 1914 Christmas Armistice: A Triumph for Common Humanity," *Financial Times,* 20 December 2013.

6. Jeremy Rifkin, *The Empathic Civilization: The Race to Global Consciousness in a World in Crisis* (New York: Jeremy P. Tarcher/Penguin, 2009), 8.

7. "The Christmas Truce," www.firstworldwar.com/features/christmastruce .html. It is likely that the website's authors meant that the truce was "widely," not "wildly," reported.

8. *Daily Telegraph,* 1 January 1915; *Manchester Guardian,* 31 December 1914; and *Morning Post,* 31 December 1914, respectively.

9. Murphy, *Truce,* 80.

10. Morley to "Eg," 29 December 1914; Gaunt to Auckland, 25 December 1914.

11. Woodward, *Great Britain and the War of 1914–1918,* xxxii.

Bibliography

Primary Sources

Newspapers

Daily Mail
Daily Telegraph
Illustrated London News
Manchester Guardian
Morning Post
Times

Soldiers' Letters, Diaries, Memoirs, and Interviews

Acton, J. H. 1st Devonshires. Interview, 1975. Imperial War Museum Collection No. 24881.

Archibald, Stanley. 1st East Kents (the Buffs). Interview, 1990. Imperial War Museum Collection No. 11340.

Armes, R. J. 1st North Staffordshires. Private Papers of R. J. Armes. Imperial War Museum Collection No. 16576.

Ashurst, George. *My Bit: A Lancashire Fusilier at War 1914–1918.* Wiltshire, U.K.: The Crowood Press, 1987.

———, 2nd Lancashire Fusiliers. Interview, 1987. Imperial War Museum Collection No. 9875.

Asquith, Raymond. *Raymond Asquith: Life and Letters.* Edited by John Jolliffe. 1980. Reprint, London: Century Hutchinson, 1987.

Atkins, Harold. 1/5th London Rifle Brigade. Private Papers of Harold Atkins. Imperial War Museum Collection No. 16505.

Bairnsfather, Bruce. *Bullets & Billets.* London: Grant Richards, 1916. Available at www.gutenberg.org/files/11232/11232-8.txt.

Bates, Arthur. 1/5th London Rifle Brigade. Ms. letter. Imperial War Museum Collection No. 10083.

Bell, Douglas Herbert. *A Soldier's Diary of the Great War.* London: Faber & Gwyer, 1928.

Berryman, Edward R. P. 2/39th Garhwal Rifles. Private Papers of E. R. P. Berryman. Imperial War Museum Collection No. 17257.

Black, Frank H. 1st Royal Warwickshires. Private Papers of F. H. Black. Imperial War Museum Collection No. 4333.

Blewitt, Ralph. 39th Brigade Royal Field Artillery. Private Papers of R. Blewitt. Imperial War Museum Collection No. 8469.

Brookes, Bernard J. 1/16th Queen's Westminster Rifles. Private Papers of B. J. Brookes. Imperial War Museum Collection No. 10825.

Brown, Frederick A. 2nd Monmouthshires. Private Papers of F. A. Brown. Imperial War Museum Collection No. 4401.

Bryan, H. D. 1st Scots Guards. Private Papers of H. D. Bryan. Imperial War Museum Collection No. 13833.

Burgoyne, G. A. 4th Royal Irish Rifles. Private Papers of G. A. Burgoyne. Imperial War Museum Collection No. 12484.

Burke, A. P. 20th Manchesters. Private Papers of A. P. Burke. Imperial War Museum Collection No. 1665.

Chandler, F. G. 2nd Argyll and Sutherland Highlanders. Private Papers of F. G. Chandler. Imperial War Museum Collection No. 15460.

Chappell, H. J. 1/5th London Rifle Brigade. Private Papers of H. J. Chappell. Imperial War Museum Collection No. 1674.

Chater, Alfred Dugan. 2nd Gordon Highlanders. Private Papers of A. D. Chater. Imperial War Museum Collection No. 1697.

Chennell, William J. 2nd Queen's Royal West Surreys. Private Papers of W. J. Chennell. Imperial War Museum Collection No. 16627.

Colquhoun, Iain. 1st Scots Guards. Private Papers of Iain Colquhoun. Imperial War Museum Collection No. 6373.

Cook, Arthur Henry. *A Soldier's War (Being the Diary of the late Arthur Henry Cook, . . . during the Great War, 1914–18)*. Taunton, U.K.: Goodman & Son, 1957.

Coppard, George. *With a Machine Gun to Cambrai: The Tale of a Young Tommy in Kitchener's Army, 1914–1918*. London: Her Majesty's Stationery Office, 1969.

Cox, Edgar W. Intelligence Section. Private Papers of E. W. Cox. Imperial War Museum Collection No. 8548.

Cuthbert (last name unknown). Regiment unknown. Ms. letter. Imperial War Museum Collection No. 15241.

Daniell, E. H. E. 2nd Royal Irish. Ms. letter. Imperial War Museum Collection No. 1329.

Davey, J. 1st Royal Irish Rifles. Private Papers of J. Davey. Imperial War Museum Collection No. 3643.

Diggle, W. H. HQ 8th Division. Private Papers of N. Noble. Imperial War Museum Collection No. 854.

Dillon, Harry M. 2nd Oxfordshire and Buckinghamshire Light Infantry. Private Papers of H. M. Dillon. Imperial War Museum Collection No. 4430.

Drummond, Cyril A. F. 32nd Brigade Royal Field Artillery. Private Papers of C. A. F. Drummond. Imperial War Museum Collection 1694.

Dunn, J. C. *The War the Infantry Knew: 1914–1919, A Chronicle of Service in France and Belgium with the Second Battalion His Majesty's Twenty-Third Foot, the Royal Welch Fusiliers*. 1938. Reprint, London: Jane's, 1987.

Edmonds, Charles. *A Subaltern's War, Being a Memoir of the Great War from the Point of View of a Romantic Young Man.* 1929. Reprint, New York: Minton, Balch, 1930.

Ewart, Wilfred. *Scots Guard.* London: Rich & Cowan, 1934.

Fenton, J. S. 2nd Field Company Royal Engineers. Private Papers of J. S. Fenton. Imperial War Museum Collection No. 12033.

Fisher-Rowe, Laurence. 1st Grenadier Guards. Private Papers of L. Fisher-Rowe. Imperial War Museum Collection No. 16978.

Foxx-Pitt, W. A. F. 2nd Cheshires. Private Papers of W. A. F. Foxx-Pitt. Imperial War Museum Collection No. 18386.

French, Sir John. *1914.* Boston: Houghton Mifflin, 1919.

Garrod, R. G. 20th Hussars. Private Papers of R. G. Garrod. Imperial War Museum Collection No. 6677.

Gaunt, Kenneth M. 1/16th Queen's Westminster Rifles. Private Papers of K. M. Gaunt. Imperial War Museum Collection No. 7490.

Goodman, Frederick Charles. 2/1st London Field Ambulance, R.A.M.C. Interview, 1986. Imperial War Museum Collection No. 9398.

Graves, Robert. *Good-bye to All That: An Autobiography.* 1929. Revised edition, New York: Doubleday, 1957.

Greenwell, Graham Hamilton. 4th Oxfordshire and Buckinghamshire Light Infantry. Interview, 1985. Imperial War Museum Collection No. 8766.

Grigg, J. Selby. 1/5th London Rifles. Private Papers of J. Selby Grigg. Imperial War Museum Collection No. 3881.

Haldane, James Aylmer. *A Soldier's Saga: The Autobiography of General Sir Aylmer Haldane.* Edinburgh: William Blackwood & Sons, 1948.

Hancock, J. 1st Royal Fusiliers. Private Papers of J. Hancock. Imperial War Museum Collection No. 8146.

Henderson, Kenneth. 1/39th Garhwal Rifles. Private Papers of K. Henderson. Imperial War Museum Collection No. 10942.

Holbrook, William George. 4th Royal Fusiliers. Interview, 1986. Imperial War Museum Collection No. 9339.

Holdsworth, E. E. 110th Battery Royal Field Artillery. Private Papers of E. E. Holdsworth. Imperial War Museum Collection No. 17028.

Holroyd, Michael. 1st Hampshires. Private Papers of M. Holroyd. Imperial War Museum Collection No. 7364.

Horne, Henry S. (Baron Horne of Stirkoke). I Corps Royal Artillery. Private Papers of H. S. Horne. Imperial War Museum Collection No. 12468.

Hulse, Edward Hamilton Westrow. *Letters Written from the English Front in France between September 1914 and March 1915.* 1916. Reprint, Miami: HardPress Classics, n.d.

———. 2nd Scots Guards. Private Papers of Edward Hulse. Imperial War Museum Collection No. 2621.

Hutchinson, Graham Seton. *Warrior.* London: Hutchinson, 1932.

Jack, James L. *General Jack's Diary, 1914–1918.* 1964. Reprint, Princeton: Collectors Reprints, 1997.

Jackson, Peter. Interview, 1963. Imperial War Museum Collection No. 4138.

Jameson, George Brummel. 1/1st Northumberland Hussars. Interview, 1984. Imperial War Museum Collection No. 7363.

Jones, Percy H. 1/16th Queen's Westminster Rifles. Private Papers of P. H. Jones. Imperial War Museum Collection No. 12253.

Lack, Ted. Regiment unknown. Collection of Documents relating to Croydon Branch of the Old Contemptibles. Imperial War Museum Collection No. 9646.

Laffin, John. *Letters from the Front, 1914–1918.* London: J. M. Dent & Sons, 1973.

———. *On the Western Front: Soldiers' Stories from France and Flanders, 1914–1918.* Gloucester, U.K.: Alan Sutton, 1985.

Lane, Sam. 2nd Wiltshires. Private Papers of S. Lane. Imperial War Museum Collection No. 11686.

Lawson, Cuthbert G. 3rd Royal Horse Artillery, 2nd Calvary Division. Private Papers of C. G. Lawson. Imperial War Museum Collection No. 7834.

Lewis, Harold Essex. 240th Royal Field Artillery. Interview, 1986. Imperial War Museum Collection No. 9388.

Liddell, John Aiden. 2nd Argyll and Sutherland Highlanders. Private Papers of J. A. Liddle. Imperial War Museum Collection No. 11126.

Lintott, Richard. 1/5th London Rifle Brigade. Private Papers of R. Lintott. Imperial War Museum Collection No. 3394.

Lloyd-Burch, D. Ambulance Corps. Private Papers of D. Lloyd-Burch. Imperial War Museum Collection No. 1423.

Lucey, S. Thomas. 1st Loyal North Lancashires. Private Papers of S. T. Lucey. Imperial War Museum Collection No. 15331.

Mascall, Maurice. Royal Garrison Artillery. Private Papers of E. M. Mascall. Imperial War Museum Collection No. 11163.

Moren, Albert. 2nd Queen's Royal West Surreys. Interview, n.d. Imperial War Museum Collection No. 30546.

Morley, Ernest G. 1/16th Queen's Westminster Rifles. Private Papers of E. G. Morley. Imperial War Museum Collection No. 2450.

Neame, Philip. 15th Field Company Royal Engineers. Interview, 1974. Imperial War Museum Collection No. 48.

Nesham, Félicité, ed. *Socks, Cigarettes and Shipwrecks: A Family's War Letters, 1914–1918.* Gloucester, U.K.: Alan Sutton, 1987.

Nicholson, Cecil Lothian. 2nd East Lancashires. Private Papers of Cecil Lothian Nicholson. Imperial War Museum Collection No. 9975.

Packe, F. E. 2nd Welch. Private Papers of F. E. Packe. Imperial War Museum Collection No. 1653.

Pelham-Burn, Arthur. 6th Gordon Highlanders. Scrapbook of Claude Buckingham. Imperial War Museum Collection No. 8632.

Quinton, W. A. 2nd Bedfordshires, Machine Gun Section. Private Papers of W. A. Quinton. Imperial War Museum Collection 6705.

Ray, John. 1st Duke of Cornwall's Light Infantry. Private Papers of J. Ray. Imperial War Museum Collection No. 4652.

Richards, Frank. *Old Soldiers Never Die*. 1933. Reprint, East Sussex, U.K.: Naval and Military Press, n.d.

Ridsdale, H. 76th Field Company Royal Engineers. Private Papers of H. Ridsdale. Imperial War Museum Collection No. 5186.

Self, A. 2nd West Yorkshires. Private Papers of A. Self. Imperial War Museum Collection No. 7753.

Seymour, John. Army Service Corps. Interview, 1986. Imperial War Museum Collection No. 9543.

Smith, Gilbert H. 1st Queen's Royal West Surreys. Private Papers of G. H. Smith. Imperial War Museum Collection No. 11396.

Spencer, Wilbert B. P. 2nd Wiltshires. Private Papers of W. B. P. Spencer. Imperial War Museum Collection No. 1684.

Squire, E. W. 1/13th London Kensingtons. Private Papers of E. W. Squire. Imperial War Museum Collection No. 369.

Tate, W. 2nd Coldstream Guards. Private Papers of W. Tate. Imperial War Museum Collection No. 4520.

Tennant, C. G. 1/4th Seaforth Highlanders. Private Papers of C. G. Tennant. Imperial War Museum Collection No. 8046.

Unknown soldier (1). 1/16th Queen's Westminster Rifles. Manuscript diary of unidentified soldier. Imperial War Museum Collection No. 1552.

Unknown soldier (2). 2nd Borders. Transcription of diary of unidentified soldier. Imperial War Museum Collection No. 8631.

Walkinton, M. Leslie. 1/16th Queen's Westminster Rifles. Interview, 1979. Imperial War Museum Collection No. 4519.

———. Interview, 1985. Imperial War Museum Collection No. 9132.

———. Private Papers of M. L. Walkinton. Imperial War Museum Collection No. 12061.

———. *Twice in a Lifetime*. London: Samson Books, 1980.

Wedderburn-Maxwell, John. 45th Brigade Royal Field Artillery. Interview, 1985. Imperial War Museum Collection No. 9146.

———. Private Papers of J. Wedderburn-Maxwell. Imperial War Museum Collection No. 9362.

Wellesley, C. G. V. 2nd Lincolnshires. Private Papers of C. G. V. Wellesley. Imperial War Museum Collection No. 15579.

Williams, Ernie. 6th Cheshires. Interview, n.d. Imperial War Museum Collection No. 25228.

Williams, H. G. R. 1/5th London Rifles. Interview, n.d. Imperial War Museum Collection No. 30545.
Williamson, Henry. 1/5th London Rifles. Interview, 1964. Imperial War Museum Collection No. 4257.
———. Private Papers of Henry Williamson. Imperial War Museum Collection No. 1724.
Wilson, Colin. 1st Grenadier Guards. Interview, 1975. Imperial War Museum Collection No. 9083.
Withall, Martha. Territorial Force Nursing Service. Private Papers of Martha Withall. Imperial War Museum Collection No. 17423.

Government Publications

General Staff, War Office. *Field Service Pocket Book*. London: His Majesty's Stationery Office, 1914.
General Staff, War Office. *Field Service Pocket Book: 1916*. Revised edition. London: His Majesty's Stationery Office, 1917.
House of Commons Hansard, George V year 20, 920–981, 5th ser., vol. 237. 1930.

Official War Diaries

2nd Argyll and Sutherland Highlanders, WO 95/1365, National Archives
1st Bedfordshires, WO 95/1570/1, National Archives
2nd Bedfordshires, WO 95/1658/2, National Archives
2nd Borders, WO 95/1655, National Archives
2nd Cameronians, WO 95/1715/1, National Archives
5th Cameronians, WO 95/1366, National Archives
1st Cheshires, WO 95/1571, National Archives
6th Cheshires, WO 95/1572, National Archives
1st Devonshires, WO 95/1565/1, National Archives
2nd Devonshires, WO 95/1712, National Archives
1st East Kents (the Buffs), WO 95/1608, National Archives
1st East Lancashires, WO 95/1498, National Archives
2nd East Lancashires, WO 95/1719/2, National Archives
2nd Essex, WO 95/1505, National Archives
1/39th Garhwal Rifles, WO 95/3945/3, National Archives
2/39th Garhwal Rifles, WO 95/3945/3, National Archives
2nd Gordon Highlanders, WO 95/1656/2, National Archives
6th Gordon Highlanders, WO 95/1657, National Archives
1st Grenadier Guards, WO 95/1657, National Archives
2/3rd Gurkha Rifles, WO 95/3946/1, National Archives
1st Hampshires, WO 95/1495, National Archives

2nd Lancashire Fusiliers, WO 95/1507, National Archives
1st Leicestershires, WO 95/1611/2, National Archives
2nd Leinsters, WO 95/1612/2, National Archives
1/13th London Kensingtons, WO 95/1730/3, National Archives
1/5th London Rifles, WO 95/1498, National Archives
2nd Manchesters, WO 95/1564, National Archives
2nd Monmouthshires, WO 95/1506, National Archives
1st Norfolks, WO 95 1573/1, National Archives
2nd Northamptonshires, WO 95/1722, National Archives
1st North Staffordshires, WO 95/2213/1, National Archives
2nd Queen's Royal West Surreys, WO 95/1664, National Archives
1/16th Queen's Westminster Rifles, WO 95/1616, National Archives
1st Rifle Brigade, WO 95/1496, National Archives
2nd Rifle Brigade, WO 95/1731, National Archives
3rd Rifle Brigade, WO 95/1613, National Archives
2nd Royal Berkshires, WO 95/1729, National Archives
2nd Royal Dublin Fusiliers, WO 95/1481/4, National Archives
1st Royal Fusiliers, WO 95/1613/2, National Archives
1st Royal Irish Fusiliers, WO 95/1482, National Archives
1st Royal Irish Rifles, WO 95/1730/4, National Archives
8th Royal Scots, WO 95/1663/3, National Archives
1st Royal Warwickshires, WO 95/1664, National Archives
2nd Royal Welch Fusiliers, WO 95/1365, National Archives
1st Scots Guards, WO 95/1219, National Archives
2nd Scots Guards, WO 95/1657, 1223, National Archives
2nd Seaforth Highlanders, WO 95/1483, National Archives
1st Sherwood Foresters, WO 95/1721, National Archives
2nd Sherwood Foresters, WO 95/1616, National Archives
1st Somerset Light Infantry, WO 95/1499, National Archives
2nd West Yorkshires, WO 95/1714, National Archives
2nd Wiltshires, WO 95/1659, National Archives
1st Worcestershires, WO 95/1723/1, National Archives
2nd York and Lancasters, WO 95/1610, National Archives
2nd Yorkshires, WO 95/1659, National Archives
10th Brigade, WO 95/1477, National Archives
11th Brigade, WO 95/1486, National Archives
12th Brigade, WO 95/1501, National Archives
14th Brigade, WO 95/1560, National Archives
15th Brigade, WO 95/1566, National Archives
16th Brigade, WO 95/1605, National Archives
17th Brigade, WO 95/1612, National Archives
19th Brigade, WO 95/1364, National Archives
20th Brigade, WO 95/1650, National Archives

21st Brigade, WO/95/1658/2, National Archives
22nd Brigade, WO 95/1660, National Archives
23rd Brigade, WO 95/1707, National Archives
24th Brigade, WO 95/1716, National Archives
25th Brigade, WO 95/1724, National Archives
Garhwal Brigade, WO 95/3930, National Archives
4th Division, WO 95/1440, National Archives
5th Division, WO 95/1510, National Archives
6th Division, WO 95/1581, National Archives
7th Division, WO 95/1627, 1634, National Archives
8th Division, WO 95/1671, National Archives
Meerut Division, WO 95/3943, National Archives

Secondary Sources

Fiction and Poetry

Blackall, C. W. *Songs from the Trenches.* London: Bodley Head, 1915. Available at http://archive.org/stream/songsfromtrench00blacgoog/songsfromtrench00blacgoog_djvu.txt.
Ewart, Wilfred. *Way of Revelation: A Novel of Five Years.* New York: D. Appleton and Company, 1922. Available at http://books.google.com/books?id=wAIoAAAAMAAJ&printsec=frontcover&source=gbs_ge_summary_r&cad=0#v=onepage&q&f=false.
Graves, Robert. "Christmas Truce." In *The Shout and Other Stories.* New York: Penguin Books, 1965. Originally published as "Wave No Banners," *Saturday Evening Post,* 15 December 1962.
Remarque, Erich Maria. *All Quiet on the Western Front.* 1928. Reprint, New York: Ballantine Books, 1982.
Sassoon, Siegfried. *The Complete Memoirs of George Sherston.* 1937. Reprint, London: Faber and Faber, 1980.
Sherriff, R. C. *Journey's End.* 1929. Reprint, London: Penguin Books, 2000.
Williamson, Henry. *A Fox under My Cloak.* London: Macdonald & Co., 1955.

Regimental Histories

Atkinson, C. T. *The Seventh Division, 1914–1918.* London: John Murray, 1927.
Berkeley, Reginald. *The History of the Rifle Brigade in the War of 1914–1918,* vol. 1, *August 1914–December 1916.* London: Rifle Brigade Club, 1927.
Bolitho, Hector. *The Galloping Third: The Story of the 3rd the King's Own Hussars.* London: John Murray, 1963.
Boraston, J. H., and Cyril E. O. Bax. *The Eighth Division in War, 1914–1918.* London: Medici Society, 1926.

Brett, G. A. *A History of the 2nd Battalion the Monmouthshire Regiment*. Pontypool: Hughes and Son, 1933.

Burrows, A. R. *The 1st Battalion: The Faugh-a-Ballaghs in the Great War*. Aldershot, U.K.: Gale & Polden, 1926.

Burrows, John W. *The Essex Regiment, 2nd Battalion (56th) (Pompadours)*. Southend-on-Sea: John H. Burrows & Sons, 1927.

Capper, Sir John Edward. *History of the 1st & 2nd Battalions the North Staffordshire Regiment (the Prince of Wales), 1914–1923*. Staffordshire: Hughes & Harper, 1932.

Evatt, J. *Historical Record of the 39th Royal Garhwal Rifles*, vol. 1, *1887–1922*. Aldershot, U.K.: Gale & Polden, 1922.

Falls, Cyril. *The History of the First Seven Battalions, The Royal Irish Rifles in the Great War*. Aldershot, U.K.: Gale & Polden, 1925.

Gillon, Stair. *The K.O.S.B. in the Great War*. London: Thomas Nelson and Sons, 1939.

Gleichen, Edward. *The Doings of the Fifteenth Infantry Brigade: August 1914 to March 1915*. Edinburgh: William Blackwood & Sons, 1917. Available at http://archive.org/stream/thedoingsofthefi22074gut/pg22074.txt.

Harris, Henry. *The Irish Regiments in the First World War*. Cork, Ireland: Mercier Press, 1968.

Henriques, J. Q. *The First Battalion Queen's Westminster Rifles, 1914–1918*. London: Medici Society, 1928.

Kipling, Rudyard. *The Irish Guards in the Great War, Edited and Compiled from Their Diaries and Papers*. 2 vols. London: Macmillan, 1923.

Latter, J. C. *The History of the Lancashire Fusiliers, 1914–1918*, vol. 1. Aldershot, U.K.: Gale and Polden, 1949.

Martin, David, ed. *The Fifth Battalion the Cameronians (Scottish Rifles), 1914–1919*. Glasgow: Jackson, Son & Co., 1936.

Maurice, Sir Frederick. *The History of the London Rifle Brigade, 1859–1919*. London: Constable, 1921.

Molony, C. V. *"Invicta": With the First Battalion, the Queen's Own Royal West Kent Regiment in the Great War*. London: Nisbet, 1923.

Moody, R. S. H. *Historical Records of the Buffs, East Kent Regiment (3rd Foot), Formerly Designated the Holland Regiment and Prince George of Denmark's Regiment*. London: Medici Society, 1922.

Nicholson, C. Lothian, and H. T. MacMullen. *History of the East Lancashire Regiment in the Great War, 1914–1918*. Liverpool: Littlebury Bros., 1936.

O'Neill, H. C. *The Royal Fusiliers in the Great War*. London: William Heinemann, 1922. Available at http://archive.org/stream/royalfusiliersin000nei /royalfusiliersin000nei_djvu.txt.

Pearse, H. W., and H. S. Sloman. *History of the East Surrey Regiment*, vol. 2, *1914–1917*. London: Medici Society, 1923.

Petre, F. Loraine. *The History of the Norfolk Regiment, 1685–1918.* Norwich, U.K.: Jarrold & Sons, 1924.

Petre, F. Loraine, Wilfred Ewart, and Sir Cecil Lowther. *The Scots Guards in the Great War, 1914–1918.* London: John Murray, 1925.

Ponsonby, Sir Frederick. *The Grenadier Guards in the Great War of 1914–1918,* vol. 1. London: Macmillan, 1920.

Popham, Hugh. *The Somerset Light Infantry (Prince Albert's; the 13th Regiment of Foot).* London: Hamish Hamilton, 1968.

Stacke, H. Fitz M. *The Worcestershire Regiment in the Great War.* Kidderminster, U.K.: G. T. Cheshire & Sons, 1928.

Story, H. H. *The History of the Cameronians (Scottish Rifles), 1910–1933.* Aylesbury, U.K.: Hazell Watson & Viney, 1961.

Whitton, Frederick Ernest. *The History of the Prince of Wales' Leinster Regiment (Royal Canadians),* pt. 2, *The Great War and the Disbandment of the Regiment.* Aldershot, U.K.: Gale & Polden, 1924.

Wylly, H. C. *The Border Regiment in the Great War.* Aldershot, U.K.: Gale & Polden, 1924.

———. *Crown and Company: The Historical Records of the 2nd Batt. Royal Dublin Fusiliers, Formerly the 1st Bombay Regiment,* vol. 2, *1911–1922.* Aldershot, U.K.: Gale & Polden, 1923.

———. *The 1st and 2nd Battalions the Sherwood Foresters (Nottinghamshire and Derbyshire Regiment) in the Great War.* Aldershot, U.K.: Gale & Polden, Ltd., 1925.

———. *History of the First and Second Battalions the Leicestershire Regiment in the Great War.* Aldershot, U.K.: Gale & Polden, Ltd., 1928.

———. *The York and Lancaster Regiment, 1758–1919,* vol. 1. London: N.p., 1930.

Wyrall, Everard. *A History of the 14th, the Prince of Wales' Own (West Yorkshire Regt.) and of Its Special Reserve, Territorial and Service Battns. in the Great War of 1914–1918.* London: John Lane, 1924.

Books, Articles, and Films

Abbot, Willis J. *Pictorial History of the Great War.* New York: Doubleday, Page, 1918.

Ashworth, Tony. *Trench Warfare, 1914–1918: The Live and Let Live System.* London: Pan Books, 1980.

Attenborough, Richard, director. *Oh! What a Lovely War.* Accord Productions, 1969.

Birkenhead, Frederick Edwin Smith, Earl of. *The Five Hundred Best English Letters.* London: Cassell, 1931.

Bond, Brian, ed. *The First World War and British Military History.* Oxford: Clarendon Press, 1991.

————. *The Unquiet Western Front: Britain's Role in Literature and History.* Cambridge: Cambridge University Press, 2002.

Booth, Arthur H. *The True Book about the First World War.* London: Frederick Muller, 1958.

Bourke, Joanna. *An Intimate History of Killing: Face-to-Face Killing in Twentieth-Century Warfare.* London: Granta Books, 1999.

Bridge, F. Maynard. *A Short History of the Great World War.* London: H. F. W. Deane & Sons, 1919.

Brophy, John. *The Five Years: A Conspectus of the Great War Designed Primarily for Study by the Successors of Those Who Took Part in It and Secondarily to Refresh the Memory of the Participants Themselves.* London: Arthur Barker, 1936.

Brown, Malcolm. "Peace in No Man's Land." BBC, 1981.

————. *Tommy Goes to War.* London: J. M. Dent & Sons, 1978.

————. "When Peace Broke Out." *Guardian*, 23 December 2001.

Brown, Malcolm, and Shirley Seaton. *Christmas Truce.* London: Pan Books, 1984.

————. *Christmas Truce: The Western Front, December 1914.* Rev. ed. Oxford: Pan Macmillan, 1999.

Buchan, John. *Nelson's History of the War*, vol. 5, *The War of Attrition in the West, the Campaign in the Near East, and the Fighting at Sea Down to the Blockade of Britain.* London: Thomas Nelson and Sons, 1915.

Cameron, James. *1914.* New York: Rinehart, 1959.

Carey, G. V., and H. S. Scott. *An Outline History of the Great War.* 1928. Reprint, Cambridge: Cambridge University Press, 2011.

Carion, Christian, director. *Joyeux Noel.* Sony Picture Classics, 2005.

Clark, Alan. *The Donkeys.* London: Pimlico, 1961.

Cooper, Caroline Ethel. *Behind the Lines: One Woman's War, 1914–1918, The Letters of Caroline Ethel Cooper.* Edited by Decie Denholm. Sydney: Collins, 1982.

Corrigan, Gordon. *Mud, Blood and Poppycock: Britain and the First World War.* London: Cassell Military Paperbacks, 2003.

Cruttwell, C. R. M. F. *A History of the Great War, 1914–1918.* Oxford: Clarendon Press, 1934.

Curtis, Richard, and Ben Elton. *Blackadder Goes Forth.* BBC, 1989.

Deary, Terry, and Martin Brown. *The Frightful First World War* [1998] and *The Woeful Second World War.* London: Scholastic, 2003.

De Groot, Gerard. *The First World War.* New York: Palgrave, 2001.

Doyle, Arthur Conan. *The British Campaign in France and Flanders*, vol . 1, *1914.* 1916. Reprint, Newcastle: Cambridge Scholars Publishing, 2009.

Edmonds, Sir James E. *History of the Great War, Based on Official Documents, by Direction of the Historical Section of the Committee of Imperial Defence, Military Operations: France and Belgium, 1914: Mons, the Retreat to the*

Seine, the Marne and the Aisne, August–October 1914. Woking, U.K.: Shearer, 1922.

Edmonds, Sir James E., and G. C. Wynne. *History of the Great War, Based on Official Documents, by Direction of the Historical Section of the Committee of Imperial Defence, Military Operations: France and Belgium, 1915: Winter 1914–15: Battle of Neuve Chapelle: Battle of Ypres.* London: Macmillan, 1927.

Eksteins, Modris. *Rites of Spring: The Great War and the Birth of the Modern Age.* Boston: Houghton Mifflin, 1989.

Ellis, John. *Eye-Deep in Hell: Trench Warfare in World War I.* Baltimore: Johns Hopkins University Press, 1976.

Essex, Tony, Gordon Watkins, John Terraine, Ed Rollins, and Tom Manefield, producers. *The Great War.* BBC, 1964.

Falls, Cyril. *The Gordon Highlanders in the First World War, 1914–1919.* Aberdeen: University Press, 1958.

———. *The Great War.* New York: G. P. Putnam's Sons, 1959.

———. *War Books: A Critical Guide.* London: Peter Davies, 1930.

Ferguson, Niall. *The Pity of War.* London: Penguin Press, 1999.

Ferro, Marc, Malcolm Brown, Remy Cazals, and Olaf Mueller (with translations by Helen McPhail). *Meetings in No Man's Land: Christmas 1914 and Fraternization in the Great War.* London: Constable, 2007.

Fletcher, Anthony. "Between the Lines: First World War Correspondence." *History Today* 59 (November 2009): 45–51.

Fletcher, C. R. L. *The Great War, 1914–1918: A Brief Sketch.* London: John Murray, 1920.

Foreman, Michael. *War Game: Village Green to No-Man's-Land.* 1993. Reprint, London: Pavilion Children's Books, 2006.

Fussell, Paul. *The Great War and Modern Memory.* New York: Oxford University Press, 1975.

Gibbs, Philip. *Realities of War.* London: Heinemann, 1920.

Gilbert, Martin. *The First World War: A Complete History.* London: Orion Books, 1994.

Gopnik, Adam. "The Big One: Historians Rethink the War to End All Wars." *New Yorker,* 23 August 2004.

Graham, Stephen. *The Challenge of the Dead: A Vision of the War and the Life of the Common Soldier in France.* London: Cassell, 1921.

Gregory, Adrian. *The Last Great War: British Society and the First World War.* Cambridge: Cambridge University Press, 2008.

Groom, Winston. *A Storm in Flanders: The Ypres Salient, 1914–1918.* New York: Grove Press, 2002.

Gullace, Nicoletta F. "Allied Propaganda and World War I: Interwar Legacies, Media Studies, and the Politics of War Guilt." *History Compass* 9, no. 9 (2011): 686–700.

Hanna, Emma. *The Great War on the Small Screen: Representing the First*

World War in Contemporary Britain. Edinburgh: Edinburgh University Press, 2009.

Hartesveldt, Fred R. van. *The Battles of the British Expeditionary Forces, 1914–1915: Historiography and Annotated Bibliography*. Westport, Conn.: Praeger, 2005.

Haste, Cate. *Keep the Home Fires Burning: Propaganda in the First World War*. London: Penguin Books, 1977.

Home, William Douglas. *A Christmas Truce*. London: Samuel French, 1990.

Horne, John. *A Companion to World War I*. Malden, Mass.: Blackwell, 2010.

Hussey, A. H., and D. S. Inman. *The Fifth Division in the Great War*. London: Nisbet, 1921.

Hynes, Samuel. *A War Imagined: The First World War and English Culture*. New York: Atheneum, 1991.

Keegan, John. *The First World War*. London: Hutchinson, 1998.

———. *An Illustrated History of the First World War*. New York: Random House, 2001.

Liddell Hart, B. H. *The Real War, 1914–1918*. Boston: Little, Brown, 1930.

———. *Through the Fog of War*. New York: Random House, 1938.

Lipson, Ephraim. *Europe, 1914–1939*. Revised edition. London: Adam & Charles Black, 1944.

Lloyd, Alan. *The War in the Trenches*. London: Hart-Davis, MacGibbon, 1976.

Löhrke, Eugene, ed. *Armageddon: The World War in Literature*. New York: Jonathan Cape and Harrison Smith, 1930.

Macdonald, Lyn. *1914: The Days of Hope*. London: Penguin Books, 1987.

———. *1915: The Death of Innocence*. London: Headline, 1993.

Macdonald, Lyn, with Shirley Seaton. *1914–1918: Voices and Images of the Great War*. London: Penguin Books, 1988.

MacMillan, Margaret. "The 1914 Christmas Armistice: A Triumph for Common Humanity." *Financial Times*, 20 December 2013.

Marwick, Arthur. *The Deluge: British Society and the First World War*. New York: Norton, 1965.

Meyer, Jessica. *Men of War: Masculinity and the First World War in Britain*. New York: Palgrave MacMillan, 2009.

Middlebrook, Martin. *The First Day on the Somme: 1 July 1916*. London: Penguin Books, 1971.

Montague, C. E. *Disenchantment*. 1922. Reprint, London: MacGibbon & Kee, 1968.

Morrow, John H., Jr. *The Great War: An Imperial History*. New York: Routledge, 2004.

Murphy, Jim. *Truce: The Day the Soldiers Stopped Fighting*. New York: Scholastic Press, 2009.

Neiberg, Michael S. "Revisiting the Myths: New Approaches to the Great

War." *Contemporary European History* 13, no. 4 (November 2004): 505–515.

Perris, George Herbert. *The Campaign of 1914 in France and Belgium.* London: Hodder and Stoughton, 1915.

Ponsonby, Arthur. *Falsehood in War-Time: Containing an Assortment of Lies Circulated throughout the Nations during the Great War.* New York: E. P. Dutton, 1928.

Renault, Mary. *The Charioteer.* 1953. Reprint, New York: Bantam Books, 1959.

Richards, Irene, J. B. Goodson, and J. A. Morris. *A Sketch-Map History of the Great War and After, 1914–1935.* London: George G. Harrap, 1938.

Rifkin, Jeremy. *The Empathic Civilization: The Race to Global Consciousness in a World in Crisis.* New York: Jeremy P. Tarcher/Penguin, 2009.

Robbins, Keith. *The First World War.* Oxford: Oxford University Press, 1984.

Roper, Michael. *The Secret Battle: Emotional Survival in the Great War.* Manchester, U.K.: Manchester University Press, 2009.

Schama, Simon. "No Downers in 'Downton.'" *Daily Beast,* 16 January 2012.

Sheffield, Gary. *Forgotten Victory, the First World War: Myths and Realities.* London: Headline, 2001.

———, ed. *War on the Western Front.* Oxford: Osprey, 2007.

Simkins, Peter. *Chronicles of the Great War: The Western Front, 1914–1918.* Godalming, Surrey, U.K.: CLB International, 1991.

Simpson, John. *Unreliable Sources: How the Twentieth Century Was Reported.* London: Macmillan, 2010.

Stapleton, Stephen. "The Relations between the Trenches," *Contemporary Review* 111 (January–July 1917): 636–644.

Stephen, Martin, ed. *Never Such Innocence: Poems of the First World War.* 1988. Reprint, London: J. M. Dent, 1991.

The Story of the Great War, vol. 3. New York: Collier, 1916.

Strachan, Hew. *The First World War.* London: Penguin Books, 2003.

Taylor, A. J. P. *A History of the First World War.* New York: Berkeley Medallion, 1963.

———. *Origins of the Second World War.* Middlesex, U.K.: Penguin Books, 1961.

Terraine, John. *The Western Front, 1914–1918.* London: Hutchinson, 1964.

Theatre Workshop. *Oh, What a Lovely War.* Edited by Joan Littlewood, with commentary and notes by Steve Lewis. 1965. Reprint, London: Methuen, 2006.

Thompson, P. A. *Lions Led by Donkeys: Showing How Victory in the Great War Was Achieved by Those Who Made the Fewest Mistakes.* London: T. Werner Laurie, 1927.

The Times History of the War, vol. 4. London: The Times, 1915.

The Times History of the War: The Battlefield of Europe. New York: Woodward & Van Slyke, 1914.

Todman, Daniel. *The Great War: Myth and Memory.* London: Hambledon Continuum, 2005.

Tuchman, Barbara W. *The Guns of August.* 1962. Reprint, New York: Presidio Press, 2004.

Watson, Janet S. K. *Fighting Different Wars: Experience, Memory, and the First World War in Britain.* New York: Cambridge University Press, 2004.

Weintraub, Stanley. *Silent Night: The Story of the World War I Christmas Truce.* New York: Penguin, 2002.

Williamson, Anne. *A Patriot's Progress: Henry Williamson and the First World War.* Stroud, Gloucestershire, U.K.: Sutton, 1998.

Wilson, H. W. *The War Guilt.* London: Sampson Low, Marston & Co., 1928.

Winter, Denis. *Death's Men: Soldiers of the Great War.* London: Allen Lane, 1978.

Winter, J. M. *The Great War and the British People.* New York: Palgrave Macmillan, 1985.

Winter, Jay, and Blaine Baggett. *The Great War and the Shaping of the Twentieth Century.* New York: Penguin Books, 1996.

Woodward, Sir Llewellyn. *Great Britain and the War of 1914–1918.* 1967. Reprint, Boston: Beacon Press, 1970.

Young, Nic, director. *Days That Shook the World: The Christmas Truce.* BBC, 2004.

Permissions

"The Gates of Delirium": Words and music by Jon Anderson, Steve Howe, Chris Squire, Alan White, and Patrick Moraz/© 1974 Topographic Music Ltd. All rights administered by WB Music Corp. All rights reserved. Used by Permission of Alfred Music.

Thanks to the following copyright holders for their kind permission to quote from the following letters, diaries, and memoirs lodged with the Imperial War Museum:

Suzanna Alexander, for permission to quote from the papers of R. J. Armes.

Charles Oliver-Bellasis, grandson, for permission to quote from the papers of Arthur Bates.

Tamsin Baccus, granddaughter, for permission to quote from the papers of Edward R. P. Berryman.

Mrs. H. M. Black, daughter, for permission to quote from the papers of Frank H. Black.

Charles and Liz Bazeley, great-nephew and great-niece, for permission to quote from the papers of Ralph Blewitt.

Dr. Robert C. Brookes, son, for permission to quote from the papers of Bernard J. Brookes.

Vanod Brown, daughter-in-law, for permission to quote from the papers of Frederick A. Brown.

Chris Brady, grandson, for permission to quote from the papers of H. D. Bryan.

Lady Chandler, daughter-in-law, for permission to quote from the papers of F. G. Chandler.

The Royal Green Jackets (Rifles) Museum, through the courteous agency of Mrs. Christine Pullen, for permission to quote from the papers of H. J. Chappell.

Simon Chater, grandson, for permission to quote from the papers of Alfred Dugan Chater.

Paul Chennell, grandson, for permission to quote from the papers of William J. Chennell, 2nd Queen's Royal West Surreys.

Sir Malcolm Colquhoun of Luss, grandson, for permission to quote from the papers of Iain Colquhoun.

Jo Cox, granddaughter, for permission to quote from the papers of Edgar W. Cox.

Malcolm Drummond, son, for permission to quote from the papers of Cyril A. F. Drummond.

Dorothy Griffiths, niece of Hancock's school-age pen pal, for permission to quote from the papers of J. Hancock.

Beryl Howe, daughter, for permission to quote from the papers of Sam Lane.

Gillian Clayton, niece, for permission to quote from the papers of John A. Liddell.

Hazel Lucey, daughter-in-law, for permission to quote from the papers of S. Thomas Lucey.

Brian Waite for permission to quote from the papers of Ernest G. Morley.

Mrs. Nicola C. H. Kent, niece, for permission to quote from the papers of Wilbert B. P. Spencer.

Elizabeth Ray for permission to quote from the papers of E. W. Squire.

Imperial War Museum for permission to quote from the papers of W. Tate.

Sara Glover, granddaughter, for permission to quote from the papers of M. Leslie Walkinton.

Sylvia Hollands for permission to quote from the papers of C. G. V. Wellesley.

Anne Williamson, daughter-in-law, for permission to quote from the papers of Henry Williamson.

These copyright holders granted permission to quote from the following collections, although for reasons of space, no quotations were used. I am, however, very grateful for their kind offers for use of this material, and I certainly used these works for general information:

Fiona Armitage, granddaughter, for permission to quote from the papers of G. A. Burgoyne; Tina and Howard Sleight, granddaughter and grandson, for permission to quote from the papers of F. Douglas; Barbara Jones, granddaughter, for permission to quote from the papers of E. E. Holdsworth; Madame Jean de Roany, granddaughter, for permission to quote from the papers of Henry S. Horne (1st Baron Horne of Stirkoke); Edward Hulse for permission to quote from the papers of Edward Hamilton Hulse; Rodney Stubblefield, son, for permission to quote from the papers of James Stubblefield; Charles Clarke, nephew, for permission to quote from the papers of Martha Withall.

Every effort has been made by the Imperial War Museum to trace the

copyright holders of the records listed below, and both the author and the Imperial War Museum, where these collections are preserved, would be grateful for any information that might enable them to get in touch with the current copyright owners:
Harold Atkins, 1/5th London Rifle Brigade; E. H. E. Daniell, 2nd Royal Irish; J. Davey, 1st Royal Irish Rifles; W. H. Diggle, HQ 8th Division; Harry M. Dillon, 2nd Oxfordshire and Buckinghamshire Light Infantry; R. G. Garrod, 20th Hussars; Kenneth M. Gaunt, 1/16th Queen's Westminster Rifles; J. Selby Grigg, 1/5th London Rifles; D. Lloyd-Burch, Ambulance Corps; Maurice Mascall, Royal Garrison Artillery; F. E. Packe, 2nd Welch; Arthur Pelham-Burn, 6th Gordon Highlanders; John Ray, 1st Duke of Cornwall's Light Infantry.

Although the copyright owners for the following Imperial War Museums collections were contacted in an effort to obtain permission for use of the letters, diaries, and memoirs cited, no response was received. Both the author and the Imperial War Museum, where these collections are preserved, would be grateful for any information that might enable them to get in touch with the current copyright owners of the collections listed below:
J. S. Fenton, 2nd Field Company Royal Engineers; Laurence Fisher-Rowe, 1st Grenadier Guards; W. A. F. Foxx-Pitt, 2nd Cheshires; Kenneth Henderson, 1/39th Garhwal Rifles; Michael Holroyd, 1st Hampshire; Percy H. Jones, 1/16th Queen's Westminster Rifles; Ted Lack, regiment unknown; Cuthbert G. Lawson, 3rd Brigade Royal Horse Artillery (2nd Calvary Division); Richard Lintott, 1/5th London Rifle Brigade; Cecil Lothian Nicholson, 2nd East Lancashires; H. Ridsdale, 76th Field Company Royal Engineers; A. Self, 2nd West Yorkshires; Gilbert H. Smith, 1st Queen's Royal West Surreys; John Wedderburn-Maxwell, 45th Brigade Royal Field Artillery.

Thanks to the Imperial War Museum for permission to use quotations from the following interviews preserved by the museum:
J. H. Acton, 1st Devonshires, interview, 1975; Stanley Archibald, 1st East Kents (the Buffs), interview, 1990; George Ashurst, 2nd Lancashire Fusiliers, interview, 1987; Peter Jackson, interview, 1963; Harold Essex Lewis, 240th Royal Field Artillery, interview, 1986; Albert Moren, 2nd Queen's Royal West Surreys, interview, n.d.; Philip Neame, 15th Field Company Royal Engineers, interview, 1974; M. L. Walkinton, 1/16th Queen's Westminster Rifles, interviews, 1979 and

1985; John Wedderburn-Maxwell, 45th Brigade Royal Field Artillery, interview, 1985; Ernie Williams, 6th Cheshires, interview, n.d.; H. G. R. Williams, 1/5th London Rifles, interview, n.d.; Henry Williamson, 1/5th London Rifles, interview, 1964; Colin Wilson, 1st Grenadier Guards, interview, 1975.

Index

CPSIA information can be obtained at www.ICGtesting.com
Printed in the USA
BVOW02*0344051015

420785BV00001B/1/P